A GUIDE TO LIVING AND WORKING IN
SPAIN 2.0

Santiago · San Fermin · Dalí · Calçot · Pintxos · Tapas · Toros · Madrid · Gaudi · Barcelona · Sangria · Serrano · Paella · Ensaimada · Fiesta · Flamenco · Vino

THE GUIDE TO HELP YOU EARN A LIVING IN EUROPE

HOW TO TEACH ENGLISH & MOVE TO SPAIN

Colin Rivas & Sean Dykes

EXTENDED VERSION
400+ PAGES WITH
PHOTOS & WEBSITES

COLIN & SEAN

THIS BOOK IS DEDICATED TO THE MEMORY OF EDY, ANDREW KLINE, RUSSELL PINE, JOAQUIN OUBIÑA AND ALL THE OTHERS WHO SPENT THEIR LIVES MAKING THE HUMAN FAMILY BETTER. THANKS TO ALL THE FRIENDS WE LOST ALONG THE WAY AND ALL THE FRIENDS WE STILL HAVE.

PRINTED IN THE UK AND SPAIN
FIRST EDITION: OCTOBER 2018 ~

ISBN 9781072197553

COLIN & SEAN

COLIN & SEAN

TABLE OF CONTENTS

Ernest Hemingway, pictured here with his wife Mary Welsh, had plenty to say about Spain. Photo: AFP

"I WOULD SOONER BE A FOREIGNER IN SPAIN THAN IN MOST COUNTRIES. HOW EASY IT IS TO MAKE FRIENDS IN SPAIN!"
–GEORGE ORWELL TRAVELLED TO SPAIN AS A VOLUNTEER FOR THE REPUBLICAN CAUSE AGAINST FRANCO DURING THE CIVIL WAR. HIS EXPERIENCES OF THE TRENCHES, THE ANARCHIST MOVEMENT AND REVOLUTIONARY BARCELONA WOULD FORM THE BASIS FOR HIS 1938 BOOK HOMAGE TO CATALONIA.

WHO SAID AFRICA BEGINS IN THE PYRENEES, AND WHAT IS THE THING THAT GEORGE ORWELL FOUND SO EASY TO COME BY DURING HIS SPANISH SOJOURN? FIND OUT MORE ABOUT TEACHING AND TRAVELING SPAIN TO THE FULLEST INSIDE THIS BOOK.

INTRO : SPAIN 101

Back in the fall of 1999, my senior year of college in California, I decided I wanted to move to Spain after graduation **to teach English** for a few years before traveling around the world. I was working at the Whole Foods Store on Lincoln Avenue in Santa Monica when I overheard one of the customers talking about the *auxiliar de conversación* program. I thought to myself **Hell Yeah!** That's my chance to move to Spain and perhaps traveling around Europe without asking my parents for money! **Duh!**

I had asked Spanish people and other American friends before but no one could come up with solid answer or plan about getting a job in Spain, doing the paperwork required, the how's and where's, the pros and cons etc.... friends just looked at me and pointed out that I should just marry a **Spanish señorita** and that was basically it.

So, I started going to the local library in Santa Monica, read some books about Spain, do a few internet searches here and there but zero, zilch, zip, nada, nothing... checking books and websites about how to work and live in Spain was not useful at all. I was getting more freaked out. So, I arranged to meet this customer of mine for a coffee at the 3rd promenade local coffee house and that was the best decision of my life. She gave me a briefing of how her daughter went to teach English in Spain and how she was having a hell of a great time there, she had a rich Spanish boyfriend, about to get the Spanish green card etc. etc....

She really was very helpful; I took lots of notes, headed to the Spanish consulate next day in down town LA to get all details about entering the **auxiliares program**. So I got ready to move to Spain to get a visa for Spain, I applied with enthusiasm as soon as the application opened.

"Are you telling me it was that easy?"

Nope. Well I'm trying to tell you that by then, there was no websites in Spain like there is now, there were no direct flights from LAX to Spain either. I didn't know what to pack; where to go in Spain or who I was gonna meet there. Note this is the turn of the last century -2000/2001. These English teaching programs in Spain were just starting off and there wasn't much information circulating around. It was basically a lot of word of mouth going around.

"Was I a certified teacher or pretty fluent in Spanish?"

Nope. At the time, I was hanging out with Spanish people in Los Angeles and my girlfriend was from Barcelona. So, I pretty much got by in Spanish but my teaching skills were bare to a minimum and I did not have a certificate or any credentials to teach English except for my degree in Theoretical Linguistics.

"So, Why did I write this e Book?"

This eBook is for people who either want to move to Spain. You want to just live and travel around Spain and Europe, lets say, for a year, and have fun and learn some Spanish and maybe have some different experience than living in the US. Well this book is definitely for you.

On the other hand, lets say, you are a teacher or you just completed your degree, no matter whether it be in Sciences or Humanities, but you really want to move to Spain and live there and learn the language.

You want to stay there for a while, get to know the Spanish culture, even travel around Europe, and maybe you meet a **señorita or señorito** and want to live there with them on a long-term basis. Make Spain your base country, your headquarters.

This book is definitely for you, too!

What I'm basically saying is that I wrote this book, so you don't make the same mistakes that I made when I moved to Spain whether it be packing wise, workwise, visa wise or even going to the wrong places in Spain and Europe. You'll find this eBook very helpful. It will help you avoid all the wrongs and will lead you to a high quality life or travelling in Europe and more specifically in Spain.

Besides, when you graduate from university in the U.S or Great Britain, the societal pressure to get a corporate job is in the air. However, it maybe just doesn't sit right with you. Thus, teaching English as a second language in Spain is a great way to explore the local culture, travel while earning good money, and gain a new experience. For example, for British people and wanna-be-teachers from the UK, Spain has an added value, and that is the sun. It is warm, which doesn't happen in the UK since it's an awful cold and rainy weather most of the year.

Teaching in Spain was, then, my second time teaching English as second language- the other being at Santa Monica College library to students taking Spanish 101- and from the very beginning, it was a rollercoaster of emotions. But, I wouldn't change any part of it for anything. In fact, I highly recommend the experience to anyone looking for a way to travel and explore Spain.

Spaniards are probably the closest -culturally speaking- in the western world to Americans. I did check the possibilities to go and teach English in Korea, Japan or even in China. But close friends and relatives that had already been there in the past told me not to.

WHAT CAN YOU EXPECT FROM THIS BOOK?

The book is divided into four parts; I'll now give you a quick overview of each.

PART 1: THE ENGLISH TEACHER ECOSYSTEM IN SPAIN

This part covers all of the English Teacher's basics in Spain that you need to know. If you're new to Spain you'll get a crash course in what teaching English is, the different terminology and generally get you up to speed on everything about Spain, its private sector and its socialist public educational system. This part also covers the different paperwork and documents you need to do before and after you arrive in Spain. The first chapters deal mainly with the US teachers assistant program and how to apply to it.

How to apply for a Spanish visa, getting your Spanish ID card and temporary residence in Spain, the overview the living cost in the different regions of Spain and how to get stable accommodation, how to get health care insurance and a bank account set up to start working and living safely in Spain.

PART 2: MAKE A DECENT LIVING AND SETTLE DOWN IN SPAIN

This part also covers the different opportunities that are hiding inside the English teaching business and school system in Spain and how to come up with new teaching business ideas. Also, for those of you who are from the US, how to sort out your taxes and make some extra bucks teaching and applying to other more profitable teaching assistant programs and perhaps even traveling cheaply and safely around Spain.

The final chapter in this part talks about my own dirty little secrets about how I became a permanent resident and how I made money from privately teaching English in Spain without working too hard and being able to travel around Europe, too.

PART 3: SPAIN AND BEYOND

This part has been updated from previous volumes. I talk about dealing with pregnancy in Spain, process, benefits and registration of the child and documents. There are 2 very practical chapters about packing and removal tips, how to get a driving permit and even buying a vehicle in Spain. I delve much deeper into gastronomy, culture and also what things you should say or not in Spanish if you don´t have a good command of the language.

PART 4: APPENDIX-WEBSITES-GLOSSARY

In the last part of this book I'm going to show a glossary and a listing of helpful websites about how to sell and buy stuff you need or not. If you already live in Spain you could jump straight on to the second part, but I highly recommend going over the entire book before doing so.

SOME THOUGHTS ABOUT TEACHING AND TRAVELING SPAIN

+Live in Spanish Regions Where You Can Experience the Real Culture schools are mainly placed in main Spanish cities, and in rural and pueblo locations in different areas of Spain, some may be pretty remote. Transportation doesn't get there. But since Spaniards are fairly nice and kind people, school teachers always offer themselves to give you a ride early in the morning, - Note there will be some kind of cultural exchange to return this "favor." Both options are good ways to experience Spanish life, due to cultural and economic factors: - It's a great opportunity to completely be immersed in the culture of Spain and get to know the wonderful people who live there. Discover local festivals, try new and unfamiliar dishes made by those who know it best, learn about traditions and the history of the people, and truly come to understand the Spanish people. - Both options are affordable in terms of living. Rent can be up to half the cost of inner city living and life is generally more relaxed. At the same time, Spain public transportation system is well known due to its low cost and convenient network.

+Teach in Public Schools: the Best Way to Experience True Spanish Education

Over the last 20 years, Spanish Education has improved greatly and more recently, bilingualism has become an important issue. Spain is putting a lot of energy into bringing native English speakers to teach the new generations and provide them with exciting, international opportunities.

Get Out of the Comfort Zone and Learn Life Skills

Those who teach English in Spain place themselves outside of their comfort zone and become more than an ESL teacher. Although taking a step into the unknown can be daunting, there is a good support network on the internet Facebook and Instagram and lots of blogs with auxiliaries supporting each other and bringing new ideas and ways to better their life in Spain. Moreover, participants become ambassadors of their culture, **assisting with so much more than just teaching English as a second language.**

Learn a new language, Spanish, while Living in Spain - Why Not?

As previously mentioned, **knowledge of the Spanish language is not a requirement to teach English in Spain.** It will be the responsibility of the participant to decide the extent of which to improve one's Spanish. It is very easy to arrange conversation classes or tandem exchanges with friends or fellow teachers. Spanish is one of the most popular languages to be learning. With over 400 million native speakers across the globe, **Spanish is the second more commonly spoken language after Mandarin and before English.** Learning this language will certainly open doors and create opportunities not only in Spain but also across Latin America and the USA. Those with a real interest in learning Spanish can apply to the Escuela de Idiomas in Spain, once you have arrived in the country. It is located in every county or region [**provincia-Sp**] and it's very cheap. Around $80 per year. My best bet is that you get to live with Spanish people rather than with Americans or other English-speaking teachers.

Gain International Experience to Boost Future Employability

Gaining valuable experience abroad and in an international setting is extremely valuable nowadays. **Employers not only look for work-related skills and educational background but for life skills.** By teaching English in Spain, living in another country, embracing another culture, and placing themselves outside of their comfort zone participants gain so many other transferable skills for their résumés. These range from **improving cultural awareness to working in a team from preparing classes and presentations to demonstrating intercultural skills. Even babysitting in English or doing private tuition is a great asset you should not miss.**

PART 1: THE ENGLISH TEACHER ECOSYSTEM IN SPAIN

CHAPTER 1
THE AUXILIARES PROGRAM
YOUR GOLDEN TICKET TO SPAIN

Well, you made the decision. You want to move to Spain. Your girlfriend lives there, you got close friends there, you just don't like Donald Trump or simply you just wanna see and live new experiences.

Gee!

This is where the thing starts getting trickier...

Your only one-way-ticket to Spain legally is the auxiliares programs or what they call the North American cultural ambassador program!

Want a practically guaranteed 12-hour a week job that lets you live in Spain? That's what the Auxiliares Language & Culture Assistants program promises. It's geared towards young Canadians, Americans or even some of the citizens from the British common wealth- check ahead in later chapters- who want to go to Spain for a year.

They get jobs teaching English in Spain, and it's pretty impossible to get a visa for that otherwise. So I probably don't have to spell it out for you – it's **a golden ticket** for a lot of people.

"So, What is the Auxiliares Program all About?"
The basis behind the Auxiliares Program is that Native English speakers, even those who are not necessarily teachers or come from a teaching ecosystem, can teach English in Spain as language and cultural ambassadors in public schools all across Spain.

This book, therefore, strives to unite Language Assistants with a suitable school and region in Spain, in which they can come together and build a strong teaching relationship. The relation with the schools and placements within the program are fully managed by the regional government.

So far, sounds alright? Huh?

So, What are the Conditions?

Positions managed by the regional Governments Schools placed in metropolitan areas of any region, and in rural and pueblo locations in other Spanish areas are based on,

+8 and 9-month placements (October to May or June)
+Paid school holidays (Christmas, Easter, and local festivities), except for the summer period – I'll talk about this later in the summer camps section.

+ 12-16 teaching hours per week

+4 consecutive teaching days a week

+Stipend: €875/month (for example Galicia) and €1,000/month (for example Barcelona or Madrid) – in the **extra work section**, I´ll talk about how to double or better your income without working too hard in Spain while doing these programs.

+Activities are to be held under the supervision and guidance of schoolteachers

+No lesson planning is involved

+No homework or grading is required

+ Health insurance included – full coverage

What are the requirements, then?

Well this is a grey area sometimes. At first you don't have to have a teaching background or experience with children, though, it´s highly valued by the ministry of Spanish education and the public schools.

–Native-level English speaker
–University degree or high school diploma
–No age limit
–Spanish skills are not required
–Some experience with children will be valued

I know! You still think it´s too good to be true. There ain't no such thing as a free lunch. Yeah Right!

Well, Now you're too lazy... umm. And don't feel like working. You guys perhaps thought about studying rather than working in Spain. You really want to have fun and lots of fiesta feeeeeastaaaa Si! Not have any responsibility if you happen to be around children. Here, I have made a comparison between studying and working in Spain. Economically speaking is more viable to work than to study in Spain. And, for sure more fun! Here´s why...

So, What about study vs. work in Spain?

+ More responsibility is good. You´re a grown up now!

Those days of skipping school for an extended weekend escapade or turning up to class still plastered from a night of binge drinking Leave those behind; you're a grown up now! Going to Spain as a teaching assistant rather than a student brings with it more responsibility: you have to show up to work on time, pay the bills, and present yourself as a good role model for your students. Don't worry; with a 12 (16 in Madrid) hour a week work schedule, you'll still have plenty of money, time for traveling and partying.

+ Making new foreign acquaintances. What a pain in the ass!

It's a pain in the ass to make real friends, let alone, Spanish friends, if you spend countless hours around fellow Americans. And when you're studying abroad is even seemingly worse — just turn to your large group of fellow students, all with similar backgrounds and goals (not to mention they all speak your language!).

As an auxiliar de conversación, you won't have organized group excursions or get-togethers, so it's a bit more work to find your own friends. If you're lucky, you'll click with other teachers at your school (whether Spanish or **guiris-foreign anglosaxon people or WetBacks in Spanish**), and be sure to make an effort to befriend other locals, but auxiliar Facebook, twitter or instagram groups can also be a tremendous help when it comes to finding people to hang out with.

+ Location Location Location. Not your choice in Spain

As a student, you can choose your place of study, and most stick to major Spanish cities like Sevilla, Compostela, Barcelona, Valencia or Madrid, or at least smaller ones with a large student population, like Salamanca. As an auxiliary de conversación, you have less say in where you'll be working and living, which means you could find yourself in a Micky Mouse tiny pueblo in the middle of nowhere in the Spanish countryside with no sign of native English speakers for miles.

This may sound daunting to some, but how better to learn Spanish language and culture than being surrounded by true, unadulterated Spaniards? If you do get placed in a small town, it may be positive or negative! You can always travel to major cities on weekends, and, in the meanwhile, you'll have an incomparable experience. But in the end, if you wanna learn, it's all up to you!

Money, money, money

One of the best differences between being a student and being an auxiliar is that, as a teacher assistant, you'll be taking home a paycheck. The wages may not be large sums of cash, but living in Spain is a lot more fun when you're not watching your bank account dwindle away every day. Plus, Spain is very cheap unless you live in touristy large cities like Madrid or Barcelona. And if your auxiliary de conversación salary doesn't seem to be enough for your kicks, you can do extra work such as private lessons, which are fun; easy, and pay surprisingly well. English private tuition in Spain pays you about $20-35 [18-25 euros] dollars per hour. That is, One 2 One class, I used to have groups in my home and at a coffee house in Madrid, my second year of being auxiliar, and I would cash in over $50-60 dollars an hour [group of 3-4, each pay 8 to 10 euros an hour, total= 30-40 euros/hr.]

If you get to do 4 or 5 of these group classes a week, your income could boost greatly. Remember, I got to earn some months over 3,500 dollars [2,800-3,000 euros a month, working no less than 30-30-35 hours a week plus the auxiliary of conversacion job which accounts for 12 hours and over 800-1,000 euros per month]

So, as a rough estimate of my earnings monthly was 800 euros PdA + 2,200 euros PT of particulares, that is private tuition...

That's a whopping figure monthly of 3,000 euros=$3,800. Dollars!!!

And yes! I had plenty of time to travel and do some sports on the weekend and throughout the week, too!!!!!!!!

Grow Up. Make a Decision!

As an auxiliar, you'll be finding your own apartment, opening a bank account in Spain, living on your own or with other roommates, managing your personal finances, shopping and cooking for yourself, and performing all the other responsibilities that come with being a real grown up. It may sound nicer to have a host family do all that for you, but being independent is empowering and comes with a lot of freedom... and responsibility, of course!!

Plenty of time to travel Spain and Europe.

As an auxiliar, you'll get three-day weekends (in some cases, even four-day weekends!), plus countless Spanish holidays. Between your long weekends and inexpensive bus, train, and discount airline deals, you can easily spend your weekends gallivanting around Europe.

Spanish Nightlife is Great!

Yep, that hasn't changed one bit since you studied abroad. Tapas crawls, pinchos, amazingly cheap cañas and vino, discotecas [clubs], and nights that don't end until 6am at the earliest can still be a big part of your life in Spain. Just maybe not on Monday nights.

It's all up to you!

Just like when you studied abroad, when you become a teacher or a teacher assistant in Spain, the extent to which you blend into Spanish culture is up to you. It's easy to surround yourself with American friends, speak English, eat American food, and ignore Spanish traditions.

However, with just a bit of effort, you can develop a deep understanding of Spanish culture and improve your language skills rapidly. It's all about how you decide to spend your time abroad. There's no denying that Spain is a laid-back country. You've likely already noticed the country's "mañana, mañana" culture and general goodwill. As an auxiliar, you are in this relaxed culture, and, since you'll be working only 12 to 16hours a week in a job with minimal responsibilities, you'll have plenty of time to chill. It's a good life. Trust me! Spain is the perfect cure for your stressful sick city life.

So far So good?

Have you already made a decision based on what I've told you?

Have I convinced you yet? ... Or you already had a vague idea that things were in Spain as I'm telling you here. Right?

You really wanna move to Spain and enjoy traveling and working there?

Don't worry! I will tell you the good and bad things about Spain.

So, chill, sit back cuz this is gonna be one hell of a bumpy ride!

The next chapter, I will cover how to apply for the auxiliar program in a very simple manner with real life examples.

AUXILIARES TIMELINE

EARLY-MID JANUARY

APPLICATION PERIOD OPENS! MAKE SURE YOU HAVE YOUR LETTER OF RECOMMENDATION AND COLLEGE TRANSCRIPT/DIPLOMA IN ORDER TO APPLY QUICKLY!

FEBRUARY - MARCH (ISH)

YOU WILL HEAR BACK FROM THE PROGRAM AND YOUR STATUS IN PROFEX WILL CHANGE TO ADMITIDA (ONCE YOU'VE BEEN ACCEPTED) THIS CAN TAKE A MONTH OR SO!

(THE WAITING HERE TAKES A WHILE)

MID-MAY - JUNE (ISH)

IF YOU HAVE A RELATIVELY LOW INSCRITA NUMBER (BELOW 1,500), THIS WILL BE ABOUT THE TIME YOU START HEARING BACK FROM THE SCHOOLS AND FINDING OUT IN WHICH REGION YOU HAVE BEEN PLACED! IF YOU HAVE A NUMBER BELOW ABOUT 4,000, BE PATIENT! YOU WILL HEAR BACK, JUST LATER (SOMETIMES UP UNTIL SEPTEMBER!) - FROM HERE YOU HAVE **THREE DAYS** TO ACCEPT OR REJECT YOUR REGIONAL PLACEMENT!

JUNE - JULY

ONCE YOU HAVE ACCEPTED YOUR REGIONAL PLACEMENT, YOU WILL BE ASSIGNED A SCHOOL! YOUR SCHOOL WILL SEND YOU YOUR **CARTA DE NOMBRAMIENTO** WHICH YOU WILL NEED TO APPLY FOR YOUR VISA! SOME CARTAS COME A WEEK AFTER YOU ACCEPT YOUR REGION, OTHERS CAN TAKE A COUPLE MONTHS...

JUNE - AUGUST

AS SOON AS YOU RECEIVE YOUR CARTA, YOU SHOULD GO AND GET YOUR **BACKGROUND CHECK** AND **MEDICAL CHECK**! YOU WILL NEED THESE TO APPLY FOR YOUR VISA (AND NEITHER CAN BE MORE THAN 90 DAYS OLD AT THE TIME OF YOUR VISA APPLICATION)

JULY - AUGUST

TIME TO **APPLY FOR YOUR VISA**! CHECK YOUR CONSULATE. SOME REQUIRE APPOINTMENTS (WHICH CAN BE BOOKED OUT FOR MONTHS), BUT YOU'LL WANT TO HAVE YOUR APPLICATION IN NO LATER THAN AUGUST (EARLY-MID) BECAUSE IT CAN TAKE A MONTH OR SO TO GET IT MAILED BACK!

EARLY - MID SEPTEMBER

HEAD TO SPAIN! OLÉ! MOST SCHOOLS START OCT 1ST, BUT SOME START IN MID SEPTEMBER (YOUR CARTA WILL TELL YOU). SO YOU SHOULD ALLOW YOURSELF AMPLE TIME TO GET SETTLED, FIND AN APARTMENT, APPLY FOR YOUR NIE/TIE, GET A BANK ACCOUNT, ETC. LOTS TO DO BEFORE YOU BEGIN TEACHING!

CHAPTER 2
AUXILIARES PROGRAM
APPLICATION PROCESS TUTORIAL

HOW TO APPLY FOR THE AUXILIARES DE CONVERSACIÓN PROGRAM IN SPAIN

Alright, if you got here, it means you've decided to take a step forward, become a grown up and teach English in Spain!!! Or, you're considering but are still unsure if this is right for you. Well, either way, I'm going to break down how to apply for the **Auxiliares de Conversación** program [www.mecd.gob.es/eeuu/convocatorias-programas/convocatorias-eeuu/auxiliares-conversacion-eeuu.html]

In Spain (the program that I was part of for many years). When I first applied to the program, I scoured the Internet for "how to's" and complete directions to correctly fill out the form because I could barely understand what I was reading. I had to use, at times, Google Chrome to translate bits and pieces the application said, just to make sure I was doing this right!

First things first.

Before You even sit down at the computer desk and start applying, check this list of requirements and see if you´re eligible or even capable first Here are the requirements for applying for this program (hint: they're very minimal):

+**You must be American or Canadian.** (British and Common wealth citizens have another different program which is run by the British council and I'll be covering that in a later chapter)

+**A college senior** in their last year or a college graduate.

+**English or French are your first language.**

+**Good physical and mental health** (you need to complete a physical and have your doctor state that you are in good health for the visa – this is a requirement for the visa, but does not automatically disqualify you from the program)

+**Clean criminal records** (this is also a requirement for the visa, but does not automatically disqualify you from the program)

+There is also **no age limit** to the program, although the guidelines state that most participants are between the ages of 21-35 years old.

+**If you are older than 35,** it depends on if your school if they would like an older candidate or not. I have an American friend from New York who is 62 years old and applied even after the deadline and got in, no problem.

+**The deadlines** vary but from experience they range **from February to April,** early applicants get in first provided you meet their requirements and have all documents done in time. Example: if you want to apply to start in October 2018, you must apply no later than April 2018.

+**Some times people turn down their auxiliares job** and what it happens is that, though, it doesn´t say anything about it on their program website that you can apply after the deadline because some accepted candidates fell through... Most likely, you should apply after the deadline above since you have a high probability of being accepted due to these program dropouts.

They would notify you if you applied very late or after the deadline, probably by August and in some odd cases around September. So, if you really want to get in the program apply early, but you will have a chance, too if you decide to apply late, for example, after April or even in June.

I have even heard, first hand, about cases of auxiliares applying in September and starting 4 or 6 weeks after they´d applied!!!!

So, Don't Despair and Be patient. Things go very slow in Spain.

Spaniards have a saying "Las cosas de palacio van despacio..."
[Sp lt trans.Things at the Royal palace go very slowly = *Things grind slowly*]

+Through **traveling and interacting with other auxiliares**, I've seen that most fall between the ages of 21-26 years old. The guidelines also state that a **basic level of Spanish is required**, but they never test you on that.

So, if your Spanish skills are super simple, like mine were, you'll be learning fast!

Before we really get started off applying, I would suggest reading the guidelines here (www.mecd.gob.es/eeuu/dms/consejerias-exteriores/eeuu/auxiliaresusa/APPLICATION_GUIDELINES_2016_15-12-16/APPLICATION_GUIDELINES_2016_15-12-15.pdf) to understand what is needed and how do you apply. Now, on to Profex (the program used for applicants

www.mecd.gob.es/eeuu/dms/consejerias-exteriores/eeuu/auxiliaresusa/PROFEX_MANUAL_2016_16-12-15.pdf). The Profex doesn't get updated at all and nor does the application guidelines. It's confusing and it crashes plenty of times in the first few days that the application opens (I have enclosed the ones for the academic term 2016-2017 school year the application opens, January 12th, 2016). Now, after going through the above mentioned requirements, and you're still sure you'd like to apply.

North American Language and Culture Assistants in Spain

APPLICATION GUIDELINES

WARNING : The Ministry of Education, Culture and Sport programs as well as the future programs that I´ll cover later on are FREE and THEY WILL NEVER ASK FOR OR REQUIRE ANY FINANCIAL INFORMATION ABOUT BANK CARDS AND/OR ACCESS CODES NOR WILL THEY DEMAND ANY PAYMENT IN ADVANCE through electronic mail or any other means. Please remember that all the email addresses that belong to the Ministry of Education of Spain end for example with @mecd.e and the regional governments with xunta.es junta.es yunta.es or they will be embedded in the domain edu or education.

 North American Language and Culture Assistants

CHECKLIST FOR APPLICANTS
LANGUAGE AND CULTURE ASSISTANTS PROGRAM FOR SCHOOL YEAR 2016-17
IMPORTANT: PRINT THIS DOCUMENT AND MAIL IT ALONG WITH THE REST OF DOCUMENTS TO THE
REGIONAL EDUCATION ADVISOR
DO NOT SEND DOCUMENTS SEPARATELY OR UNTIL YOU HAVE OBTAINED AND UPLOADED ALL OF THEM.

Last name, First name, MI: State/Province of origin:

Please, initialize after each applicable category. Once you have completed all these sections, your application will be considered.

Here is a list of more paperwork that you need for your actual application form on Profex:

+This checklist [www.mecd.gob.es/eeuu/dms/consejerias-exteriores/eeuu/auxiliaresusa/CHECKLIST_CONTENIDOS_2016.pdf]

+A copy of the main page of your passport (color if possible)
+A copy of either your college transcripts or diploma (some people I know sent a scanned copy of their diploma. I downloaded the unofficial transcripts and submitted it onto Profex)
+A signed and dated Statement of Purpose as to why you'd like to be part of this program (it can be in either English or Spanish)
+A letter of recommendation (on your college's or company's letterhead) from a professor or supervisor (this also needs to be signed and dated, I would ask for an electronic copy and a physical copy)

DOCUMENTS TO BE MAILED INTO YOUR STATE'S CONSULATE

+**The generated PDF document from Profex** (after you've completed and submitted all the required documents)

+**A signed and dated copy of the checklist [SCREENSHOT ABOVE]**

SCHOOL YEAR 2018-2019

North American Language and Culture Assistants in Spain

List of contacts in the US and Canada

PROFEX

To actually apply, you must apply through Profex. It can get a bit tricky and confusing, sometimes even it can give you a protocol error message or after hitting the enter button, it might have expired the page and you must refresh it and start all over again. However, you'll be successful at completing the form in the end. No worries. Here are most of the materials you will need to get through and understand what you are doing!

These are links provided for the 2016-2017 application: [In 2018, last time I checked to update this second edition eBook, the materials were pretty much the same but it just said 2018.]

+North American auxiliares website

[www.mecd.gob.es/eeuu/convocatorias-programas/convocatorias-eeuu/auxiliares-conversacion-eeuu.html]

+List of contacts USA & Canada

[www.mecd.gob.es/eeuu/dms/consejerias-exteriores/eeuu/auxiliaresusa/List-of-contacts-in-the-US-and-Canada/List%20of%20contacts%20in%20the%20US%20and%20Canada.pdf]

+Profex   Manual   [www.mecd.gob.es/eeuu/dms/consejerias-exteriores/eeuu/auxiliaresusa/PROFEX_MANUAL_2017.pdf]

+Application   Guidelines   [www.mecd.gob.es/eeuu/dms/consejerias-exteriores/eeuu/auxiliaresusa/APPLICATION_GUIDELINES_2017.pdf]

+Frequently Asked Questions

+Checklist (to print)   [www.mecd.gob.es/eeuu/dms/consejerias-exteriores/eeuu/auxiliaresusa/CHECKLIST_2018.pdf]

 North American Language and Culture Assistants

LETTER OF RECOMMENDATION GUIDELINES

Please, share this document with the person who will write the letter of recommendation that will support your participation in this program.

To whom it may concern,

Thank you for making the time to create a letter for one of the candidates to the *Language and Culture Assistants Program* from the *Spanish Ministry of Education, Culture and Sport*. The person you are writing the letter for has applied for a scholarship within the program. If the applicant is selected, he/she will be offered a position to support the teaching of English or French in a K-12 school in Spain for one academic year. Therefore, the candidate must be responsible, open to new ideas and cultures, and have good social and communicative skills. The candidate will be assisting the English or French teacher in classes by means of oral practices and conversation techniques to improve the students' speaking performance. It is essential that your ***letter is SIGNED and DATED***.

+For review before submitting application

[http://www.mecd.gob.es/eeuu/dms/consejerias-exteriores/eeuu/auxiliaresusa/For_review_before_submitting_application.pdf]

+Guidelines For The Reference Letter

[www.mecd.gob.es/eeuu/dms/consejerias-exteriores/eeuu/auxiliaresusa/REFERENCE-LETTER-GUIDELINES-2016/REFERENCE%20LETTER%20GUIDELINES%202016.pdf]

+ Regional Contacts in Spain

[http://www.mecd.gob.es/eeuu/dms/consejerias-exteriores/eeuu/auxiliaresusa/Contacts_in_Spain_-2017/Contacts_in_Spain_%202017.pdf]

+Profex app

[www.educacion.gob.es/profex/jsp/login/login.do?identificadoEnLaAplicacion=n]

The first thing you'll have to do is make sure you have a valid US Passport (Canadian Passport if you're from there, obviously). You'll need to use your passport number when creating a username for PROFEX, the online application system used to apply to the program. Make sure your passport is valid at least 6 months after you move to Spain! That is a requirement when applying for your visa in the future. If you don't have a passport, **you're going to need to get one here** [**travel.state.gov/content/travel/en/passports/apply-renew-passport/how-to-apply.html**] Assuming you do have a passport, you'll have to click the Access PROFEX button.

If it is open season for applications (between January and April- You can even try applying out of season, sometimes they have accepted auxiliares way after the admissions deadline), you should see the year and program link. When I first got on the site, it was too early and the only thing I could see was the "Mantenimento del CV" button. If you are early like I was, start filling out the CV info! Make sure you have the required documents *before* the application period opens, that way you can apply the first day! Spots are given out on a **first come, first serve basis**, like I said above. So your best bet is to apply as early as possible!

Once you have these four things, you can start uploading them online. For a step-by-step guide on how PROFEX works, click on this one

[www.mecd.gob.es/eeuu/dms/consejerias-exteriores/eeuu/auxiliaresusa/APPLICATION_GUIDELINES_2017.pdf]

Or on this outdated one

[mecd.gob.es/eeuu/dms/consejerias-

exteriores/eeuu/auxiliaresusa/PROFEX_MANUAL_2016_16-12-15.pdf].

These two PDFs are magic if you follow them through properly
when applying through PROFEX! (Seriously, whoever made this, was
an amazing person) The only thing I have found to be wrong in the
PDF guide is that you DO need to submit a small passport photo of
yourself; you won´t be able to continue applying without one. Some
people have told me that if you take a photo on your cell phone and
upload it within 2-3 minutes will work out, too. No big hassle! So, it
isn't too big of a deal.

There will then be a few other things you'll need to fill out. You can
select your regional preferences (which I´ll cover in depth later on
about the **living costs of each region and other minutia**) along with
information about the age of students you prefer to teach, the size
of the city or pueblo you prefer to live in, and whether or not you
are applying with a partner. Make sure you've done some research
on the different regions of Spain! Keep in mind that you might find
old information online that says certain regions are not
participating. As of 2018-9, *they all are!*

**And that is why I wrote this book. Because, I know, much of the
information going around on the Internet is either misleading or
outdated!**

APPLICATION STEPS

There are a total of 5 STEPS of the application process: inscrita, registrada, admitida, adjudicado/candidato seleccionado, and **aceptada (*YOU'RE IN, FOR REAL!*).** The process to becoming *aceptada* is long, and calls for a lot of patience. For example, the auxiliares that applied back in February/March of 2017, they did not receive their a*djudicado/candidato seleccionado* until the beginning of May, some people even June July. And some weren't told where they would be placed [living] until the beginning of August! [**Double check often your spam folder, if you haven't gotten an email from the ministerio, most likely, it has ended up in your junk mail tray**]

INSCRITA

Basically, the Auxiliares program is first come first serve. Your *inscrita*, is your application number in the process. People get a little bit crazy for this part, freaking out that if they have an extremely high number, they won't have a work placement. Not true. Maybe, if you're in the 4,000's your chances are a bit lower, but this past year, people in the 3,000's were getting placed at a normal time. Also, the lower your inscrita number, the higher chances you'll have for receiving the region that you picked. Although, the Spanish government is a hazy about it, and sometimes people are placed in areas that they never even listed. It's really "luck of the draw" and I can see them throwing darts as to where we'll end up! (Although, I definitely recommend getting a lower *inscrita* number to receive your placement sooner.)

Keep checking the website to see how far they are along the application process. This will let you know if they've passed your inscrita number and let you see when the first round ends. In 2016, it ended on June 10.

Last update: June 10, 2016

ASSIGNMENTS

We have reached application number 16_2AXC00**4255** and have assigned all available positions. The first round of assignments is now over. Starting June 13th, we will be offering those positions that become available as a result of candidates declining them. This second round may well last into the summer. Please stay tuned to this website, as we update it on a regular basis. All assignments are sent by email, so please check your inbox for new mail frequently. You can also check your status by accessing Profex. Remember you have three days from the moment you receive an offer to either accept or decline the assignment.

To receive your *inscrita* number, you'll need to fill out your basic information on, add your CV, and choose which region you'd like to be part of! For the school placement, you can choose to work with children or teenagers, and decide whether you'd like a rural area or an urban area. For your region selection, you will have to choose one region, from six, and they are divided into three groups. [**Go to the next chapter to learn more about regions**] You'll need to rank your top three choices from highest to lowest. The groups are:

Group A: Asturias, Ceuta y Melilla, Extremadura, La Rioja, Navarra, País Vasco

Group B: Aragón, Cantabria, Castilla-La Mancha, Cataluña, Galicia, Islas Canarias

Group C: Andalucía, Castilla y León, Islas Baleares, Madrid, Murcia, Valencia

In the past, some regions were not available to North American auxiliares such as Cantabria, Melilla and Catalunya. I'd suggest reading the manual to see which regions are available to you, now- *for all I know they all are.* After doing all of that, **you will receive an email with your *inscrita* number**!! You're almost there! Now, you can go back into the application and upload all of the required documents. **This can be found under** *curriculum > documentos anexos.*

WARNING : If you decide to stay and apply for a second year. All first year or new auxiliares applying will have priority. You'll be put on a wait list.

Since all regions will be open to the North Americans! As you may (or may not) know, when **applying to the auxiliaries program**, you will have to choose your top three *regions* in which you'd like to be assigned. You do not have the option of picking a specific city. That being said, if you haven't visited Spain before, you may be wondering what each region is like and curious as to which regions you should list in your application. We'll take a look at each region and break it down in the next chapter!

If it's application season and you're freaking out because you are missing one of your required documents, **DO NOT PANIC!** As long as you have created a login with your passport number, you can submit the documents later! You may be thinking to yourself, *"Why is this so important? I have months to apply to this program, who cares if I do it the first day or the 20th?"* Well, yes, the application period is open for a long time, but if you have your heart set on a particular region, especially if it's competitive, you'll want to apply early! Unless you are a second year renewal (and if you are, why are you reading this book? You already know what the application is like!), assignments are handed out in order of your *inscrita* number.

NOTE : If you misplace, lose or get your passport stolen and get a different number on the new passport from that one you originally typed in the profex. **DO NOT WORRY!** Just write a note on the printed PDF on the profex. Usually, you have to email it to the contact at your regional office-Ministry of Education [Galicia-Xunta, Andalucia-Junta o Catalunya-generalita...] to get a different "carta de nombramiento" with the right passport number as they always send you one with the old number.

Sometimes, you'll email Profex tech support to no avail, but be patient and ask them to change it and they will.

Número de solicitud	16_2AXC000775	Resumen digital	d143826314ae6d79f742f178899f3812121e1c9e

YOUR INSCRITA NUMBER IS AUTOMATICALLY GENERATED BY PROFEX ONCE YOU SUBMIT YOUR APPLICATION!

Once you have changed the status of your application from **borrador** (rough or first draft) to **inscrita** (submitted) you will be given a digital PDF. On the top left hand corner, there will be the year (19 for 2019) followed by some numbers and letters. **The LAST 4 NUMBERS** represent **your inscrita number,** and this is the order you are in to have your application requests met. Make sure that you are confident in your decisions before you submit the application, because **once the status has turned out to be inscrita, you can't edit any preferences (like region or grade level, etc.).**

Now, back to the missing documents situation … Say you don't have your letter of recommendation yet, but you're confident in your selections of regions and filled all of the other important information out in **PROFEX**… That's fine because while you may no longer be able to change your preferences, *you are still able to submit important documents after submitting your application!* There is a section labeled **"Curriculum: Documentos anexos"** that you can use to upload important documents later- the one I mentioned at the beginning o this chapter. This allows you to get the coveted lower inscrita number! Just be aware that **you must** *eventually* **turn in all of the documents to be fully accepted into the program!**

Example: let's say that you applied on the *first* *day* at about 10:30am Mountain Time, and *still* got an inscrita number in the high 700s!

I've been assigned a region! How do I accept?

There was a little bit of confusion in the 2016/2017 and 2017-18 school years, as many of the emails assigning positions did not go through to applicants. Seeing as how you only have three days to accept or decline your position, this leaves you no time!

A few people miss their deadline and have to email regional coordinators explaining the situation (don't worry, it is a common problem and all are given another opportunity to accept). Basically, to accept your position, you log in to your Profex Account. (Note: don't worry if it says "Número total de solicitudes: 0" as that is normal. Your application is still there, I promise).

Where to accept your placement in Profex. Here is where you can see if you have a position waiting for you. Open the Auxiliares de Conversación tab then Gestión solicitudes and Aceptación y renuncia candidatos. Make sure your drop down menu is set to the correct year – 2016 en España in this case – and hit "Buscar." Now, if you have a position waiting for you, it will be available and a button saying Aceptada will be there. Once you've accepted, your status will change from admitida to plaza aceptada (as pictured above).

To view your regional placement, you'll click on the same tab on the left, but this time go to the bottom to find Gestión de plazas y profesores and then Consulta plazas. Where to check your regional placement in Profex?

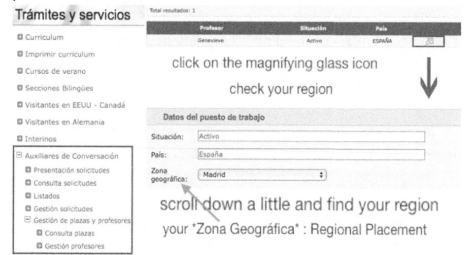

Like above, make sure your year/en España is selected and hit Buscar. You will then see your name and a little magnifying glass icon. Click it and it will take you to a page where you will be able to see your regional placement.

You must apply ASAP!

Please people apply early!

DONE WITH PROFEX? SO, NOW WHAT?

So you've finally completed the freaking PROFEX application! That wasn't so hard, was it? Now that you've followed the guided PDF and reached the end of the PROFEX application, you can print the generated PDF with your inscrita number and preferences and hand sign and date it. That, along with this checklist here [**www.mecd.gob.es/eeuu/dms/consejerias-exteriores/eeuu/auxiliaresusa/CHECKLIST_2018.pdf**] will be mailed to your corresponding consulate here [**www.mecd.gob.es/eeuu/dms/consejerias-exteriores/eeuu/auxiliaresusa/Contacts_in_Spain_-2017/Contacts_in_Spain_%202017.pdf**]

Now the really fun part... The waiting game! Some consulates take longer than others to respond to you and change the status of your application.

Remember, you have THREE DAYS to log into PROFEX and accept your position before it is forfeited to the next person in line. Assignments are given out starting with inscrita #1!

PROFEX should automatically generate an email saying you've been offered a regional placement, and if you've received PROFEX emails in the past, there should be no worries it will go to your spam folder (still, if you're worried, it doesn't hurt to check!).

Once you get your region you can accept and then wait to be assigned to a school (ugh, more waiting?). The school will send you a **carta de nombramiento** with all of your information: location, hours, pay, health coverage info, etc. At this point, you can contact your school and get in touch with a local who should be able to help with some things like finding a place to rent for the year or putting you in contact with current/former auxiliares who have taught there. Remember to contact them before school is out for the summer, however! Otherwise you might not get help.

Finally, you will need this carta from the school in order to move onto the next step, Applying for your Visa! We´ll cover this next...

REGISTRADA

To get to the *registrada* (registered) stage, you will need to mail in your PDF version of your application form, from Profex (after completed), and the signed and dated copy of your checklist. In the Profex Manual, you can find the person to whom you should send your information to, and the address for the Spain consulate in your state.

ADMITIDA

After all of your paperwork has been reviewed, you'll be admitted!! **Yeah baby!!** You have made it to the final step and closer to Spain! When you are admitted, this just means that all of your paperwork was done correctly. Now comes the most fun part, waiting for your actual placement in Spain. **This, dude, will take a wee while!**

ADJUDICADA/CANDIDATO SELECCIONADO

After waiting, waiting, and even more waiting (it takes between 2 weeks to about 3 months), you will FINALLY receive your regional placement in your email. [Again check your junk mail or spam tray, you might not find it and its right there!] You, then, have 7 days to accept or decline your offer to work in the program. Placements start in early May, beginning with second year renewals and then first year auxiliares in order of their *inscrita* number. If you choose to decline your offer, your place will, then, be offered to someone else.

ACEPTADA

If you've accepted your offer, you're admitted! Which means, **CONGRATULATIONS YOU'RE GOING TO SPAIN!!!**

Trámites y servicios   Gestión de personal de programas en el exterior

Gestión solicitudes: Aceptación y renuncia candidatos

- Curriculum
- Imprimir curriculum
- Cursos de verano
- Secciones Bilingües
- Visitantes en EEUU - Canadá
- Visitantes en Alemania
- Interinos
- Auxiliares de Conversación
  - Presentación solicitudes
  - Consulta solicitudes
  - Listados
  - Gestión solicitudes
    - Aceptación y renuncia candidatos
- Gestión de plazas y profesores

Ayuda   Ir al inicio   Salir

Por favor, introduzca las condiciones de búsqueda de solicitudes y pulse sobre el botón "Buscar"

Convocatoria:	2016 - Auxiliares de conversación extranjeros en España
Destino:	Todos
Nombre:	James Skywalker
Tipo documento:	Todos
Id documento:	
Situación solicitud:	Todos
Número solicitud:	

Buscar   Limpiar

Solicitudes con información complementaria

Total resultados: 1

Profesor	Número solicitud	Situación solicitud	Destino
James Skywalker	16_2AXC000775	Plaza aceptada	ESPAÑA

CARTA DE NOMBRAMIENTO

Your "*carta*" is the email/letter you get that tells you specifically which city or pueblo you'll be working in and your school/s! For my very first year, this didn't arrive until June! [And there was no Profex system in place yet] This is the exciting part, and probably the most surreal. You'll get your school's email and can finally start discussing with them about the upcoming year and getting to know them better. The process for receiving your "*carta*" can vary, because, well... it's Spain, and things are a bit chaotic on this end.

... Veni Vidi vici...

... You got this in the bag, dude!

You've applied, been accepted, and are now thinking on what to pack, how to polish on your Spanish, and dreaming about those Tapas and Sangría under the Spanish sun.

Don't get carried away, just yet!

The process to get into Spain is not over. You will still need to apply for your student VISA to get into Spain, look for a piso -An apartment or flat for the Brits in Spanish- and ultimately start a new life in an unknown beautiful country. So the next 2 chapters, I will cover the Region options and the VISA process back in the States.

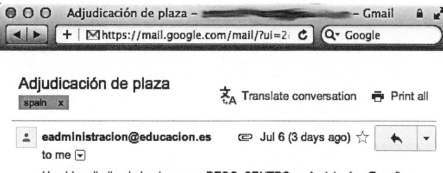

○ ○ ○   Adjudicación de plaza – ━━━━━━━━━ - Gmail

◀ ▶   +   ✉ https://mail.google.com/mail/?ui=2   C   Q▾ Google

Adjudicación de plaza
spain x

文A Translate conversation   🖶 Print all

▪ **eadministracion@educacion.es**   ✉ Jul 6 (3 days ago) ☆   ↩ ▾
to me ▾

Ha sido adjudicada la plaza en <DESC_CENTRO> - Andalucía - España a su solicitud 12_2AXC001429 del programa de Auxiliares de Conversación en España.

Si desea ACEPTAR, hágalo a través de la aplicación Profex en el plazo de SIETE (7) días naturales a partir de la recepción de este mensaje. Para ello deberá seguir los siguientes pasos:

A **CARTA DE NOMBRAMIENTO** will look something like the document below,

XUNTA DE GALICIA
CONSELLERÍA DE CULTURA, EDUCACIÓN E ORDENACIÓN UNIVERSITARIA

Edificio Administrativo San Caetano
15781 – Santiago de Compostela

D. MANUEL CORREDOIRA LÓPEZ, DIRECTOR XERAL DE EDUCACIÓN, FORMACIÓN PROFESIONAL E INNOVACIÓN EDUCATIVA DA CONSELLERÍA DE CULTURA, EDUCACIÓN E ORDENACIÓN UNIVERSITARIA DA COMUNIDADE AUTÓNOMA DE GALICIA

CERTIFICA

Que, D./Dª. ███████████, de nacionalidade estadounidense, provisto/a de pasaporte nº S52651790774, foi seleccionado/a para participar no programa "**Auxiliares de Conversa MINISTERIO DE EDUCACIÓN, CULTURA E DEPORTE – CONSELLERÍA DE CULTURA, EDUCACIÓN E ORDENACIÓN UNIVERSITARIA DA COMUNIDADE DE GALICIA**", programa que se desenvolve mediante convenio entre o Ministerio de Educación, Cultura e Deporte de España e a Consellería de Cultura, Educación e Ordenación Universitaria da Comunidade Autónoma de Galicia, concedéndoselle unha axuda económica, para exercer as funcións de auxiliar de conversa en centros de educación infantil e primaria, institutos de educación secundaria ou escolas oficiais de idiomas da Comunidade de Galicia (todos eles incluídos no Rexistro Estatal de centros docentes non universitarios do Ministerio de Educación, Cultura e Deporte) por unha contía mensual mínima de setecentos euros (700 €), do 1 de outubro de 2013 ao 31 de maio de 2014, ambos inclusive. Esta Consellería de Cultura, Educación e Ordenación Universitaria ten tamén subscrita unha póliza de seguro médico, accidentes e repatriación a favor deste/a auxiliar desde o 1 de outubro de 2013 – mes no que deberá desprazarse a España e realizar o curso de orientación para a súa incorporación ao programa – ao 31 de maio de 2014, ambos inclusive.

Centro educativo de destino:
CEIP Plurilingüe Infante Felipe de Borbón
Enderezo: Rúa da Escola, s/n - 36450 Salvaterra de Miño - Pontevedra
Tfno.: 986658011
Correo electrónico: ceip.infante.felipe@edu.xunta.es

Os/as participantes neste programa exercen as súas funcións de auxiliar de conversa, durante un mínimo de 12 horas á semana, nos centros docentes onde desenvolven a súa actividade.

E, para que conste para os efectos oportunos, expídese a seguinte certificación en Santiago de Compostela, a 18 de abril de 2013.

Asdo.: Manuel Corredoira López

Este documento foi asinado dixitalmente, pode verificar a súa validez introducíndo o código CVE da marxe esquerda en www.xunta.es/cve

CHAPTER 3
REGIONAL CHOICES
LIVING COST, EXPENSES & CULTURE

This section is designed for you to make a decision before you fill out the part of the Profex in which you will have to enter you Regional choice. Remember that in order to get your *inscrita* number, you'll need to fill out your basic information on which region you'd like to be part of!

For the school placement, you can choose to work with children or teenagers, and decide whether you'd like a rural area or an urban area.

For your region selection, you will have to choose one region, from six, and they are divided into three groups. You'll need to rank your top three choices from highest to lowest.

The groups are:
Group A: Asturias, Ceuta y Melilla, Extremadura, La Rioja, Navarra, País Vasco
Group B: Aragón, Cantabria, Castilla-La Mancha, Cataluña, Galicia, Islas Canarias
Group C: Andalucía, Castilla y León, Islas Baleares, Madrid, Murcia, Valencia

Deciding to move to Spain is easy; but figuring out how you can afford it is a totally different issue altogether. That's why I've asked many auxiliares who have been around for years and lived in all the regions to get to the bottom of exactly how different expats around the country see the Spanish regions, their cultures, languages, dialects, food, and most importantly the **Cost of Living in Spain**.

In Spain, actually, they have many languages besides Spanish. Gallego, Basque- Euskera, Catalonian, Valenciá and Mallorquín, which shape the landscape of the nations or **autonomous communities** as they call it-**autonomías- in Spain**.

PLEASE DO NOT FREAK OUT JUST YET!!! CHILL OUT!!

DO I HAVE TO LEARN THE LOCAL LINGO BESIDES SPANISH?

NOPE! Most Spaniards are not gonna talk to you in their local language. They will notice right away you are Giris –foreigners- and they will surely address to you only in Spanish.

Generally speaking, larger cities are more expensive in terms of rent and transportation, being Madrid, Barcelona and Bilbao the most expensive ones and with a skyrocketing cost of living, and cities in the north are often (but not always) pricier too. Living the pueblo life may mean spending less on living costs, but more to get out of town. Everyone budgets differently, but the following data about regions is a rough but close estimate how other foreign residents in Spain *spend their money on a monthly basis.*

Galicia is located in the Northwest coast of Spain. Some Spaniards call it **Gali-fornia**. It does resemble parts of Northern California at times. It is also referred to as the "Switzerland or Ireland of Spain" because of how green everything is! It can be a bit far away from the rest of Spain, so a lot of auxiliares get placed in Galicia as a last resort. That being said, most people seem to really enjoy their time in Galicia! The two most common destination cities are **Santiago de Compostela** or **Vigo**. The program is efficient, people are paid on time, and the scenery is beautiful! If you end up in Galicia, you won't be disappointed. They have great food, lots of fish, seafood, pork and potatoes. If your a vegan or vegetarian you're gonna have a hard time finding veggie dishes in Galicia. I worked in both Compostela and Vigo, and definitely they're very different cities. If you like the beach, the sun, sports and the big city, Vigo is the place for you, though, it's rainy for about 3 months a year. Compostela is a more touristy, small and easy to reach everywhere. You won't even need to get on a bus or a train in Compostela. Pontevedra and Coruña are less popular with auxiliares, but very warm small cities with a great nightlife, too.

Tapas are very popular and cheap in Galicia. Sometimes you don't even have to buy lunch or dinner since Bars and Coffee Houses in Galicia have the habit of giving away lots of food when you order any type of beverage.

Average auxiliary de conversación salary : €700-800
Average Rent in Compostela: €175 (in shared piso) €40 utilities
Average Rent in Vigo: €150 (in shared piso) + €35 utilities
Average Cost of 3 meals/day at a restaurant or bar (Breakfast/Lunch/Dinner) in Galicia [price all of meals combined on a single day]: €12

Asturias is also on the coast, neighboring Galicia. Like Galicia, Asturias is also very green. Because the region is smaller and there are fewer cities that participate, this region is pretty competitive. You will most likely end up in either Oviedo or Gijón. Mostly, second years in the auxiliares program are placed here. A very dear friend of mine Andrew spent 2 years here and I went visit him very often. It is rainy too and the beaches are not as great as the Galician ones.

Average Rent in Oviedo: €220 (in shared piso) + €45 utilities
Average Rent in Gijón: €215 (in shared piso) + €45 utilities
Average Cost of 3 meals/day at a restaurant or bar (Breakfast/Lunch/Dinner) in Asturias [price all of meals combined on a single day]: €18-20

Cantabria is located on the northern most area of Spain. It's another overlooked area, but it truly is nice! There are gorgeous mountains, forests, and of course a beautiful sea line. The typical local dish is anchovies and baby eels. The cities here can be a bit smaller, but the region itself is beautiful. Most auxiliares in Cantabria end up in Santander.

Average Rent in Santander: €230 (in shared piso) + €50 utilities
Average Cost of 3 meals/day at a restaurant or bar (Breakfast/Lunch/Dinner) in Cantabria [price all of meals combined on a single day]: €12-15

Update: Cantabria pulled out of the program in late 2016-7... No word yet as to why, but rumors seem to think it's due to a lack of funding... Auxiliares assigned to this region were switched to other regions.

País Vasco borders the east of Cantabria. País Vasco is the heart of **Basque Country,** an autonomous region of Northern Spain. Basque has it's own language too-**Euskera,** but have no fear! Spanish is still spoken in País Vasco as well. It's a beautiful area, with the sea and France located not too far away. This area actually has the highest earning per capita out of all of Spain, so it can be a bit more expensive to live here! One of the major cities, San Sebastián, is located here, making País Vasco a popular choice for many auxiliares.

Average Rent of San Sebastián: €415 (in shared piso) + €50 utilities

Average Cost of 3 meals/day at a restaurant or bar (Breakfast/Lunch/Dinner) in San Sebastián or Bilbao [price all of meals combined on a single day]: €25-35

Navarra is located just south of France and hosts the annual Running of the Bulls in its city of Pamplona during the <u>San Fermín Festival</u>. Over 1,000,000 people come to participate in this festival! Navarra is a bit modern and has a lot of automobile manufacturing. Its largest city, Pamplona, is also home to two universities, so you can be sure there is a good bit of nightlife and fun to be had here!

Average Rent of Pamplona: €275 (in shared piso) + €50 utilities
Average Cost of 3 meals/day at a restaurant or bar (Breakfast/Lunch/Dinner) in Navarra [price all of meals combined on a single day]: €15-20

Aragón is a larger, landlocked region of Spain, located just south of France. This region can be more competitive for auxiliares because they only accept a small amount of individuals. More than half of Aragón's population lives in the large city of Zaragoza. The only other city in Aragón that has a population of over 50,000 is Huesca. Through the trains, you can get to Barcelona and Madrid fairly easily, as well as the rest of Europe with the Zaragoza airport. It's not quite as touristy as other large cities in Spain, so if you live here, you'll have an authentic Spanish year abroad!

Average Rent in Zaragoza: €210 (in shared piso) + €65 utilities
Average Cost of 3 meals/day at a restaurant or bar (Breakfast/Lunch/Dinner) in Navarra [price all of meals combined on a single day]: €12-18

Cataluña is one of the regions that are having problems with Spain. Have you checked the news lately? Yep, the bad news is that Catalonians want to be independent from Spain. The good news is that the auxiliary salary has gone up and ever since they wanted to become a country of their own, the cost of living is gone down a bit. It's been always a great region for auxiliares. Cataluña is home to Barcelona, the second largest city in Spain, located on the coast. Unlike the majority of Spain, most people in this region speak Catalán rather than Spanish. They'll still understand you (most likely) if you speak Spanish, but many prefer to speak Catalán. This could make your experience in Spain a bit different than if you choose an area where Spanish is mainly spoken, but there's no doubt that Cataluña is a beautiful region.

Average auxiliary de conversación salary: €1,000-1,200
Average Rent in Barcelona: €405 (in shared piso) + €45 utilities
Average Cost of 3 meals/day at a restaurant or bar (Breakfast/Lunch/Dinner) in Barcelona [price all of meals combined on a single day]: €25-35

Castilla Y León is a large region located east of Portugal. Much of the region consists of a large, central plateau – the Meseta. Río Duero is a large river that flows through the region. The weather here tends to be cold in winter and warm and dry in the summer. Salamanca is a large university town and capital of this region.

Salamanca attracts thousands of international students, generating a diverse environment! Salamanca is located about 120 miles (200 kilos) west of Madrid, making an easy commute to the country's capital city. El Camino de Santiago also runs through this region in the north.

Average auxiliary de conversación salary: €700-800
Average Rent in Salamanca: €200 (in shared piso) + €50 utilities
Average Cost of 3 meals/day at a restaurant or bar (Breakfast/Lunch/Dinner) in Castilla & Leon [price all of meals combined on a single day]: €8-15

La Rioja is a small, landlocked region of northern Spain. Its capital is Logroño, a popular area for auxiliares to end up. The region is well known for its wines under the brand Denominación de Origen Calificada Rioja. This area is relatively cheap compared to other areas of Spain, and the food in Northern Spain is supposed to be delicious! If you end up here, you'll have a blast from the past!

Average auxiliary de conversación salary: €700-800
Average Cost of 3 meals/day at a restaurant or bar (Breakfast/Lunch/Dinner) in La Rioja [price all of meals combined on a single day]: €10-18
Average Rent in Logroño: €250 (in shared piso) + €50 utilities

The country's capital, Madrid! Madrid is a region as well as a city, so note that if you select Madrid as your preference, you are selecting the *region*, not the capital city. Madrid, the city, is one of the largest in the world, with about 3.2 million people living there. In the EU, it is the third largest city, behind London and Berlin. As such, there is a huge amount of auxiliares who get placed in Madrid. If you've selected Madrid as your #1 region and you have an inscrita number below 1,200, you're most likely ending up in this region. The cost of living is a bit higher here than the rest of Spain. You do work 16 hours (instead of 12) and make €1,000/month (instead of the usual €700). You also work until the end of June in Madrid instead of the end of May. Móstoles and Alcalá de Henares are the next two largest cities in this region, with just over 200,000 people in each. Because the capital city is so huge for tourism, you do run the risk of having Spaniards want to practice their English with you, which can make an "authentic Spain experience" more difficult. Commuting is also fairly common for people in this region.

Average auxiliary de conversación salary: €1,000-1,200
Average Cost of 3 meals/day at a restaurant or bar (Breakfast/Lunch/Dinner) in Madrid [price all of meals combined on a single day]: €15-25
Average Rent in Madrid: €440 (in shared piso) + €50 utilities
Average Rent in Alcalá de Henares: €300 (in shared piso) + €50 utilities

Castilla La Mancha is located just east of Madrid. Historically, this region is very significant to Spain. The historical battles between Christian crusaders and Muslim forces during the period from 1000 to the 13th century occurred in Castilla La Mancha. It is also the land of Don Quixote and windmills! <u>Albacete</u> is the largest and most populous city here, and its capital city is <u>Toledo</u> (a beautiful city in Spain, worth visiting while you're here!)

Average auxiliary de conversación salary: €700-800
Average Cost of 3 meals/day at a restaurant or bar (Breakfast/Lunch/Dinner) in Castilla [price all of meals combined on a single day]: €8-15
Average Rent in Castilla: €315 (in shared piso) + €45 utilities
Average Rent in Toledo: €300 (in shared piso) + €50 utilities

Valencia is also a city as well as a region of Spain. Valencia is the third largest city in Spain, after Madrid and Barcelona. Valencia is the home of the famous dish **Paella**; they speak Spanish as well as Valenciá, a variety of Catalán. Before the region was cut some years ago, it was very popular amongst students! Mainly 2nd years were placed here because of the competitiveness. It will be interesting to see how this region plays out in the years moving forward!

Average Rent in Valencia: €250 (in shared piso) + €35 utilities
Average auxiliary de conversación salary: €700-800
Average Cost of 3 meals/day at a restaurant or bar (Breakfast/Lunch/Dinner) in Valencia [price all of meals combined on a single day]: €10-20

Extremadura is located east of Portugal and west of Madrid. This region is important for the wildlife of Spain. Wild <u>Black Iberian pigs</u> roam in the area and consume acorns from oak groves here! They're called Pata Negra or Jamón Serrano. It's a Spanish deli dish. The human population density is relatively low compared to the rest of Spain in Extremadura. This can make cities in Extremadura much cheaper compared to the rest of Spain! Some of the possible cities you could get placed in here are Badajoz, Cáceres, or Mérida.

Average Rent in Badajoz: €150 (in shared piso) + €45 utilities
Average Rent in Cáceres: €160 (in shared piso) + €50 utilities
Average auxiliary de conversación salary: €700-800
Average Cost of 3 meals/day at a restaurant or bar (Breakfast/Lunch/Dinner) in Extremadura [price all of meals combined on a single day]: €5-15

Andalucía is located in the southern most part of Spain. A *lot* of auxiliares end up here. It's thought of as "traditional Spain" which can be great for a year abroad. Here, you will find beautiful flamenco dancing and wonderful Spanish music.

Seville, Granada, Córdoba, Málaga, Almería, and Huelva are some major cities in Andalucía in which you may be placed. *Semana Santa* or Holy Week is especially festive in Andalucía! There is an incredibly heavy Spanish accent in the south, which can make it difficult to understand the locals (a lot of it sounds slurred together, heave *ssssth* sounds for c and z), so that's something to be aware of! Also, this region is the hottest of mainland Spain, so take that into considerations when finding a *piso* to live in!

Average auxiliary de conversación salary: €700-800
Average Cost of 3 meals/day at a restaurant or bar (Breakfast/Lunch/Dinner) in Andalusia [price all of meals combined on a single day]: €5-25
Average Rent in Seville: €285 (in shared piso) + €35 utilities
Average Rent in Granada: €200 (in shared piso) + €45 utilities
Average Rent in Córdoba: €240 (in shared piso) + €35 utilities

Murcia is located to the east of Andalucía and south of Valencia. It is also a region as well as a city. Like Andalucía, the traditional Spain setting is found, with big cathedrals and a lot of history. There also exists the heavy southern Spanish accent here, which again makes it difficult to understand the natives. It is a beautiful region, but has had a lot of problems with auxiliares in the past. This area seems to be the most notorious for paying auxiliares late (sometimes even a few *months* late), which can make your Spain experience quite tainted. The city of Murcia is the most common location auxiliares get placed in this region.

Average Rent in Murcia: €215 (in shared piso) + €40 utilities
Average auxiliary de conversación salary: €700-800
Average Cost of 3 meals/day at a restaurant or bar (Breakfast/Lunch/Dinner) in Murcia [price all of meals combined on a single day]: €5-12

Las Illas Baleares or the <u>Balearic Islands</u> is a region located east of Valencia in the Mediterranean Sea. The four largest islands are <u>Majorca</u>, <u>Minorca</u>, <u>Ibiza</u> and <u>Formentera</u>. Only a small amount of auxiliares is placed here. The most famous pastry here is the ensaimada and the sobrasada is a spicy red sausage spread. They're both yummy and delicious for breakfast, lunch or dinner! They speak both Spanish and Mallorquín, which is a dialect of Catalonian here.

The famous tennis player and champion of 11 French Opens-Roland Garros, Rafa Nadal is from these tiny bucolic islands. The cost of living is a bit higher here than the rest of Spain because the islands are quite touristy! There are plenty of flights going on and off the islands, however, so your opportunities for traveling around Europe are great!

Average Rent in Palma de Mallorca: €280 (in shared piso) + €50 utilities

Average Rent in Ibiza: €460 (in shared piso) + €30 utilities

Average auxiliary de conversación salary: €700-1,000

Average Cost of 3 meals/day at a restaurant or bar (Breakfast/Lunch/Dinner) in Majorca [price all of meals combined on a single day]: €15-25

Las Islas Canarias or the Canary Islands are a region very far south of Spain, located west of Morocco and Western Sahara in Africa! The main islands are (from largest to smallest) Tenerife, Fuerteventura, Gran Canaria, Lanzarote, La Palma, La Gomera and El Hierro. This region is hugely popular for travel and tourism. Because they're located so far away from Spain, it can make travel around the rest of Europe a bit time consuming and pricey. Spanish is the main language on the islands, but because they're so popular for tourism, you can often find English, German, and Italian speakers with relative ease! The climate here is subtropical and the average high is about 75°F (24°C) while the low averages 64°F (18°C). So yeah, this is an ideal vacation spot, especially during winter months!

Average Rent in Tenerife: €220 (in shared piso) + €30 utilities
Average Rent in Gran Canaria: €200 (in shared piso) + €25 utilities
Average auxiliary de conversación salary: €700-800
Average Cost of 3 meals/day at a restaurant or bar (Breakfast/Lunch/Dinner) in the Canaries [price all of meals combined on a single day]: €12-25

(**Note:** Pricing information on rent is based on a 3 bedroom shared piso in the city center. Pricing may change dramatically if you choose to live alone or outside of the city center! I used information from www.numbeo.com/cost-of-living/ to get these numbers. It's always a good idea to talk to current auxiliares and see what they're paying, too!)

Cat of Sunshine and Siestas December 5, 2013 at 2:02 AM #

I miss my job as an auxiliar. Coming in 2007 meant there was little competition for the position, no stupid online process, and I never had any late payments. I also worked just three days a week, and I was treated as an equal in the school I worked for. It's a shame that so many people seem to get taken advantage of these days, or that some come expecting everything to be done for them. For me, part of the draw was having the level of uncertainty and trying to get established without knowing much Spanish or anyone else in the program.

dina January 8, 2014 at 9:32 PM #

I agree with Cat. It can be fairly disorganized, depending on your region, but I've found that it forces me to get out there and figure things out. I'm pretty sure that all the auxiliars in my region figured it out eventually, and I guess if not, they went home. This program, like life, throws us a lot of hurdles, but being able to overcome them is a huge self-esteem boost. It can be tough striking out on your own and having to meet all new friends, but forcing myself to show up to social events (many of them being all Spaniards) has been so good for me and my Spanish has greatly improved after my first few months.

Now, based on the information that I have provided in this chapter plus your own research and what you probably have heard from other people, you must return to the Profex and choose regions. I hope this chapter has helped you make a decision about where you really want to live when you move to Spain.

I´ll also cover preparing your move to Spain and how and what to pack, which cell phones and electronics you should bring to Spain in the next chapters.

Bye for now!

CHAPTER 4
VISA PROCESS IN THE US

Alright, so now you've officially applied to the Auxiliares de Conversacion Program and now it's on to the next fun step! Applying for your visa! As you must be aware of now, the program does not assist you with the visa application, so you're essentially on your own here. But have no fear! I'm here to help (if I can).

In order to apply for your **long-term visa**, you're going to need to have a few things handy. **Here check the link** http://www.mecd.gob.es/eeuu/dms/consejerias-exteriores/eeuu/auxiliaresusa/VISA_INSTRUCTIONS_FOR_US_2016_15-07-16.pdf to the Visa Application instructions for Americans, and **here** check the link http://www.mecd.gob.es/eeuu/dms/consejerias-exteriores/eeuu/auxiliaresusa/VISA_INSTRUCTIONS_FOR_CANADIANS_2016.pdf for Canadians for 2016/2017. The information I'm listing below is specific to the **Californian visa requirements**, which are where residents of California or Montana may as well apply. While most of the information is accurate for other consulates, you'll want to check your specific consulate for any variations:

1. **Your Carta de Nombramiento** (which you'll receive after successfully applying to the program and waiting for *months* – first years usually begin to receive theirs in mid-May, assuming their inscrita number is low enough. Some might not get theirs until the end of summer!) *Bring the original and a copy.*

2. **A State or FBI Background Check** – This cannot be more than 90 days old at the time of your visa application! Must be verified by fingerprints. (Update: Some consulates only require name based state background checks). Check your consulate requirements to see what your state requires. *Bring the original and a copy.*

3. **A Medical Check from a Doctor** – This also has to be less than 90 days old at the time of your visa application. It must be on a doctor's letterhead and hand signed and dated. For the San Francisco consulate, **check throughout this chapter** to see an example of what is needed. I *think* that the certificate is the same for everyone, but check your specific consulate just to be sure! *Bring the original and a copy.*

4. **Your Visa Application** – **check throughout this chapter or check the photo next** to see the Consulate Application. For the purposes of this program, you will be applying for a long-term visa (any stay greater than 90 days). *Bring the original and a copy.*

5. **Two Recent Passport Photos** – Your photos must be 2"x 2" and have a clean, white background. You can get these taken at a local Walgreens or CVS if you don't have a means to do it yourself. You can also download an app called Passport Booth if you want to try taking the photos yourself! *Remember to bring 2 pictures.*

BOSTON:
http://www.mecd.gob.es/eeuu/dms/consejerias-exteriores/eeuu/auxiliaresusa/VISADO_BOSTON_2016.pdf
CHICAGO:
http://www.mecd.gob.es/eeuu/dms/consejerias-exteriores/eeuu/auxiliaresusa/VISADO_CHICAGO_2016.pdf
HOUSTON:
http://www.mecd.gob.es/eeuu/dms/consejerias-exteriores/eeuu/auxiliaresusa/VISADO_HOUSTON_2016.pdf
LOS ANGELES:
http://www.mecd.gob.es/eeuu/dms/consejerias-exteriores/eeuu/auxiliaresusa/VISADO_LOS_ANGELES_2016.pdf
MIAMI:
http://www.mecd.gob.es/eeuu/dms/consejerias-exteriores/eeuu/auxiliaresusa/VISADO_MIAMI_2016.pdf
NEW YORK:
http://www.mecd.gob.es/eeuu/dms/consejerias-exteriores/eeuu/auxiliaresusa/VISADO_NEW_YORK_2016.pdf
PUERTO RICO:
http://exteriores.gob.es/Consulados/SanJuandePuertoRico/es/Paginas/inicio.aspx
SAN FRANCISCO:
http://www.mecd.gob.es/eeuu/dms/consejerias-exteriores/eeuu/auxiliaresusa/VISADO_SAN-FRANCISCO_2016_d.pdf
WASHINGTON DC:
http://www.exteriores.gob.es/Consulados/Washington/es/Paginas/inicio.aspx

6. **Valid Passport & Copy** – Must be good for at least 6 months after your departure date to Spain. You also need one colored copy of the information page (the one with your name and picture and signature). Your passport has to have at least one blank page to attach the visa. *Bring the original and a copy.*

7. **Copy of a Valid ID** – This can be a driver's license, state ID, current student ID card... Basically anything issued by the state with your name and picture on it. *Bring a copy.*

8. **Planned Trip/Itinerary Printout** – Don't actually purchase anything until your visa is approved! Mine was a hand typed word document. This is just so they know you're making plans. Include information like the day you'll arrive in Spain, the program start/end date, and when you'll (hypothetically) be headed back to your home country. It can be fairly simple. Include your full name and title it *Spain Itinerary* or something similar. *Bring a copy.*

9. **Self-Addressed USPS Express Mail Envelope** – This is so they can return your passport/visa/original documentation to you once everything goes through. They say you need to have $22.95 worth of stamps on it (as of 2016). Note that you *cannot* bring UPS or FedEx, it *has* to be the United States Postal Service. You may also pick up your visa in person at your consulate, in which case you won't need this.

10. **$160-180 Visa Fee Money Order** – This *must be* a money order. They will not accept checks. If you go in person, they will also accept cash, if you bring exact change. Must be made payable to the "Consulate General of Spain" in San Francisco if that is your consulate (I think it's the same for every consulate, but double check to make sure). This amount was updated as of April 2016, so check to see your specific consulate visa fees for future dates as amounts may change over time.

11. Again, while San Francisco has a selection for just the Language/Cultural Program you will be going through, you will essentially be filling out the student visa information.

How soon will my visa come back to me?

Totally depends. Factors such as your consulate, date of application, etc. all play a part. Most consulates say that it takes roughly a month to get your visa back. Personally, my mailed visa from San Francisco took only two weeks to be returned to me. Some people had even better in the 2016-2017 year! It seemed like the LA, New York, San Francisco, and Miami consulates had pretty great turnaround times with some reporting receiving their visas back in as little as a week! Always err on the side of caution, however, and plan on 4-6 weeks, just in case.

As I stated above, the information I looked into was specifically for the **California at the San Francisco or the Los Angeles consulate** because I was a resident of California. If you're too lazy to find your visa application consulate, I'll help you out with the following information:

The San Francisco Consulate – Alaska, Arizona, Northern California, Colorado, Hawaii, Idaho, **Montana**, Nevada, New Mexico, Oregon, Utah, Washington State, Wyoming (Visa Application) You can also **click here** to find out more information about the Language & Cultural Visa Application for San Francisco. **You CAN apply by mail.**

The Boston Consulate – Maine, Massachusetts, New Hampshire, Rhode Island, Vermont (Visa Application) Application for Boston. **You must apply in person.**

The Chicago Consulate – Illinois, Indiana, Iowa, Kansas, Nebraska, North Dakota, South Dakota, Ohio, Kentucky, Michigan, Minnesota, Missouri, Wisconsin (Visa Application) **You must apply in person.**

The Houston Consulate – Alabama, Arkansas, Louisiana, Mississippi, Tennessee, New Mexico, Oklahoma, Texas, (Visa Application) **You must apply in person.**

The Los Angeles Consulate – California (counties: Imperial, Kern, Los Angeles, Orange, Riverside, Bernardino, San Diego, San Luis Obispo, Barbara y Ventura), Arizona, Colorado, Utah, (Visa Application) **You CAN apply by mail.**

The Miami Consulate – Florida, South Carolina, Georgia, (Visa Application) **You must apply in person.**

The New York Consulate – New York, Connecticut, Delaware, Pennsylvania, New Jersey (Visa Application) **You must apply in person (note that you don't need an appointment to apply, however).** *Update: Applicants in the 2016/17 school year reported speaking to the consulate and being told that you may also apply by mail. I would call/email for verification beforehand, however!*

The Washington D.C. Consulate – Maryland, Virginia, West Virginia District of Columbia, North Carolina, (Visa Application) **I'm pretty sure you must apply in person (though you don't need an appointment).**

	Application for National Visa This application form is free	PHOTO

	FOR OFFICIAL USE ONLY
1. Surname(s) [1]	
2. Surname(s) at birth (previous surname(s)) [1]	Date of application:
3. Forename(s) [1]	Visa application number:

4. Date of birth (day-month-year)	5. Place of birth	7. Current nationality	File processed by:
	6. Country of birth	Nationality at birth, if different:	Documents presented:
			☐ Travel document
8. Sex ☐ Male ☐ Female	9. Marital status ☐ Single/a ☐ Married ☐ Separated ☐ Divorced ☐ Widow(er) ☐ Others (specify)		☐ Government authorisation ☐ Request for government authorisation ☐ Means of livelihood ☐ Proof of accommodation
10. For minors: surname(s), forename(s), address (if different from that of applicant) and nationality of person who exercises parental responsibility or legal guardian			☐ Medical certificate ☐ Criminal record certificate ☐ Travel medical insurance ☐ Note verbale ☐ Others:
11. Spanish National Identity Document Number, where applicable ——			
12. Type of travel document ☐ Ordinary passport ☐ Diplomatic passport ☐ Service passport ☐ Official passport ☐ Special passport ☐ Other travel document (please specify)			Decision on visa: ☐ Refused ☐ Issued:
13. Number of travel document	14. Date of Issue	15. Valid until	16. Issued by	Valid from .... until ....
17. Postal and e-mail address of applicant		Telephone number(s)	Number of entries: ☐ One ☐ Two ☐ Over Two
18. Residence in country other than country of current nationality ☐ No ☐ Yes. Residence permit or equivalent document............Nº.......................Valid until.......................			Number of days:
19. Current Profession			

---

[1]   To be completed according to data which appears in travel document.

[2]   To be completed according to data which appears in travel document.

[3]   To be completed according to data which appears in travel document.

1

The Puerto Rico Consulate – Puerto Rico, Islas de Culebra y Vieques, Virgin Islands (Visa Application)

I believe that this is a complete list of the states and their corresponding consulates! (Specific to 2017/18, though I'm sure not if it will change much soon after). It's important to know whether or not your consulate accepts applications **through mail** or if you have to **apply in person**. In San Francisco, you can apply through mail, which is a huge time saver. Check the **Language and Cultural Assistants PDF** found on your consulate's website and see whether or not yours says "Apply By Mail." As far as I know, only the California consulates let you apply through mail. Certain consulates also require you to **get your documents (such as the medical certificate/background check) translated into Spanish** (for sure Miami, I'm not sure about others), so you'll want to check requirements on that too.

Consular Services

- Passports
- Consular Registry
- Civil Registry
- Notaries, Legalizations and Translations
- Spanish Nationality
- Visas
- Other Consular Services
- Consular Fees
- Appointments
- Electoral Information
- FAQs
- Additional Information
- Legalisations
- Consular Assistance
- Passport and other documentation

News

- Ceremonia oficial de la firma del Acta de constitución de la Comisión Internacional contra la Pena de Muerte
- El ministro asiste en Madrid al funeral del presidente chileno Patricio Aylwyn
- 400 años de la muerte de Cervantes
- Actividad del Consejo de Seguridad de las Naciones Unidas

Visas

(Versión en español)

The visa department of the Consulate of Spain in San Francisco will consider applications for all kind of Visas IN PERSON AND BY APPOINTMENT, one appointment per applicant. For all appointment matters please contact VFS GLOBAL.

Due to the amount of applications received by this office, it is recommended that you plan your trip to the Schengen area with sufficient time to schedule for an appointment and to process your visa application.

> For more information about VFS GLOBAL

To make an appointment please contact VFS GLOBAL at:

1-202-684-3193 or 1-869-231-7286 (Monday - Friday 8am to 5pm)

or go to the VFS website

http://www.vfsglobal.com/Spain/usa/SanFrancisco/

For additional information and assistance on the visa process, please email VFS GLOBAL at: info.esus.sa@vfshelpline.com or by Online Chat

At the time of your appointment, you must present the following:

1. Printed confirmation of your appointment
2. Visa Fees (exact cash or money order)
3. Completed Visa application form (Photo requirements)
4. All documentation required for the visa which you are applying for

Short Stay (Tourism and Business Visa)

- Schengen Visa application
- Schengen Visa Requirements
- Table of Countries whose citizens do / not require visa
- Entry Requirements for citizens that do not need a visa

Long Stay (National Visa)

- National Visa application
- Student Visa
- Language and Cultural Assistance Visa
- Au Pair Visa
- Work and Residence Visa
- Residence for Exempt of Work Permit
- Residence for Retiree
- Residence for Religious Activities
- Residence for Non-Lucrative

CHECK THIS LINK TO SEE IF YOU ARE ABLE TO APPLY BY MAIL!

Twitter

20 Apr
@ConsuladoEspSF
@anablancagaray El Consulado General tiene cuenta oficial en Twitter. En Facebook aún no.

16 Apr
@ConsuladoEspSF
#EspañaContigo Al llegar al extranjero recibirás un sms con los números de emergencia de tu Embajada/Consulado

16 Apr
@ConsuladoEspSF
#España líder mundial en trasplantes y donaciones de órganos. Hemos superado 100.000

You can also call your consulate and ask someone if you can't find the info on your own.

Making Your Visa Appointment

Don't delay on this! If you can't mail your paperwork in, you'll want to secure an online visa appointment (from your consulate's website listed above) sooner rather than later. Often times, you'll find that your consulate won't have any "good" appointments available. Keep checking! People cancel and appointments open up all the time... It's worth checking out frequently to get a good appointment. The best time for appointments varies so much from person to person. If you have a low inscrita number and you get your school placement early, make an appointment as soon as you'll have all of your documents gathered. I know of some who got their carta and then their school placement a week later and made their visa appointments for early June. For certain regions (like Madrid), cartas come out much later.

I didn't receive my carta until mid-July, which meant I couldn't apply for my visa until after! Pretty much all regions have their cartas sent out by July's end, so if you want to be safe, make your appointment for late July or early August – that still gives you plenty of time to get your visa back before orientation in Spain in mid-late September. Again, this all varies based on your own factors: regional placement, school assignment, inscrita number, etc. You'll also need the following documents in order to apply for your visa:

WARNING: If you've lived in another country for more than 6 months in the past 5 years, you'll need a background check from that country as well. I didn't have to do this, so good luck if that's you!

The Background Check – Criminal Records Check

If you are able to, I recommend using a *state background check*. You will need a background check from every state that you have lived in for the past 5 years. If you've only lived in one state, get the state background check! (For whatever reason, I think Arizona is the only state that requires you to do the FBI check). The state check will be easier, cheaper, and much faster. If you've lived in more than a couple of states, however, getting the FBI check will be easier. Keep in mind, though, that the FBI check can take a couple of *months (or more)* to get back, so plan accordingly!

The State Background Check

You will need to go to a local police station (or other location) that can do fingerprinting. My police station charged me $11 for up to three sets of prints. You'll then use the prints to get a background check. You'll need your background check to be properly notarized in order to take/mail it to the state apostille. The state of Montana costs $10.00 to get your background check done and another $10.00 to get it apostillized. I emailed the Montana DOJ to see exactly what I needed and she told me that the easiest thing to do was to:

1. **Get fingerprinted at the local police station (in Missoula for me).**
2. **Take the prints and mail them to the Montana Criminal Records Department in Helena to complete the state background check.**
3. **Have your state Criminal Records department send the background check to the Secretary of State Apostille with a filled out form and cover letter explaining your request, saying that you need the results notarized and apostillized.**

STATE CERTIFICATION
APOSTILLE or AUTHENTICATION REQUEST FORM

1. The document(s) is/are being certified for the **country** of:

_____

2. Please include a self-addressed stamped envelope for the return of the documents.

3. Complete your contact information:

_____
Name

_____
(Area Code) Phone Number

_____
Address

_____   _____   _____
City   State   Zip Code

_____   _____   _____
E-Mail Address   Signature   Date

Filing Fee: $10.00 per document

Enclosed is a check or money order for $_____ to cover the cost of _____ documents.

Make payable to Secretary of State and mail your request to:

SECRETARY OF STATE
NOTARY AND CERTIFICATION SERVICES
PO BOX 202801
1301 6TH AVENUE
HELENA MT 59620-2801

If you have any questions please visit our website www.sos.mt.gov/Notary
Contact us at (406) 444-1877 or sosnotary@mt.gov

Example above of a certificate for the state of Montana

4. Include a $10.00 check/money order for the background check and another $10.00 check/money order for the apostille. This depends on your state.

5. Include a self addressed, prepaid envelope to have the results sent back to you.

6. Patiently wait as your request is processed and mailed back to you! *Remember, you'll need the original and a copy to get your visa.*

7. *Note: not all consulates require you to get a fingerprint-based state background check. Follow your consulate's requirements to see what yours specifies (San Francisco requires fingerprint-based checks).*

8. State Apostille

9. For any state do a quick Google search for your state's Secretary of State Apostille. The State Apostille will need your background check to be notarized before you can get it apostillized, so don't forget that step! Like I listed above, your state will most likely require you to fill out a form explaining that this is for a visa and you'll have to list the country it is for (Spain). Attach a quick cover letter explaining your needs. Here's what I used:

Secretary of State
Notary and Certification Services
P.O. Box 202801
1301 6th Avenue
Helena MT 59620-2801

To Whom It May Concern:

I am requesting that my official state background check from the Montana State Police be authenticated with the apostille of the Hague Convention. I will be using this document to apply for a visa for the country of Spain at the San Francisco Spanish Consulate. This document should be returned to me at the address listed below.

Sincerely,

It typically takes the Montana SOS Office 3-5 *days* for processing, but I'm sure that varies state to state. You can always call or email your SOS to find out turnaround time on getting yours back!

The FBI Background Check

If you've lived in more than one state in the past 5 years, you might want to consider getting the FBI Check. To get an FBI Check you will need to **visit this page** to see **https://www.fbi.gov/services/cjis/identity-history-summary-checks** what you'll need. You should also write a cover letter to let them know you are requesting a notarized background check to apply for a long term visa and that you'll need it to have a signature of the official's name, title and seal of the agency.

1. Get your fingerprints done on a **FD 258 Form**, which your local police station should be able to do.
2. Fill out an **identify form** to be sent in with your fingerprints.
3. Include a **credit card payment form**. As of 2017, it costs $18.00 to get this done.
4. Don't forget to include a cover letter explaining you'll need to have the results notarized, & the signature of the official's name, title, and seal of the agency!
5. Mail all your documents off to the following address:

FBI CJIS Division
Summary Request
1000 Custer Hollow Road
Clarksburg, WV 26306

6. Patiently wait for them to mail this back to you... It typically takes between 12 and 15 weeks (yes, 3-4 months).

The FBI check does not require you to include a self addressed, prepaid envelope. All of this information can be found on the first link I posted for the FBI Background Check. Because this process can take a long time, many people use an **FBI Channeler**, such as **My FBI Report** or **Accurate Biometrics**. Unfortunately, this can be a bit more costly! The upside is that it saves you *lots* of time, which might be important (especially if summer is already here). Instead of waiting 3+ months to get your FBI background check done, you can get it in about a week. You will still need to send it in to get it Apostillized in Washington D.C.

The FBI Apostille

You can visit **this link**
https://travel.state.gov/content/travel/en/legal/travel-legal-considerations/internl-judicial-asst/authentications-and-apostilles/requesting-authentication-services.html
To see the U.S. Department of State's webpage for Washington D.C. on how to request authentication services for your FBI checks. If you're going to mail it in, complete **the form requested.** As of 2017, this will cost you $10.00 to have it done. According to their website, you will mail your documents to the following address:

Office of Authentications
U.S. Department of State
CA/PPT/S/TO/AUT
44132 Mercure Cir, P.O. Box 1206
Sterling, VA 20166-1206

For the FBI Apostille, include a self addressed, prepaid envelope to ensure that you get your documents sent back! They say the Federal Apostille process takes about 10-15 days to complete once they start it (which may be a few days after they receive it). Plan on **about** 3 weeks to receive the FBI Apostille back.

The Medical Certificate

Like the background check, your medical certificate will need to be less than 90 days old at the time of your visa application. It must be filled out by a Medical Doctor (MD) with an official letterhead from your doctor. This letter should indicate that you have been examined and found free of any contagious diseases according to the International Health Regulation 2005. **Below** see an example of what the letter should look like. That link is specifically for the San Francisco consulate, but I *think* the medical certification is the same for all consulates. **Double check your consulate's website to see what exactly you need.** It can be in Spanish or English, but *some* consulates will require you to have the Spanish translations.

Medical Certificate of Good Health

Notes sent on prescription pad paper will not be accepted. Once the original is returned with your visa, please KEEP THE ORIGINAL FOR FUTURE VISA PROCESSING you will need in Spain. Please use the following format:

"This health certificate verifies that Mr/Ms ..... is free of drug addiction, mental illness and does not suffer from any disease that could cause serious repercussions to the public health according to the specifications of the international sanitary regulations of 2005. These contagious diseases include, but are not limited to smallpox, poliomyelitis by wild poliovirus, the human influenza caused by a new subtype of virus and the severe acute respiratory syndrome (SARS), cholera, pneumonic plague, yellow fever, viral hemorrhagic fevers (e.g.: Ebola, Lassa, Marburg), West Nile Virus and other illnesses of special importance nationally or regionally (e.g.: Dengue Fever, Rift Valley Fever and Meningococcal disease).

Mr./Ms _____ is a very healthy individual in all senses, she/he has no pre-existing medical conditions, and she/he is capable of travelling abroad".

Place and date:
Signature:
Official Physician Stamp:

A fairly generic letter, remember to keep it for getting your TIE/NIE in Spain!

If you have a typical doctor that you go to, simply call and make an appointment. The more your doctor knows you, the easier this will be to have completed. Some doctors might require a simple physical. Others will want blood work done... You might also need to get up to date immunizations, but this is a fairly simple process. Explain that you need this letter for your Spanish visa application and it must be on the MD's letterhead and hand signed and dated. If you don't have a typical doctor that you visit, just call ahead and explain what you need and ask whether or not the MD will complete this for you. I'm sure most will!

Good luck!

Last Steps to Finalize the VISA Completion

You're almost done! Now you know how to get your background check and medical certificate, so the rest is fairly simple. Scroll back up to the top to make sure you have everything (numbers 1-10) checked off your list! Don't forget to download your corresponding Visa Application form to be sent in with the rest of your documents. Personally, because I use the San Francisco Consulate, I just mailed my paperwork in.

A lot of consulates don't allow that though, so you may have to make an appointment and go in person to get your visa paperwork turned in. Visit your consulate's website (which I have listed above) to see how to go about making an appointment. Before you go, head to your local post office and make sure you bring with you a self addressed Express Mail Envelope with $22.95 worth of postage.

Make sure you get the information to track it! This is what they'll use to mail back your passport and visa, so you'll want to know where it's at, at all times! While you're there, you can also get your $160 money order made payable to "Consulate General of Spain" in most cases (check your specific consulate website to verify – listed under "Visa Fees"). You can also get your money order from a bank or bring exact change in cash if you go in person.

And that's it! Yes, it's a lot of stuff to remember, but it's really not too bad. A lot of people like to tell you how horrible and bureaucratically painful the process is, but I feel it's more about being prepared. Know what you need ahead of time, and if you're not sure, call! Someone will have the answer for you. Bring extra [colored] copies of everything (can't hurt) and double-check your consulate's visa requirements to make sure you have everything you need!

*Remember** that the turnaround time to get your passport/visa back can take around a month! The consulates are especially busy towards the end of summer, so try to get your stuff in as soon as you can to ensure that you get yours back with enough time left before you head to Spain. Keep all of your original documentation too. You'll want to have that in Spain when you apply for your TIE/NIE (which you'll need to do in order to open a bank account and set up a cell phone). But you can worry about that later!

For now, just relax and be happy because you're one step closer to Spain!

Trevor Huxham **admin** → Eric Roddy • 2 years ago
Hi Eric,

11. A DNI is something all Spaniards have, kind of like a Social Security #, so just leave it blank.
26. Leave this blank as it doesn't apply to the auxiliares situation.
27. Leave this blank since you're not applying for work authorization but for a student visa.

You do need to fill out 28 with your school's information.

BIG REMINDER: I AM WRITING THIS IN CAPITAL LETTERS, SO YOU KNOW IT'S VERY IMPORTANT. IT MIGHT SAVE YOU TIME, MONEY AND A FEW NERVOUS BREAKDOWNS.

ALWAYS MAKE 2 COPIES OF ALL YOUR DOCUMENTS, BE IT NIE, TIE, PASSPORT, CARTA DE NOMBRAMIENTO OR AUTORIZACIÓN REGRESO AND KEEP IT WITH A FAMILY MEMBER RELATIVE OR FRIEND IN A SAFE PLACE AND THE OTHER SET WITH YOU !!

IN CASE YOU LOSE THEM YOU'LL NEED THEM!!

WARNING : You don't need to translate the background check, however I would have it translate and remember whatever documents you're asked to be translated must always have a stamp or the apostille on them!

CHAPTER 5
CHECKLIST: THINGS TO DO B4 YOU MOVE TO SPAIN

Just before I was finishing up my second year working in Spain as an *auxiliar de conversación* around 2003-2004, I already had a good grasp of what was going on in Spain. I knew exactly which stores and bars to go to get nice quality cheap or even free food and other pretty amazing clothing and accommodation deals they usually have in Spain. Looking back now I wish I could punch myself at some of the big mistakes I made. There is so much stuff to learn, I wish I had known that would have saved me tons of time and money. I used get so many messages and emails from people asking me about how to get ready for moving to Spain that I have collected a few of the replies throughout the years and I may as well share it with you here.

Expenses before You Come to Spain

I'm no a stingy guy. But, when you're trying to save money to go abroad, sometimes being a bit stingy is necessary! I learned that if I wanted to make the move to Spain, some things needed to change in regards to my expenses. [Pot and Booze were out of the picture]

I went out a lot less, lived at home to save money, and worked a lot of double shifts to save money, and didn't eat out as much or waste on unnecessary items. Whatever money I spent before Spain was either on things I thought I would need (i.e.: food, clothes, shoes, etc.) Before even getting to Spain, Auxiliares will need to go and get their student visa beforehand. Below is a cost breakdown of what I had to pay for to be eligible to get my student visa and get to Spain:

Background Check – $10-20
Notary for the background check – $25
Physical and doctor's note saying I was healthy and sane – This is usually covered by your health insurance, if you have one of course.
Student Visa application – $150-200
Flight to Spain – $500-800 [Buy a one way ticket to Spain when moving first, because you wont know for sure when you'd be back home)

Timing - Come to Spain the Earliest. This depends pretty much on your assigned city, you should come at least 2 weeks or so earlier to get settled an find an apartment, [If your city is Madrid, Barcelona or Seville, one of the biggies, I suggest coming no later than the first week of September] visit your new schools, get a head start on finding private classes, or academy hopping [I'll cover this academy topic in later chapters] and adjust to your new life in Spain.

I was an airhead and decided to spend the 2 weeks with my best pal Bate in London instead, before heading down to Vigo the first year as an auxiliar. Not only did I end up spending an awful lot of money, but I also had no time to find a piso [apartment/flat in Spanish] before work started.

In a pueblo or the countryside in Spain you'll find accommodation in no time, but if you are in big cities with universities, many of them start classes at the beginning of October, which means that all of the apartments are picked over and you'll have to settle for living in the apartment from hell. Make sure to check out with other fellow auxiliares via Facebook or instagram. **Join a Facebook auxiliares local group**. Usually they start with auxiliares de conversación Madrid, Coruña, Logroño, Bilbao and so forth. Maybe, they'll lend you a hand, crash on someone's couch or they may already some looking for a roommate, though I always consider this a temporary solution. The best bet is to share a piso with the locals.

Money Money Money- HOW MUCH MONEY SHOULD I SAVE BEFORE MOVING ABROAD: AUXILIARES DE CONVERSACIÓN? Save your pennies! Spain might be one of the cheapest countries to live in in Europe, but it still ain't free. La Fiesta never stops in Spain!
One of the questions I used to get a lot was: *"How are you going to survive over there if you only get paid 700€ a month"*

However, being an American, you have a many work opportunities, too, many people will ask you for conversational lessons since the Spanish system only teaches writing and grammar. So there's great demand for speaking classes in all regions.

Let's cut to the chase!

Well, if you think about the US, one thing is very obvious: The United States is relatively expensive. Our salaries are higher than some countries to cover the cost of living in different areas.

For example, California is a pretty expensive area. If you go to the Midwest or further East or South, some areas are not as expensive. The same applies to Spain. So, how much money do you need to save before moving abroad? And how much money do you need to survive in Spain?

Note that the first payment of the auxiliares program won't come in until November or sometimes even first week in December. It just depends on the region you go to. Regions like Galicia, Andalusia or the Basque country paychecks are speedy and steady.

Can you imagine moving here in September and not getting any substantial amount of money until December? When I first came here, they recommended we come with around $600 saved up, in 2002 that was less than 400 euros. That's a joke really! You wont last a month with that amount unless you go bumming money and food around!

You should bring to Spain at least $2-3,000!

Savings for Spain			
Description	Salary		
Leftover savings from college	$1500~		
	$11/hr plus tips		
	Total tips by Sept. $500		
	Total earned by Sept. $4000		
Money from graduation	$1,700		
Going away gifts	$600		
		Total for Spain: $5000~	

You'll have to get from the airport to your city, add fares for taxis, buses, trains with all your luggage, potentially staying in a hostel or *pensión* until you find an apartment, phone credit, food until you have a kitchen, then paying for an apartment plus a deposit. Then if you need to buy things for it, like sheets, pillows, towels, etc.... then start-up groceries, installing internet [DO NOT BUY A **PINCHO-Wi-Fi usb flash drive** to connect wireless from your mac or laptop- use a regular internet home provider or many cafeterias have free Wi-Fi even large areas like the city halls or shopping malls] etc., and then to live for at least a month until you get paid. It really adds up. If you're worried about how much it can cost to start a new life in Spain, here's a rough estimate of an auxiliary or an English Teacher in Spain.

Expenses in Spain (monthly & setting up)

Description	Cost/Monthly Cost	My Payment	Notes
Security Deposit			
-- Piso #1 (Year 1) Castilla La Mancha	200€	200€	
-- Piso #2 (Year 1) Castilla La Mancha	385€	130€	
-- Piso #3 (Year 2) Andalucía	250€	125€	
Rent for a piso			
-- Piso #1 (Year 1) Castilla La Mancha	200€	200€	
-- Piso #2 (Year 1) Castilla La Mancha	385€	130€	
-- Piso #3 (Year 2) Andalucía	250€	125€	
Utilities			
-- Piso #1 (Year 1) Castilla La Mancha	100€	50€	
-- Piso #2 (Year 1) Castilla La Mancha	240€	80€	- Utilities for this piso were extremely high. This wasn't normal. We also had one heating bill that was almost as much as rent!
-- Piso #3 (Year 2) Andalucía	120€	60€	
Groceries	120-150€	30-50€/weekly	- When I lived alone, I would pay 30€/weekly for groceries. 50€/weekly or bi-weekly for groceries.
Going Out (tapas, beers, dinner, etc)		100€ 20€/weekly	
Travel Spending		150€ 150€/monthly	- I tried to plan a trip within Spain and outside of Spain once a month.
Random (clothes, gifts, etc)	50-100€	50-100€/monthly	- I never went shopping too often, but when I did see something I liked, I would buy it. Also, after the Three Kings holiday in January, there are a lot of great sales. I usually try to buy during that time.
Phone Payments		20€ 10€/monthly	- I had a pay as I go phone, that I would fill up when I ran out of data. This was probably once a month
Emergency Money		50€ 50€/monthly	- I would always make sure I had 50-100€ for just incase money. I rarely touched this, because I never needed to, but it was always there to help pay for things.

While I went out for tapas, cañas with friends, there were still times I did away with a lot of things. I wanted to save as much as possible to travel as much as possible and meet new people and other languages like French and Italian. This also meant that I took on a lot more private English classes than the average auxiliary de conversación. This is a snippet of what the income looked like while living in Spain.

Income			School year 2013-14
Description	**Income**	**Monthly Total**	**Notes**
Auxiliar de Conversación	700€	700€	
Private Lessons	€15 euros/hr		- During my first year teaching, I lived in a VERY small town. I only charged €15 euros/hr for a private lesson
	€20-25 euros/hr		- During my second year, I started to up my prices and would charge an average of €20-25 euros/hr
	15-20€/hr		- Sometimes, I gave "deals" to students who decided to take classes more than once a week. If they opted for a once a week class, there was a different price. If it was twice a week, I would give them a small discount.
	Total Year 1:	1800€ euros/m	- I worked private lessons my first year from 3:30pm-9:30pm
	Total Year 2:	2600€ euros/m	- My second year, I had private lessons from 4pm-8:30pm, and a few morning lessons depending on my schedule
Extra work /bitcoin mining	$35-75	$250-350	
Transfer to Savings	-$300-400	-$300-400	- To make sure I saved up money, and didn't spend everything I had in Spain, I would transfer $300-400/month back to my account in the United States. This helped pay for any existing credit card bills I had (ie: buying plane tickets home) or just as a savings

Some months were really good, overall, the months in Fall and Winter. Work in Spain will wane down just right after April. There were months I was raking well over $3,500 ...

I suggest transferring a 20-30% of your income to your account in the United States each month. This helps you keep track of your savings, gives you some money if you decide to come home and start job hunting, and is like an extra savings account for you!

Having 700€ a month or 1,000€ [Madrid auxiliares program] in Spain is more than enough for you to live comfortably. Of course, in different areas of the country, the cost of living varies. But, if you can supplement your income with a few extra revenue streams, you will be set!

Just don't blow your hard earned cash (or coins) on fiestas or puticlubs! I know a fistful of stories, first hand, from either American boys or girls who had to go back home with their tail between their legs due to their compulsive fiesta behavior!

Contact your schools ASAP

When I first came to Vigo in 2003, I hadn't contacted my school in advance at all, but when I found out the name of my school for the second year in Madrid, I went and visited them in June, and kept in contact with them throughout the summer. Your best bet is to contact your schools around May or June otherwise you'll have to wait later on until September 10. If you are lucky, they will answer your emails, but more than likely you have to actually call them. I'd only worked, at the beginning, at elementary schools, (*CEIP-colegio de educación infantil y primaria*), and they are usually open from 9 to 2. Once summer vacation hits at the end of June, it'll be almost impossible to talk to anyone.

Schools in Spain. What are they like?

I am of the opinion that the education is quite different in Spain compared to the schools, for example, I use to attend in California. I find that the classrooms are extremely basic here in Spain and there just isn't much funding in the way of supplies and hands-on materials for the kids. Sometimes it does feel like you're are stepping back in time with all lecture-based-classes with loads of memorization and homework. Schools in Catalunya, Basque country and Madrid are much more high tech and similar to the ones back home. Attendance is compulsory from ages 3-16, so they don't really understand or acknowledge the concept of homeschool.

If you have children and have to live with you in Spain, it is expected they will be enrolled in school. I do however know few people who are residing in Spain and are not registered with the school. This can be accomplished depending on your citizenship, visa option and/or the luck you have at your foreigner's office.

The school grounds are very basic with a blacktop/cement play area and possible a basketball hoop or fútbol [soccer] goal posts. There aren't usually many playgrounds or supplies on campus at schools. That said, they do walk too many of their field trips and they do sometimes go to the community pool or to the beach for the Physical Education class. So they do use the environment around to meet the needs rather than having it on the school grounds. This is pretty good for socialization purposes.

School Calendar

Typically the school year is from the 2nd week in September through the 3rd week in June. You may give or take a week depending on where the school is located and the type of school.

School hours in Spain

There isn't one standard across the country, so you will need to do your research based on the area you would like to live. Alternatively, you may choose to live in an area because of the school schedule they follow. Some schools have 1 continuous session during the day and others have 2 sessions, where the kids go home for a 2-3 hours in the middle of the day.

1. **School hours in Spain for primary grade levels:**

    A. From 9am – 2pm, with option for comedor (lunch and supervised play 2pm – 4pm)

    B. From 9am – 12pm and 3pm – 5pm with option for comedor
(lunch and supervised play 12pm – 3pm), the "break hours" may vary slightly in your area.

    C. Lunch is usually at home from 2pm – 4pm, so the break at school for 30-minute recess snack.

    D. International school is often a full day, from 9:45am – 5pm

2. **School hours in Spain for secondary grade levels:**

    A. From 8:15am – 2:50pm (some schools offer afternoon or night options)

    B. International school is often a full day, from 9:45am – 5pm

Spanish School Vocabulary

- **Comedor** – It's typically lunch and supervised play for 2 hours. This is an additional fee and there are options for financial assistance. In my school in 2004 this was 4.50€ per day per child. My school did not have a full kitchen, so meals were catered in each day.

- **Recreo** – Recess! Who doesn't love recess? Well, I usually just receive about 30 minutes and this includes anytime I want to take to eat a snack or have a drink. Depending on the school facilities and AMPA (Parents association, like PTA), they may or may not sell food items. Typically kids bring a snack and drink from home on a lunch box. Auxiliares sometimes start teaching at 9.00 am but then there will be some idle time in between 11-1.00 pm and may be you´ll have to teach from 3-4 again. So you´ll have plenty of free time in between sometime. Try to get your schedule and time slots as close as possible, so you can do other work and have a more efficient schedule.

Types of Schools in Spain

- **Colegios públicos** – State-funded public schools.
- **Colegios concertados** – State-funded private schools, there may be fees you need to pay in some locations, as it is not fully funded.
- **Colegios privados** – Private schools. Since some private schools are publicly funded, the line between public and private is blurred. It is common for these to be Catholic schools.
- **International Schools in Spain** – I guess this would fall into the private schools in Spain, but they are usually with a curriculum from another country, most often an English-speaking country (British, American or Australian). The International School in our town is a British curriculum. The international schools do tend to have more hands on experiences, supplies and more organized activities.

The educational system breakdown in Spain is as follows,

Primary School = CEIP [Colegio de Educación Infantil y Primaria]
- **Infantil – preschool- kindergarden ages 3-5**
- **Primary School preschool – grades 1- 6**

Secondary School = IES institutos [instituto enseñanza secundaria]
- **(Educación Segundaria Obligatoria), Second Obligatory Education.**
- Once a Spanish student graduates from ESO, students have three different choices:
  1. **Bachillerato – Grades 11-12, Junior and Senior year in high school,** but it isn't mandatory. It's intended for college prep. Students who successfully complete the requirements of the Spanish high school Baccalaureate will receive a diploma. They may then opt for vocational training, a university education, or in some cases both. In order to continue on to the university they must take an entrance exam (Prueba de Acceso a la Universidad – PAU). The test results together with the student's academic record and grades will determine not only access to the university but also which degrees the student can pursue.
  2. **FP** [Formación profesional] : **Ciclo Formativo de Grado Medio and Ciclo Formativo de Grado Superior:** Vocational/Professional training (Electrician, hairdresser, etc.)

ALWAYS ASK

Don't forget to ask for a contact email of your **coordinator** for the summer, maybe even ask the name of the auxiliar from last year to contact them yourself, get the DL on your school, maybe try to mention what your schedule might be/ask for consecutive hours. They'll probably change it around, but it can't hurt to ask. My first year **schedule** sucked because they gave me hours that weren't back to back. I had to wake up at 6:00 to work at 10 and I worked 12 hours a week but spent about 20 hours total at the school waiting for rides and the bus.

Try to get a schedule, working from 9-12 Monday to Thursday. Some people get shafted and have to work Mon, Tue, Wed and Fri, so ask about that too. But most importantly, ask what the **payment situation** was like the year before, if the auxiliares were paid on time or if the school itself pays you directly; this should help you decide on how much money to save before coming.

Transportation

To be honest, I never paid more than $600 for a one-way flight to Spain, but I am extremely stingy when it comes to shelling out for flights, and I am also flying from the west coast, So fares will apply different if you fly from Boston, New York or Los Angeles LAX. I recommend buying a one-way flight because who knows what your situation might be around May when things get wrapped up. You might wanna stay a few more months even stay the whole summer etc.... (Usually, it is not legal, you are only allowed to stay a few days after your visa expires or must obtain a prorroga from your work)

Some helpful websites for looking for cheap flights are Kayak, AerLingus, STAtravel, **Easyjet** [for domestic and European flights], **Ryanair** [international and domestic flights-the cheapest one- without a doubt] and StudentUniverse.

DO NOT ASK PEOPLE TO MAIL YOU STUFF FROM THE USA. IT´S GONNA BE VERY EXPENSIVE

Spain's customs laws are very restrictive, so now if you try to mail a lot of stuff with high value, it will get blocked in Madrid and you will have to pay a lot in import taxes. Going through this can be a nightmare, so don't count on being able to have your friends and family send you big boxes of stuff from home.

BIG REMINDER: YOU´RE BETTER OFF TO FLY INTO MADRID, THEN CATCH A BUS OR TRAIN TO YOUR NEW CITY OR PUEBLO. UNLESS YOU´RE IN BARCELONA, THE SPAIN TRAIN COMPANY IS RENFE. YOUR BEST BET IS TO BUY TICKETS ONLINE OR WAIT TILL YOU GET TO SPAIN TO BUY THEM. GET AN ALSA OR MONBUS, BUSLINK. GOOGLE **"YOUR CITY + AUTOBUS"** YOU USUALLY FIND THE COMPANY.

Save yourself the trouble and send just parcels not over 1-2 kg. Unfortunately, your also gonna have to tell lies about the contents, placing the value around $10 or less. That's how I get my stuff through without any problem, otherwise ship it with a specific international carrier designed to help you with heavy parcels and boxes [**www.themovingboxcompany.com**] overseas.

And don't even try to over pack 60-70lbs of stuff in your case on the flight back. They will make you pay a lot or give you a fine at the airport or like a friend of mine who had to throw away or leave behind some of his valuables at the airport.

The art of packing: Pack your luggage tops 40- 50lb suitcase

Let me go ahead and state the obvious. **DO NOT OVERPACK.** You are moving to Spain for a year, you are going to buy things there. You gonna get all that stuff home after a year if you show up at the airport in September with two overweight checked bags, carry-ons, and wearing all your winter clothes?

Be smart! Do you really need 5 pairs of jeans? Nope.
There are jeans in Spain, in fact, really good jeans that cost a whole lot less than ones from the US. You can pretty much find everything you need in Spain that you have back home, and most of the time it is **cheaper**. Towels and bed sheets are cheap, and you can find most of the things you need for your apartment at Spain's equivalent of **99-cent stores, the *chinos* or *cash & carry* stores.**

If you are a girl you can find tampons in Spain. YEP! *Facepalm. YESSSSS!* You're moving to Spain not to Syria. And if you are a boy and need *Trojan* condoms you can buy *Durex*, it´s same thing with a different name, and yes they have XXL American size, too!

Fit your life in **one suitcase and one carry-on.** Last time I checked they almost never weigh carry-ons on international flights from the US; you aren't flying Ryanair [this airline does not allow any bags or luggage on the plane deck.]

Put all your heavy stuff in it, wear your jeans, boots, and winter coats, the stuff that takes up the most space, and you're good to go! Throw everything else in **space-saver bags.** You'll thank yourself in June or later on in the year when you come back home.

When packing, pack up your suitcase, **unpack it, and then repack it.** Taking stuff out. Repeat as needed. The worst is waiting a few hours before your flight departs to pack and then bringing a bunch of **unnecessary** stuff. I, in fact, travel with 3 pairs of shorts, 2 Carhart hooded sweaters, a pair of jeans, 2 pairs of sneakers, some T shirts, socks and underwear and I pack it all in a backpack. I don't even bother with suitcases or carry-ons. Passport, iPhone 8, and a set of Xeroxed copies of my outmost important documents in my big jacket pocket. And my emergency cash in a special inside belt customized for the purpose of hiding money. Take a few credit cards, valid almost everywhere like VISA and MASTERCARD. That's it! Whatever else I need later, I always buy it in Spain or even Portugal-that is even cheaper and greater quality.

Layers when packing

This part is directed to women since I figure they pack a lot of layers. No matter where you are in Spain, even in Andalucía, winter is cold and people are stingy with heating. Wear lots of layers, sweaters, scarves, and boots. Are you planning to stay through the summer? If not, don't bring a lot of summer clothes because realistically, you won't start wearing them till April or later. Most of your time in Spain will be chilly or cold, so pack accordingly. Also **pack according to your regions.**

If you are in Pais Vasco-Basque Country-Euskadi, Cantabria, Asturias or Galicia, you know that it rains a lot. Bring a good raincoat and boots. In Madrid it is sunny for most of the year, so you can probably do without. Forget your UGGS, Stiletto heels or high heels. Roads and sidewalks in Spain are bumpy-some have holes in winter- and not made for these kind of shoe ware.

Also, for the most part, **you can dress however you want** to school. If you're a man, jeans, khakis, sneakers and a sweater or a jacket is okay. You don't have to wear formal. And as for women in "business casual" is okay, too. I'm Californian and for the most part I am wearing smart shorts, hoodie sweatshirts and my Nike sneakers. Talk about comfortable. In general people dress nicer here, but don't feel pressured to bring a business outfit or a tie, dress pants or button-ups because more than likely you won't have to wear them. Also, big name international brands like Northface, Wilson, Adidas, Carharrt, and Nike are **more expensive** here.

So if you need something from those brands, your better off buying it in the States. If you are curious about how men and women dress in Spain, Google work places and dress codes or men's & women's fashion in Spain. There are tons of websites and YouTube videos.

Don´t come to Spain and expect to find American Food! It´s a no-go!

There are many things you can't find easily in Spain. Every time I hop on that red-eye flight over to Barcelona, there are always a few key things I bring with me that I know are almost impossible to find (**cheaply, easily, or not at all**) in Spain. If you are living in or near Barcelona, you are lucky because there are some "American" grocery stores here, but for the rest of us, it's a lot harder!

Books and movies in English. Forget about it! I am a **BIG** reader. I always have to be read. You won´t find either movies or books in English in Spain. The TV is dubbed in Spanish. With France, Germany and Italy movies and TV sitcoms are for the most part dubbed in Spanish. No subtitles, no Original version. Also, websites like Pandora, Hulu, and Netflix don't work in Spain unless you know how to block your laptop's IP address.

If you wanna watch a movie in English, you might have to get on the Internet to watch your favorite series or go to a specialized Cines de Versión Original – OV Movie Theater in Spanish. And books weigh a lot so it's hard to bring them or ship them. You´re better off having a kindle, a tablet or your iPhone and read them from those devices like I do most of the time. When I resided in Galicia, I would cross the Spanish border down south and go to the movies in Viana do Castelo. Movies in Portugal come with subtitles. It's a worth a shot. A great site operational from Spain to watch movies is **pelispedia.tv. Or the app WISEPLAY.** I have now some girls visiting from New York and Grand Rapids at my workplace and they have told me that **American women's make-up** and some of the brands you girls buy in the States are either overpriced in Spain or nowhere to be found. They tell me also that deodorants and toothpaste suck big time in Spain. So there you go!

I also wear **contact lenses or glasses** that I can't find here in Spain, so I always make sure to stock up when I am back in the States or have a relative send them to me.

However, as a general rule, **medicine is A LOT cheaper in Spain** than back home [I'll cover this topic in the chapter Insurances, Health care and Medicare in Spain], nevertheless, it's better to wait and get stuff here that you might need. You can get a lot of stuff cheap and over the counter here without prescription.

Mc Donald's and Burger King have special deals every now and then and they have developed an app which they give away a lot of stuff and sometimes you can get several menus for peanuts. However, Mc Donald's and Burger King are still more expensive in Spain than in the USA.

Electronics, Cell Phones and Macs

While most things in Spain are cheaper than back in the States, **electronic devices** are not one of them. If you have a Mac or laptop about to crack, the LAST thing in the world you want is for it to die in Spain. There are only a few Apple stores in the 4 major cities, including Barcelona. But, its very very **"expensivo amigo!"** Get your device or gadget **checked out** before leaving for Spain and invest in a new one if you can. Unlock your American iPhone or smartphone before you come here if you can, to use while in Spain. They should be operational with the Spanish carriers **Orange, Yooigo, Vodafone, R telefonia, Movistar, Tuenti, jazztel, mobilcat, simyio, happymovil, pepephone.com, lowi.es,** etc...

iPhones, cameras, iPods and Apple products cost a lot more in Spain than back home, and you can't mail it internationally **without paying a lot of fees.**

If something gets stolen, please report it to the **Local Guardia Civil** o **Policia Nacional**, whether it be your passport, iPhone or whatever. I use my MacBook and iPad for everything here; they're my TV, my phone, my everything. It's probably the most important thing I've brought with me. Make sure it can last.

Get a sim card for your cell phone or iPhone, and top it up, buy **Pay as you go cards** or credits –**saldo** in Spanish [credit voucher from €5-10 euros] you can buy credits for your cell phone anywhere in Spain from supermarkets, shopping malls, tobacconists [tabacaleras] and even grocery stores. WhatsApp is Spain's favorite way of texting and even calling. Don't get a contract with a carrier in Spain. Just get a sim card with reusable credit. Most contracts are a rip-off. You'll spend mostly 10-20 euros a month on phone charges if you just have an unlocked cell phone. You'll save a lot of money.

For the girls, **don't bring hair straighteners or hair dryers**, you can find them in Spain very cheap and you risk breaking them on the different power outlets here. In Spain the standard voltage is 220-230V. Bring a combined power plug adapter/voltage converter. There cheaper and work fine in the States. Here, they tend to be sketchy.

MARISA K   REPLY

December 18, 2016 at 1:32 am

thanks so much for all of the information you've given! i just recently decided that i want to do the auxiliar program, and all of your Book have been so helpful. i'm a bit confused about the timeline for the background check, though. it has to be within 90 days if the appointment, but it can take 3-4 months to receive? so...i assume it's 90 days from the time i receive it? when should i request it? and also, i'm currently studying abroad in alcalá de henares, but only for 4 months. i'll be going to the chicago consulate, and it doesn't specify if i need to get a background check from here if i've only lived here for 4 months. any idea about that? from getting my visa last summer i know that the chicago consulate is a hot mess, so i know it'll be difficult to contact them. again, thanks so much for all your help!

CHAPTER 6
YOUR GOLDEN TICKET
THE NIE & TIE CONUNDRUM

How to Apply for a NIE & TIE : Residence Card (Tarjeta Comunitaria) in Spain

Congratulations! You made it to Spain! You've overcome the hurdle of applying for the program! You booked a plane ride over the Atlantic and into the land of your dreams!

Wow! What a feat! You may be asking yourself, "What comes next?"

You should probably begin the daunting task of finding an apartment (ok, I've heard that before somewhere?????). And, of course, you're going to have to apply for your TIE!

Well, Well Well!

You thought the life of pain and torture for you was over...

Well, Let me tell you...

This was probably the most painful thing of all things that I have to write about in the eBook. Why? Because, Spanish bureaucracy is one hell of a ride. I had to endure the torturous probing of the Spanish **funcionarios** [**Civil Servants**- In Spain they're unfireable- They surely don't know the catchphrase "YOU ARE FIRED!" it does not happen in Spain. They actually cannot be fired! They are very helpful at times but if you bump into one of those government dickheads...

Houston we Have a **BIG** problem!] When it came to getting my residence card. I wish you the best when it comes to the NIE & TIE nitty gritty business. They don't just hand those things out like candy in Spain! You know? You have to actually go through nine circles of bureaucratic hell. Some have decided to try, myself included, explaining it and I want to share my experience with you. I 've looked around on the internet, you have a few explanations, outlines and checklists here and there, but none of them is complete with all the info and accuracy that I'm gonna be presenting here. So, You'll be able to get it, sure, without any hassle.

You have to do this as soon as you come off the plane and arrive at your Spanish destination. I have tried to explain it and illustrate it here as best I can. Theres's no formula for this. But this will get you close enough to the finish line when you are lining up at the Brigada de Extranjería.

Should you follow my instructions word for word. You'll surely get the NIE, and thus the TIE right on 100%.

What is the tarjeta comunitaria?

Family members of a Spanish citizen or of another European Union/European Economic Area (EEA) member state, who do not hold citizenship of any of the aforementioned states and who wish to reside in Spain for a period of more than three months are eligible to apply for a 5-year residence card called the *Tarjeta de Familiar Comunitario.* For Americans, Aussies Canadians and other extra communitaries who are not married to a Spaniard must renew it each year.

This card allows you to **move and reside** freely within the member states of the European Union, show employers that you're allowed to **work in the EU and EEA member states** and qualify for certain **benefits and services.** [Ill cover some of this topic in the chapter of academics and extra work]

Peter L
March 14, 2016 12.32 pm

Your *Número de Identificación de Extranjero* (NIE) is listed in your visa. You can use it for opening a bank account, getting a library card, applying for your metro abono, etc.

Your *Tarjeta de Identificación de Extranjero* (TIE) is what you need to be a legal resident of Spain. You must schedule an appointment for your TIE within the first 30 days of your arrival in Spain. The appointment itself can be anytime before or after the 30 day window. I highly suggest everyone use this thorough walkthrough to reference how to obtain the TIE.

⟲ **REPLY**

Peter L
March 14, 2016 12.32 pm

On to the new things. Apparently starting this year, **all auxiliares will have to enroll in a Massive Online Open Course (MOOC) for language assistant training. There was also mentions of turning in some media project (website, video, portfolio, etc.) before the end of the school year.** Crazy right? Well, what's even crazier is that we didn't really get more information than that before it was on to the next topic. We were referred to check the website at a later date for more info.

💬 **REPLY**

Did You Know?

CRIS
December 7, 2015 at 11:16 pm

- The emergency phone number is Spain is 112 (and there are English speaking operators available)
- Pickpocketing is the #1 crime reported to the embassy
- Starbucks is the #1 location of pickpocketing offenses (watch your shit, people)

What else could you possibly need the embassy for? **Well, if your passport is ever lost or stolen, you can receive an emergency replacement with no hassle.** First, you have to file a police report, and then you must schedule an appointment with the embassy Monday through Fri between 8 am to 1 pm. The fee is $135, and it is due at the time of appointment. The embassy also helps with jail visits, returning bodily remains, safety/welfare checks, and etc., but that's nothing any of you good people reading this are gonna need ☺

The embassy workers also touched on the importance of using STEP (Smart Traveler Enrollment Program). It's basically is a free service that allows Americans to enroll their trips with notifications from the nearest U.S. Embassy or Consulate. **You can receive emails or texts about any danger, threats, or warnings in the vicinity of your destination.** Even better, your family can enroll and receive the same information for their peace of mind back in the states.

Holy Card Holy Grial

+ You must apply for within 30 days of arriving in Spain.

+ In many regions of Spain (such as Madrid) it can take close to three months before you're actually able to get it!

+ **Book an appointment right away**

+ **You must book an appointment at the local police station called "Policia Nacional"**

+**The Department you must go is called " Brigada de Extranjería"**

+ **Some regions like Madrid require the empadronamiento to do the NIE.** {Ill cover empadronamiento later on}

+**Some other regions don't require the empadronamiento because you will need the NIE [pink slip first to be able to "Empadronarte"]**

+If you let your temporary visa lapse before you have an appointment booked, you'll have to return to the USA (or wherever you're from) to apply for a whole new visa, so don't let this happen!

+ It is the TIE card that credits the assistant's legal stay in the country

+ The TIE card indicates the NIE number and your personal details, picture, and fingerprint

+ This is, essentially, your green card to be authorized to live and work (or study) in Spain.

+Even if the date on your NIE or TIE says June 2030 and you only come from the school year, 2018-2019. You must leave no later than June 30 of the year 2019. Get it renewed before you leave and come back. Americans, Canadians and Aussies cannot stay after the work of auxiliares is completed at the end of the academic term. That means you can't stay in Spain in summer legally.

However, there are other hacks to the system where you can stay but are very special cases and the health insurance wont cover you after the date you finish your school program.

Baby Steps to Follow When Applying for your TIE

1. Go to the **Brigada de Extranjeria** at the Local **"Policia Nacional."** If not follow step 2
2. **Make an online appointment using this website here sede.administracionespublicas.gob.es/icpplus/index.html**
   - **Select your Spanish region** [a drop down menu will appear with all the counties {provincias} in Spain, if yours is not included, go to your local police department of Brigada de extranjeria for an appointment. It´s easy ask around]
   - **Click "Aceptar"**
3. On the following page, after selecting your region, click on "TOMA DE HUELLAS (EXPEDICIÓN DE TARJETA) Y RENOVACIÓN DE TARJETA DE LARGA DURACIÓN" [This is **Taking fingerprints** for your ID.]

   [No! You're not a criminal. But in Spain is mandatory that all citizens carry a National ID with their fingerprints on it] and click accept.]
4. You'll be prompted to enter more information, including your NIE, Name, Country of origin, and current visa expiration date (typically three months from your issuance date, check your visa, enter your passport number). *(Note: When I initially tried to make this appointment with my passport number/expiration date, it said that there were no appointments available. I did it later on again with my NIE and it gave me three options.)*

5. Enter your passport number to get the NIE first.

6. Once you've finished, you'll print out your appointment slip and make sure to keep it. You'll need this when you go in to apply for your card in person – where you go varies depending on your region.

Once you've successfully completed the steps from above, it's time to prepare for your face-to-face appointment with the National Police. Here are the documents you'll need to bring with you:

- Document you printed from step 4 stating your appointment date and time
- Your carta de nombramiento (and a copy)
- EX17 Form which you can find down below or on their website here www.interior.gob.es/web/servicios-al-ciudadano/extranjeria/ciudadanos-de-la-union-europea/numero-de-identidad-de-extranjero-nie- and fill out online and then print before your appointment.

Note: the address you fill out on this form will be considered your permanent address in Spain. If you later change residence, you will be required to communicate it to the *"Brigada de Extranjería"* [Policia Nacional Station] Just walk in and let them know.

- **Proof of Payment of your TIE fees**
  - To show proof of payment, you will need to fill out the **790 Código 012 form**. After you fill out the proper form (check initial TIE and fill in the amount for €9,45 as of 2018), you'll need to bring the forms to ANY bank and they'll give you the proof of payment. This must be paid with cash. According to the TIE application instructions, you will need to go get this form at the "Brigada de Extranjería" or at a police station (I went to a police station). It's easier to just go to a police station. The downloadable form is not in color, however, and doesn't have the carbon copy receipt pages.

- **Original & Photocopies** of the following documents:

- ○ **Passport** [Xerox copy of all the pages and the binding of your passport. Yes. Photocopy all the passport just in case even the outside cover and back cover]
- ○ **Visa**
- ○ **Original Carta de Nombramiento:** You got it via email. It's the one I showed in the previous chapter.
- ○ **Entry Stamp**
  - ▪ It is mandatory to provide evidence that you arrived in Spain within a month of your initial appointment

. Con. San Francisco
to me

Dear Sir/Madam,

This Consulate General will no longer attend questions via email about the Visa application process.

For all the information and forms about Visa applications please go to our Website:
http://www.exteriores.gob.es/Consulados/SANFRANCISCO/en/ConsularServices/Pages/Visas.aspx

For questions about the process, please contact the Call Center of VFS Global. More information in our Website: http://www.exteriores.gob.es/Consulados/SANFRANCISCO/en/ConsularServices/Pages/Visas.aspx

Thank you.

Visa Department
Consulado General de España en San Francisco
1405 Sutter Street, San Francisco, CA 94109
Tel: +1 415 922 2995   Fax: +1 415 931 9706
Email: cog.sanfrancisco@maec.es
http://www.exteriores.gob.es/consulados/sanfrancisco

Do you want to bring your family to Spain? I know of an American family that has just done that. Check their blog here **https://aparentabroad.wordpress.com**

Brook Taylor • 2 years ago

I don't have any links or resources I can point you toward, but I do know for a fact that many folks do this program every year with their children (and spouses!) in tow. I can't comment on the logistical issues of having to get separate visas for your kids and being able to prove you have enough funds to support them & health insurance & all that, but I actually met a married couple last year who had brought their son with them and he seemed to fit right in at the local elementary school (and even picked up the Castilian accent in Spanish!).

Your résumé doesn't give you any advantage in getting placed...but on the flipside it doesn't detract, either. All that matters is having a completed application (admitida) by the time the application period closes, as they hand out placements first-come, first-served. Since you mentioned you have your teaching certification, you might want to bring that up with the bilingual coordinator at the school you do ultimately get assigned to, as they might be able to fit you in with more classes in "plástica" (art class) than "conocimiento del medio" (sciences) and/or might be willing to let you take the lead in lesson planning & teaching.

Estás en **PORTADA** › **DOCUMENTACIÓN** › **Extranjeros:Documentación, NIE, Indocumentados**   Martes 15 de Mayo de 2018

Documentación - Extranjeros

Documentación

Ciudadanos Comunitarios

Extranjeros
 Ámbito de Aplicación
 Documentos de viajes
 Entrada: Requisitos y condiciones
 Carta de invitación
 Salidas, prohib. y aut. regreso
 Estancia y prórroga de estancia
 Solicitud autorización residencia
 Menores extranjeros
 Número Identidad Extranjero
 Tarjeta de extranjero
 Infracciones y sanciones
 Expulsión y Denegación entrada
 Centro Internamiento Extranjeros
 Resolución procedimientos
 Oficinas Trámites Extranjería

Asilo y Refugio

Apátridas

Procedimient. Administrativos

Impreso Tasa Modelo 790 Código 012

Documentación, Nº de Identificación (NIE) y Extranjeros Indocumentados

DOCUMENTACIÓN

Todos los extranjeros que cuenten con una autorización o tarjeta para permanecer en España serán dotados de un único documento, la Tarjeta de Extranjero, en la que constará el tipo de autorización que se les haya concedido.

Los extranjeros están obligados a llevar consigo el pasaporte o documento en base al cual hubieran efectuado su entrada en España y, en su caso, el documento al que se refiere el apartado anterior, así como a exhibirlos cuando fueran requeridos por las autoridades o sus agentes.

Será aplicable al documento mencionado la normativa vigente sobre presentación y anotación en las Oficinas públicas del documento nacional de identidad, cuya normativa tendrá carácter supletorio de las normas sobre utilización en España de los documentos de identidad de los extranjeros.

El extranjero que se encuentre en territorio español tiene el derecho y la obligación de conservar la documentación que acredite su identidad, expedida por las autoridades competentes del país de origen o de procedencia, así como la que acredite su situación en España.

NÚMERO DE IDENTIFICACIÓN DE EXTRANJERO (NIE)

Los extranjeros a cuyo favor se inicie un procedimiento para obtener un documento que les habilite para permanecer en territorio español que no sea un visado, aquéllos a los que se les haya incoado un expediente administrativo en virtud de lo dispuesto en la normativa sobre extranjería y aquellos que por sus intereses económicos, profesionales o sociales se relacionen con España serán dotados, a los efectos de identificación, de un número personal, único y exclusivo, de carácter secuencial.

El número personal será el identificador del extranjero, que deberá figurar en todos los documentos que se le expidan o tramiten, así como en las diligencias que se estampen en su pasaporte o documento análogo, salvo en los visados.

El número de identidad del extranjero, NIE, deberá ser concedido de oficio, por la Dirección General de la Policía, en los supuestos mencionados en el apartado 1, salvo en el caso de los extranjeros que se relacionen con España por razón de sus intereses económicos, profesionales o sociales, que deberán interesar de dicho órgano la asignación del indicado número, siempre que concurran los siguientes requisitos:

 a. Que no se encuentren en España en situación irregular.

 b. Que se comuniquen los motivos por los que solicitan la asignación

The date will be really important for the "Brigada de Extranjería" office [Policia Nacional]. The best thing to do is to have your passport or visa stamped when you cross the border into the Schengen Zone, even better if it's into Spain. If you cross through another border, like say France or in my case Frankfurt, you must show the stamp from France/Frankfurt and keep your bus/train/plane ticket from France to Spain for proof! I kept my ticket stub and scanned it with my visa stamp, all on the same photocopy I turned in.

- **A passport sized photo**, bareheaded, on white background. It's *recommended* that you bring the picture yourself, though you can find a photo booth right outside the Policia nacional in all regions of the "Brigada de Extranjería" office. It costs €5 and takes less than 2 minutes. The pictures were actually different than my passport ones, so it was easier to just take the pics there.
- **Empadronamiento:** proof of your legal address in Spain [this is mandatory in Madrid and other regions to get the NIE, for example when I did it in Vigo, I did my NIE first, I got a pink slip then I took the pink slip to the City Hall [Ayuntamiento] and they gave me the empadronamiento, which I took back to the Brigada de Extranjeria afterwards] **I would use for my NIE as my permanent address, the school address. Ask your school first.**

Basically you take your signed lease to an **ayuntamiento-city hall**-around your city. You make an appointment to get the address official and get a sheet of paper called an **empadronamiento** that says, yes, you live there! **Note:** *I did **not** have to turn this in, which was great since I didn't have it!* On the form I mentioned above, EX-17, You fill out your address and that is it. In the appointment, the police will ask if it is your permanent address and you must say yes. However, I have heard that some students and other auxiliares needed to get their empadronamiento *for* the TIE appointment! It's really a gamble if you go without it because technically they *can* turn you away and make you come back with it in some regions.

After you've handed all of these documents over to the officers at the Brigada de Extranjería, you'll get your fingerprints scanned and you'll be given a **receipt pink slip** to come back and collect your TIE card. They say it takes about 30-45 days to process. After 30 days, take your slip & passport with you back to the "Brigada de Extranjería" department at the Policia Nacional to get your TIE card! Note that you should go back before 45 days, or the pink slip will expire… You can pretty much go anytime between 30-45 days. Below, I have enclosed a copy so if you want to print it out and practice. It's no problem. Remember this is only a copy of the real deal. It's not official though it looks like it. They'll help you fill it out at the office of Policia nacional, Brigada de Extranjería. Play the dumb American. I'm sure they'll help you out. 9 out of 10 Spaniards love the USA and Americans. Trust me! Check this website again
http://www.interior.gob.es/web/servicios-al-ciudadano/extranjeria/ciudadanos-de-la-union-europea/numero-de-identidad-de-extranjero-nie-

EX-15

GOBIERNO
DE ESPAÑA

Solicitud de Número de Identidad de
Extranjero (NIE) y Certificados
(LO 4/2000 y RD 557/2011)

Espacios para sellos
de registro

1) DATOS DEL EXTRANJERO/A

PASAPORTE _____ N.I.E. __ – _____ - ___

1er Apellido _____ 2º Apellido _____

Nombre _____ Sexo(1) H ◯ M ◯

Fecha de nacimiento(2) _____ Lugar _____ País _____

Nacionalidad _____ Estado civil(3) S ◯ C ◯ V ◯ D ◯ Sp ◯

Nombre del padre _____ Nombre de la madre _____

Domicilio de residencia _____ Nº ___ Piso ___

Localidad _____ C.P. ___ Provincia ___

Teléfono móvil _____ E-mail _____

Representante legal, en su caso _____ DNI/NIE/PAS ___ Título(4) ___

2) DATOS DEL REPRESENTANTE A EFECTOS DE PRESENTACIÓN DE LA SOLICITUD(5)

Nombre/Razón Social _____ DNI/NIE/PAS _____

Domicilio de residencia _____ Nº ___ Piso ___

Localidad _____ C.P. ___ Provincia ___

Teléfono móvil _____ E-mail _____

Representante legal, en su caso _____ DNI/NIE/PAS ___ Título(4) ___

3) DOMICILIO A EFECTOS DE NOTIFICACIONES

Nombre/Razón Social _____ DNI/NIE/PAS _____

Domicilio de residencia _____ Nº ___ Piso ___

Localidad _____ C.P. ___ Provincia ___

Teléfono móvil _____ E-mail _____

☐ CONSIENTO que las comunicaciones y notificaciones se realicen por medios electrónicos (6)

Nombre y apellidos del titular..

---

4) DATOS RELATIVOS A LA SOLICITUD[7]

4.1. TIPO DE DOCUMENTO (art. 206)

○ NÚMERO DE IDENTIDAD DE EXTRANJERO (NIE)

○ CERTIFICADO
  ○ De residente
  ○ De no residente

4.2. MOTIVOS

○ Por intereses económicos   ○ Por intereses profesionales   ○ Por intereses sociales

(Especificar)

4.3. LUGAR DE PRESENTACIÓN

○ Oficina de Extranjería   ○ Comisaría de Policía   ○ Oficina Consular

4.4. SITUACIÓN EN ESPAÑA[8]

○ Estancia   ○ Residencia

☐ NO CONSIENTO la consulta sobre mis datos y documentos que se hallen en poder de la Administración (en este caso, deberán aportarse los documentos correspondientes) [8]

...., a .... de .... de ....

FIRMA DEL SOLICITANTE (o representante legal, en su caso)

Nombre y apellidos del titular...

ANEXO I. Documentos sobre los que se autoriza su comprobación o consulta

	DOCUMENTO	ÓRGANO	ADMINISTRACIÓN	FECHA DE PRESENTACIÓN
1				
2				
3				
4				
5				
6				
7				
8				
9				
10				

ANEXO II. Documentos para los que se deniega el consentimiento para consulta

1	
2	
3	
4	
5	
6	
7	
8	
9	
10	

INSTRUCCIONES DE CUMPLIMENTACIÓN

RELLENAR EN MAYÚSCULAS CON BOLÍGRAFO NEGRO Y LETRA DE IMPRENTA O A MÁQUINA
SE PRESENTARÁ ORIGINAL Y COPIA DE ESTE IMPRESO

(1) Marque el cuadro que proceda. Hombre / Mujer

(2) Rellenar utilizando 2 dígitos para el día, 2 para el mes y 4 para el año, en este orden (dd/mm/aaaa)

(3) Marque el cuadro que proceda. Soltero / Casado / Viudo / Divorciado / Separado

(4) Indique el título en base al cual se ostenta la representación, por ejemplo: Padre/Madre del menor, Tutor.....

(5) Rellenar sólo en el caso de persona distinta del solicitante

(6) Conforme a la DA 4ª del RD 557/2011, están obligados a la notificación electrónica, aunque no hayan dado su consentimiento, las personas jurídicas y los colectivos de personas físicas que, por su capacidad económica o técnica, dedicación profesional u otros motivos acreditados, tengan garantizado el acceso y disponibilidad de los medios tecnológicos precisos. Si usted no está incluido en alguno de los colectivos mencionados, se le notificará por esta vía únicamente si marca la casilla de consentimiento. En ambos casos la notificación consistirá en la puesta a disposición del documento en la sede electrónica del Ministerio de Hacienda y Administraciones Públicas (https://sede.mpt.gob.es).
La notificación se realizará a la persona cuyos datos se indiquen en el apartado "domicilio a efectos de notificaciones" o, en su defecto, al solicitante. Para acceder al contenido del documento **es necesario disponer de certificado electrónico** asociado al DNI/NIE que figure en el apartado "domicilio a efecto de notificaciones".
Es conveniente además que rellene los campos "teléfono móvil" o "e-mail" para tener la posibilidad de enviarle un aviso (meramente informativo) cuando tenga una notificación pendiente.

(7) Marque la opción que corresponda.

(8) Los interesados no están obligados a aportar documentos que hayan sido elaborados por cualquier Administración o que hayan sido ya aportados anteriormente en un procedimiento administrativo. A tal fin, deberá enumerar en el anexo I los documentos en cuestión. Se presumirá que esta consulta es autorizada, salvo que conste su oposición expresa, debiendo cumplimentar el anexo II.

La información específica sobre trámites a realizar y documentación que debe acompañar a este impreso de solicitud para cada uno de los procedimientos contemplados en el mismo, así como la información sobre las tasas que conlleva dicha tramitación (HOJAS INFORMATIVAS), se encuentra disponible en cualquiera de las siguientes direcciones Web:
 http://extranjeros.empleo.gob.es/es/.
 http://extranjeros.empleo.gob.es/es/InformacionInteres/InformacionProcedimientos/.

Los modelos oficiales podrán ser reproducidos por cualquier medio de impresión.
Estarán disponibles, además de en las Unidades encargadas de su gestión, en la página de información de Internet del Ministerio de Empleo y Seguridad Social
 http://extranjeros.empleo.gob.es/es/.

IMPRESO GRATUITO. PROHIBIDA SU VENTA

Final NIE+TIE Checklist

+Make an appointment online

+Or Make a physical appointment at the Brigada de Extranjería

+Go early. If you can show up by 6.30-7.00 am. Right on!!

+It is located at your Policia Nacional station in your locality

+Take with you all documents and copies of your passport

+Take with you the original or a copy of your carta de nombramiento

+Go to the nearest Photo Booth and take 4 ID photos.

+Get the print out of the NIE

+Pay the **790 Código 012 form** tax required it's about 10 euros

+You can use as your permanent address, your school address. Ask your school first though.

+Take your empadronamiento slip with you if required.

+You'll be given a pink slip after the finger printing (make a Xerox copy of this pink slip just in case and keep it in a safe place)

+Do not forget to come back 30-45 days later to the Policia nacional and collect your TIE card

Fingers crossed now and sleep tight for 30 days and 30 nights!

CHAPTER 7
APARTMENT HUNTING
TO SHARE OR NOT TO SHARE
THAT IS THE QUESTION!

The first year I got to Spain, a day just right after I arrived in Spain, I booked a cheap *pension* (student hostel) for a week and I also made, that same very same day, the earliest appointment available for my TIE card (even though it was in a pueblo outside of Vigo), paid the *tasa* (form tax payment) and went straight to the police station to have my fingerprints done. I remember those days being very hectic because I had a small time frame to do all the hard paper work. But something happened. It was my lucky day! As I was being assisted by the *funcionaria*, the status of my residence card application changed to *Resolución Favorable*! She discarded the paperwork for the student TIE and got the documents for the *tarjeta comunitaria*! Cool! I had everything! Sometimes it pays to be an over thinker. I left with a *resguardo-justificante* (receipt-pink slip) with the number of processing days before I could collect my card.

Bingo! The Golden Card Finally Arrived!

I counted around 30 processing days from my *comisaría* appointment and I picked up my card...

Above picture of a British or EU citizen Spanish TIE, different from those of extra communitaries. Below, a picture of an American student or auxiliares TIES. Yours will look just like these.

Finding an apartment (*piso*)

It ain´t easy to go apartment hunting in Spain. One rule of thumb is to talk to other auxiliares or Spanish people that are looking for roommates already and announce themselves on Facebook in the auxiliares groups or instagram. Ask around on these blogs and websites first. [At the end of this book you have a list of websites where you can interact with tenants and apartment block or piso managers. In my first two years here, I went from having the worst apartment to the best apartment because I knew exactly what I needed and wanted after suffering through 10 months of no central heating, cold showers, and the loudest and dirtiest roommates in Spain. So by trial and error, here are some tips for finding an awesome, affordable apartment here in Spain.

Apartment hunting for a *piso* can be tricky if your level of Spanish isn't high; when I first moved to Spain, nothing scared me more than having to talk on the phone in Spanish! Don't be shy, be a go-getter! I would suggest asking your school coordinator or 2nd year auxiliares in your town to help you calling. They might even have some leads on *pisos* for you!

+**You don´t wanna move in with other auxiliares** or English-speaking people. You´ve moved to Spain to learn Spanish. So blend in!

+ **If you go to a real estate agency.** Don´t pay any finders fee upfront. No Way José! You only pay a deposit and the first month rent.

+**Tell them you're an English teacher** in a school not a student. Managers in Spain don't want students.

+ Check the **easypiso, idealista,enalquiler, fotocasa.es** websites.

+ **Never, Ever, Ever** agree to an apartment you find online or pay by wire transfer, without seeing it in person and don't pay anything until you have seen it yourself.

+**Pay,** if so, **a deposit** once you agree in person to reserve it and promise the apartment manager or owner you will pay the rest once you move in.

+**Ask for a receipt and contract** or paper with a signature and the name of the person and their DNI (Spanish ID) printed in capital letters and visible. Oral agreements are rarely binding in Spain.

+ **Look for *anuncios* (listings) at the local college or university**

+**Contact Erasmus people** in your area. They have reps in every region. And they're not American. They're from other European countries and South America, so you'll brush up on your Spanish real good!

+ **A good idea is to ask your school.** Maybe one of the teachers or students parents is renting a piso.

+ You have to **decide if you want to live alone or share** an apartment. I have shared an apartment many times before, and it has been so bad sometimes that I swore also many times I would live alone. But I am socialite and I always like to share a piso in the end. Perhaps, after you have made some Spanish acquaintances or friends, have some real residual income, and you're already fluent in Spanish, maybe then, you can live on your own in Spain.

+ Note that **many owners** or apartment block managers **rent by room,** so your contract might just be for you rather than for the whole apartment, and then you might be able to sign it till June and not for a full 12 months. Also many people rent rooms illegally (it's totally normal in Spain) and you don't have a "real" contract. It is actually illegal to sublet rooms in Spain, but then again, it's Spain, so no one really cares.

+ This is not usually a problem unless to need to be *empadronado* (registered living there) for some reason, like getting a student bus pass, joining the local gym, utility bills or if you need it for certain paperwork, but even then there are ways around it.

+ **Having Spanish roommates is a great** way to **improve your Spanish** and **meet new people/locals,** get work easily and do some networking. Thanks to my Spanish friends I always make an extra $1,000-1,500 month through their acquaintances and contacts.

+ **Try to move in with people who actually are working professionals,** lawyers, teachers, yoga instructors… not party goers or Erasmus students.

+ Around most of Spain, with the exception of bigger, wealthier cities, living alone with probably cost around **400 euros**, give or take, while sharing an apartment will cost around **150-200 euros,** usually less. The majority of auxiliares share pisos, since you only earn **700 euros** a month except for Madrid and Barcelona that can cash you in at least 1,000 euros a month.

+Factor in a month's rent deposit, and you're good to go! But trying to afford living alone in a city like Madrid would be almost **impossible.** I know many people who have signed legit apartment contracts there, and they are asked to pay several months rent as a deposit.

+**If they ask you to sign with a guarantor or a bank sponsor** (*abal* in Spain). Don´t do it. Pass on the deal and move on to another apartment.

+ **You shouldn't pay more than 20-25%** of what you earn in renting a piso in Spain. Financially, it makes more sense to share places. It can be hard to afford to live **alone** on your salary, especially in large cities like Madrid, Barcelona, Bilbao or Valencia.

Now, Let´s see the benefits of living in a ciudad or a pueblo in Spain…

Small town vs. city life in Spain

So, now that everything has been signed, sealed, and delivered and I have all the paperwork required to be a legal alien in Spain, I'm settling down in Spain for a teacher's lifestyle in favor of greener pastures (but later on, if you decide to stay longer, say 3 years, I could have the same benefits as the Spaniards, say: social security, permanent residency, and the ability to apply for actual jobs. But this is the first step for you of not-so-long- a -journey).

But, Now, Do you really want to live in a Pueblo or a City? Let's check it out!

Small Town

+Lets say you been **placed in a tiny little village** called Cambados (population 9,500something) in the province of Pontevedra, Galicia. I'm saying you must live in the largest possible nearby town, Vilagarcia, for example (population 30,000 something), and commute to and from work every day with other teachers via carpooling or similar. You can also take a bus. That is about $2 dollars.

+**Small town means small school**. There are maybe, at most, 200 students in the entire high school. You will only work with the bilingual group of each grade level and keep the same schedule all the time.

+Your **Work schedule will be 12 hours** spread out over 3 days: Tuesday, Wednesday, and Thursday. The principal of the school, your boss will tell you herself that she wants you to have time to get out of town and travel due to the fact that there isn't much going on in that area.

+ **The Work ecosystem** being at such a small school means that you are going to be able to **get to know your students as well as your co-workers personally** as well as academically. It is going to be much easier for you to memorize students' names (since there aren't as many of them), and hardly a few days are gonna go by when you run into one of them around town. (This wont happen in major cities) There are also fewer teachers at the smaller school, and You'll be able to make some great friendships with some of your colleagues. The fact that you are going to commute to work with several of them will surely help you bond with them, too.

+ **When it boils down to your classroom experience and quality of teaching,** you are going to work in bilingual math, science, and social studies classes, as well as the English language classes. Auxiliares at bilingual schools in Galicia or Barcelona, for example, typically don't assist with English language classes, but there are so few bilingual classes at the school that they'll have to put you somewhere. The English classes will end up being your favorite for many reasons: You're a native and you're getting paid for talking in your mother tongue, which didn't require any teaching training, and if you're passionate about language learning, and the classes provide a great deal of opportunities for active games and fun group discussions. That won't happen in maths or sciences, which are not tailored around English.

+**Living in a small town whether it be in Spain or in America** isn't easy, since you sometimes can't find people your own age to live with in a small, non-college town. You end up spending the year living by yourself in a 3-bedroom, 2-bathroom townhouse or apartment in Cambados or a Micky Mouse tiny village. While there are times you wish there could be someone else your age around, I loved living by myself for the most part. It really makes me feel more independent and helps me learn how to take responsibility for things. The only negative here is, loneliness, and sociability, which are two factors you must consider when living in such a small town. The positive fact is how cheap a little town in Spain is, that the entire rent payment (250-300€ a month – that was half of my share of rent at my college apartment in Pico Blvd. in California in the year 1998) and all the bills are included. Very cheap!!!

+ **Fiestas in small towns usually take place during the summer or Easter break when you're not around**. The rest of the year is boring. There isn't going to be much to do in your little Mickey Mouse town, and not many private classes either. Locals are too old and less eager to learn English. They probably wont even speak Spanish correctly. However, I had the greatest stroke of luck just a few weeks after I arrived, a group of *españoles* from Madrid came down to the pueblo to check their real estate investments in this bucolic coastal town. And we would soon become my closest friends. I also became good friends with the other handful of auxiliares who lived in the region and the surrounding villages. But, coming from Los Angeles, I didn't have the feeling for a small town.

The Big city

I am a person who doesn't like comparing people or places. All places have good and bad things about them, just like people. Lets say you live and work in a place like Vigo (population 300,000 something), a much larger and better-known city. I live in the city center and either walk or get the bus to work, depending on time/weather/how lazy I feel that day. I could even take a taxi to work for only $3 dollars. It was cheap, big and the living conditions were awesome. The beach is close and it has a kind of Californian vibe to it.

+ **Big town means Big school**. You'll be teaching a school with well over 1,000 students. You still work only with the kids in the bilingual program, but since it's a much larger school, each grade level has multiple bilingual groups. You are going to have a rotating A-and-B-week schedule, which allows you to have several classes a week with each group, too. However, You'll be able to talk to the principal and fit your schedule to your private lesson needs, though you shouldn't mention that as a cause of your schedule modifications. Tell them you live far and have problems with transportation to reach the school. They'll understand. Even if you are a stones throw away from the school like I used to.

+ **Your work schedule** will be 12-16 hours spread out over 4 days: Monday-Thursday with Fridays off. This is a more realistic auxiliar schedule...

+ **Your school, I'm sure, will be awesome** as well. Big schools in large cities in Spain have a nice playground, a teacher's canteen, meeting room, lockers, football pitches and tennis courts. Children, generally, in Spain are great, though, there are few exceptions but in the largest Spanish inner cities only, which have a lot of immigration from countries not bonding with local Spanish culture- this is a problem that is been widespread to all western countries worldwide, including the US. You know what I'm talking about!! However, the fact that it's a much larger school means that you wont be able to bond as much with the students and colleagues. You'll see each group for about two hours a week tops (and sometimes even less), so, you'll have to make the most of the time you have with them. On a similar note, your colleagues will also be nothing but kind to you, but it'll be harder for you to get to know them better due to the sheer fact that there's just so many of them. While in the small town school there are maybe only 8-10 teachers. In the big city school, there will be well over 30-40 teachers.

+**The classroom experience and quality of teaching** depends pretty much on teachers and how well the school is managed by the principal and the budget allocated by the ministerio to that public high school-*instituto*. There will be a much larger variety of bilingual subjects at the school. In addition to the courses, you'll also help out in more specialized classes such as technology and citizenship.

Although, you won't probably work in any English language classes, you might spend an hour each week helping the students in **ESO** (the equivalent of American **intermediate school** or **junior high school**/the old American middle school) and **segundo de bachillerato** (senior high school) prepare for the oral interview part of the Cambridge (British exam) Trinity English (British Exam). These are writing and reading British English classes and not as active as an actual English class, **Note:** if you don't know about British English and grammar, either do a crash course online or stay away from it. British English is very different from American English regarding grammar, writing and pronunciation. You are going to get to talk to the children one-on-one or in small tutorial groups about a variety of different topics and get to know them a little better. Most of Spanish children are very witty, thoughtful and insightful and they come with awesome answers (and their English, in large cities, is good). In the end, you'll look forward to the more conversational classes. You Betcha!

+**Living cost** was a bit **higher** than the *pueblo.* And you know, the rent will be a bit higher too, instead of having a solo gig-apartment with 2 bedrooms like in the pueblo, here you'll be sharing a piso, though, some cities have great deals for large apartments in the city down town. Only problem is that they'll be a bit old and not as cozy. The highest rent I've paid, sharing a piso, has been 200€ a month. That was in Madrid. Even with bills, it doesn't even come close to what I was paying in a small town.

But, you'll find more private tuition clients and be able to charge more for private classes (my little town price was 8-15 euros but in the city I'd always charge at least 20-30 for a one2one class), which certainly helps as well. You'll be depositing more money into your bank account every month, and have plenty of residual income to spend on your traveling or bad habits.

Peter L
March 14, 2016 12.32 pm

If you ever have someone who is looking to teach English in the Ribeira area nearby, there is enough opportunity for that here and I can put that person in touch with a parents association who foots the bill usually. There is such a shortage of English teachers here that many kids get sent abroad to learn it as it is a required language on their exams.
Generally opportunities one finds best by oneself in Galicia. The informal communication is super fast here. Another good way of finding work is domestiko.es. Got tons of reactions for a good cat sitter through that one, all from locals nearby. Of course it is used mostly by young people. Oder people are more into the informal network.

⬡ **REPLY**

CHAPTER 8
BANKING, INTERNET, AND PHONE!

Now, in this chapter we'll deal with with **3 key main issues, that is opening a bank account**-to receive and withdraw your money, **setting up a phone**-to communicate with people around and **getting internet** connection- to keep in touch with relatives back home and make some money, use email or simply for mere entertainment, once you arrive in Spain as a worker, a student, a teacher, a cultural ambassador or an *auxiliar de conversación*.

Chose a big, well-known bank

You'll need a bank account to receive the money from your employers. If you're in the auxiliary program send an email and inform your principal, boss of your account number and name of the bank. Use the IBAN and SWIFT code to provide your banking details to your regional teaching office or business if you're simply working as a teacher.

For a country with quite literally a million local and national banks to choose from, it can be a real pain in the ass dealing with them. One of the first things you will want to do when you arrive in Spain is to **open a bank account**; you'll need one for any **contract** you might have to set up. But **choose carefully**. I learned the hard way at first by choosing the first bank I saw in Vigo, A caixa. A caixa is a local bank, which meant that it was only found really in Vigo and Galicia, but not nationwide.

As an *auxiliar*, I can safely assume that you will want to **travel** a lot around Spain and probably Europe too. Chose a big bank that you can find all over Spain, like **"la Caixa," Santander, ING, or BBVA**. I chose first BBVA when I arrived first but when I met my girlfriend, she was working at "la Caixa" that year, and I couldn't be happier. They have locations everywhere, at least in all city centers. They also have **free and "youth" accounts if you are less than 26 years old**. So no fees. A lot of banks in Spain do this, so make sure to ask first.

It is easy to set up **online banking** with "la Caixa," and make sure you ask for the SWIFT, IBAN and the BIC codes if you are planning to buy or sell things online. Many banks in Spain will give you a card with a grid of letters and numbers, codes that will be prompted when you try to buy something like a train ticket or a flight online. Antiquated, but effective against fraud. Many banks have deals and let you use partner or foreign ATM's without fees if you set it up in advance.

You will need a bank account for when you get paid, in all the Regions you'll receive direct deposits into your account. You might also need a bank account to sign a lease, set up a cell phone, and get Internet. Just go into the bank, take the program letter with you and explain that you need to set up an account. Say that you will be a **resident**. There are more fees if you set up with your passport as a tourist. If you don't have your **NIE** number yet, explain that you will receive it soon and they can change the type of account opened.

On a daily basis, No bank will deal with you until you have a NIE or TIE, so worry about getting that first. Then, once you have the actual number – NIE- (the pink slip with number on the top will suffice), you can go in and apply for a bank account. If you're under 26 or sometimes 30 you may be eligible for a youth account at certain banks, which waives fees/requirements and all that nonsense.

Online banking would be CRITICAL especially since banks are only ever open until 2pm on weekdays and ATMs are few and far between. I wouldn't worry about closing your bank account when you leave for good as long as you've withdrawn all your euros before you leave (or using Transfer Wise to take them out when you're back home). Also I would recommend going with a national bank like BBVA, Banco Santander, Unicaja, etc. because you will probably be doing a lot of travel around Spain and you don't want to have to get charged out-of-network ATM fees every damned time you need 10€.

I Got My iPhone Stolen!!! OMG 😱 !!!!

Now that you have settled down in Spain and have all your legal stuff sorted out. You have your house, your school, your friends, your monthly paycheck and you're starting to make new friends *españoles*. It so very happens, that one fateful day the whole world comes falling down on you. Where is the cell phone? Texts, pdfs, whatsApps messages, Apple wallet, credit card numbers, your Google history searches, bitcoin private keys, emails... and all of that stored on your iPhone.

A fucking Greek tragedy!!!!

What are you gonna do now? Your iPhone is nowhere to be found!

So, you suspect that somebody has stolen your iPhone or perhaps, you just lost it on a wild **fiesta** night of *sangria* and *señoritas* the day before!

First of all, you must report it lost or stolen ASAP to the local Police Department- Policia Nacional or Policia Municipal. A terrorist could use nationally or internationally that iPhone to either steal information or for an imminent attack. So, it´s your duty to report it stolen in Spain, for your own security and the others´. A cell or mobile phone (un móvil) can be purchased in any major city and even in many small towns and pueblos. The major mobile phone companies in Spain where to get a new phone are **Phone House Vodaphone, Movistar, Orange, and Yoigo.**

Each company has individual stores where you can buy a phone from any high street or promenade. Stores like **Phone House** and Corte Inglés sell phones from many different companies, which make it easy to compare brands and find a good deal. Of course, I would go to El Corte Inglés first [a bit too expensive] just to browse cell phones but may be later head directly for the Phone house to actually buy it.

Unlockable or Not?

There are two network types:

- **Global System for Mobile communication (GSM)**

GSM phones use SIM cards and **can be unlocked.**

- **Code Division Multiple Access (CDMA)**

CDMA phones **cannot be unlocked.** If you live in the US, you can tell which type your phone is based on your carrier.

How to Unlock a Phone

If you have a GSM phone, get it unlocked before arriving in Spain.
Call your provider and ask them for the code. Explain that you're going to Europe for X amount of time and they should give you the code, though it may take a bit of persistence. There are stores in Spain that unlock phones if you absolutely cannot unlock it before hand. Look for signs that say *"Se liberan móviles"* in store windows. This might cost from 30-50 euros.

Finding the Right Deal

There are two types of plans:

- **Contract (Contracto)**

This means signing a contract to a fixed monthly rate. Contract plans usually come with a free or lower-cost phone. Most contracts are good for a certain amount of time such as a year or 2 years. **DON´T DO IT!**

- **SIM Card (Tarjeta SIM)**

This is the best option if you're a teacher and don´t want to waste money on unnecessary calls. If you're moving to Spain for a short amount of time such as studying abroad or working as an auxilar. This is also what you should do if you're bringing an unlocked phone to Spain.

If you're not bringing a phone to Spain, buy a non-contract phone (móvil libre) and a SIM card (Tarjeta SIM) separately. A SIM card is a prepaid card that you reload money onto.

These phones have also **European Roaming**, which means you can use it anywhere in Europe at the same price you pay in Spain per outgoing call made. Ask your local phone store, just in case. SIM cards can be reloaded at any phone store, most grocery stores, and online. You simply tell them your phone company, phone number, and the amount of credit (saldo) you want to add. Credit can only be added in increments of 5€- 10€- or 20 at a time, so for example if you need 11€ more for the next month, you have to put at least 15€ on.

Your phone number is usually written on the SIM card. Also given to you is your PIN and PUK numbers. Write these down, they'll be needed to unlock your phone when you turn it on and off.

Understanding the Plan

Contracts and SIM cards usually list the price of 4 things:

Cuota mensual/semanal (Monthly/weekly payment)

This is the base price that you are charged each month or week. If you have a SIM card, it will automatically be deducted from your credit (saldo). If you don't have enough credit (saldo) on your SIM card, you won't be able to make calls or send texts.

SMS (Text messages)

Some plans have unlimited (ilimitados) text messages, others list the price per text message, and others have a set number of free texts included.

Elizabeth Carlson August 7, 2012 at 8:19 am

yeah it really really sucks. I had to wait a month last year for internet in cordoba, and another month this year in logroño. its because they have to have a technician come and install the cables, if your piso doesn't have them, it's complicated ☐

Reply

Amanda Prisco
1 comment · 0 votes

Many people do **pay as you go**, adding 5 or 10 euros on the phone whenever you want. This what I have been doing. I usually spend 25-30 euros a month. Usually you go and buy the SIM card, for a few euros and it includes money on it. For example when I bought mine at Vodafone, it was 9 euros for the SIM and it came with 9 euros of *saldo* (credit). If you don't care about your phone, then you can buy a cheap, basic phone to use here. That's what I have done in the past. You won't need a bank account for this option, and you can top up your phone at grocery stores, online, phone shops, tobacco shops, and at special phone machines.

Llamadas (Calls)

Calls typically have a connection fee (establecimiento de llamada) plus a per minute price. Some plans instead have an amount of free minutes included.

Internet

Most plans have a set amount of data per payment period you can use. 1GB-3GB

Phone Habits in Spain

Most plans charge either per minute and per text messages, or you have a limit of 300-500 minutes at a flat rate and then they start charging you double for calls and internet hook-up, sending lots of texts or having long chats on a mobile phone is not very common. What is common is using **WhatsApp**. Usually, people have even started using a new verb- ***"whatsappear."***

People say **dame un toque** ("give a touch" literally in Sp. that is playing **phone tag- give me a buzz**), also called *"enviar una llamada perdida"* (*"send a missed call"*). This is done by calling and immediately hanging up, so a missed call shows up on your phone screen. People will sometimes ask you to "dar un toque" in place of an "I'm here" text or an "I got home OK text."

Tips:

- Phone numbers that start with a 9 are landlines and numbers that start with a 6 are mobile phones.
- Spain's emergency number is **112** (the equivalent of 911 in the US)
- Remember that in Spain "," is a decimal point and. is used to separate digits. So "1.000" means one thousand

Setting up Internet quickly

Maybe not everyone is as addicted to being online as me, but having Internet in my apartment was crucial to me. My MacBook is my lifeline here. I use it for everything. From planning my classes, to Google hanging out with my family, to watching TV and movies. For me, it is very important that I have a fairly fast Internet connectivity in my apartment in Spain.

Look for a piso that already has Internet installed. In Spain it takes around **a month to install Wi-Fi**, which for me, is sometimes a bummer. If you can't find a **piso** with wifi, then look for companies that **don't require a 12-month contract**, like Jazztel, R or KNET. In 2010, I made a mistake signing a-year-long-contract for Internet with Orange.

I had to pay 35 euros a month and then when I tried to cancel it in June, they made me jump through so many hoops with sending letters and faxes and calling an expensive number, that eventually I had my Spanish girlfriend fix it with Orange.

You don't wanna end up in someone's hit list next time around!

Even though it takes around a month to install Wi-Fi. Which is why you should start the process as soon as you find a piso-apartment if you need to. In that time it takes to install it, you can go to coffeehouses, cafes and local libraries to use Wi-Fi.

ANNA   Reply

⊙ *June 10, 2016 at 7:59 AM*

Your time at that school seems to have been pretty exciting and great! When I was younger I always thought about taking part in such a program but not being the best with kids I was always hesitant. I hope you enjoy your next adventure and I'm excited to read more about it

★ Like

Jessi July 8, 2013 at 6:47 pm

I had the same problem when I had internet with Vodafone – they practically refused to terminate my contract, so I had no choice but to just close my bank account and leave. (In fact, when I talked to co-workers about this, they SUGGESTED that I do that … apparently it's somewhat common even among locals if companies are being unreasonable.) I was nervous I'd be blacklisted somehow, but… no issues with credit at all. Phew.

CHAPTER 9
HEALTHCARE, MEDICARE AND INSURANCE

Now, you fell from the horse and broke your leg and don't know what to do! Call the horse back, call a friend or call you mom back home!

No, this is not Who Wants to Be a Millionaire! Call always 112!

112 is the emergency number in Spain and Andorra equivalent to the 911 number in the US or the 999 in the UK. Overall, the Spanish healthcare system works well, and it is often even possible to find English speaking medical staff. However, before moving to Spain you need to be sure that the costs of future medical treatment will be covered. The Insurance companies are called in Spain Seguros de Salud. They usually cover Medicare and healthcare plus some dental and eye problems. The best bet if you happen to get sick in Spain, even if you consider it to be a minor injury, just go to the emergency room, even if it's a simple cold or a migraine. Don't Worry, Spaniards do that a lot. Even if they redirect you to a public hospital, you should go always to the *Seccion de* **Urgencias**. [U.S. **ER**- UK **Casualty Department**]

R b rt S b o ro ▸ Auxiliares de •••
conversación

3 hrs ·

I had to take an ambulance to the hospital to get an IV a couple of weeks ago, and today I got a bill for 361 Euros. Unfortunately it's not itemized, so I can't see what it's for beyond "services." This is unusual, right? I've seen people paying way less or even nothing for medical services, so this feels really high. I have Adselas if that makes a difference.

👍 Like   💬 Comment

😢 1

I used an ambulance last year, also with adeslas, I didn't have to clear it first, and adeslas covered it, including the visit to the ER at a different place other than adeslas! I would say contact the hospital and ask if you can pay with your adeslas insurance and then just send them send the information. Feel free to PM if you want!

2 hrs   Like   Reply   More

View previous replies

I don't think you'll have a problem! We have great insurance; they even sent a doctor to my house once, and I paid nothing. Good luck! & hope you're feeling better!

1 hr   Like   Reply   More

The Auxiliares program, for example, has a very efficient and different private insurances depending on the region with full coverage. Most of the HealthCare Insurance companies if you choose to do the auxiliares program will be Cigna. Asisa, Adeslas, DKV, Mapfre or Sanitas. They´re great companies. Spaniards in spite of having a socialist Healthcare, they tend to buy a private health insurance, too. It has been estimated that more than 10 million Spaniards hold a private healthcare insurance card.

NOTE: if you are with any of the government teaching programs as an auxiliar, the British Council or Ministry of Education. Make sure you follow the instructions from the orientation and order your card. I suggest giving your school address as your address and the delivery of the health card will be safe and speedy.

Spanish healthcare is not free since it comes out of the Spaniards´ paychecks in form of a tax monthly. And they could pay up to 180-200 euros a month tops for the socialist government insurance over. So it is not free, though some Spaniards think so! It´s free, obviously, if they dodge taxes. In Spain it is mandatory to assist the sick and injured. It is considered a felony or a minor crime not to stop and help even people that had an accident in the street. So you know! So, individuals who are covered by the State system pay a contribution towards the cost, depending on their personal circumstance or how much they earn.

On the other hand, I love Spain for their accessibility to healthcare, dental, eye care, affordable pharmaceuticals and educated pharmacists. For the most part I have had great experiences. Normally, in the states I'd have to make an expensive eye appointment to even see an optometrist to get my prescription information and they'd try to corner me into buying something new and if I were to see an ophthalmologist the price escalated.

Here you can walk into an optometrist's office, bring them your script or if you're a regular they will pull up your file on the computer and order your contacts or give you your script for no added cost, no sales spiel, nada;

You'll be able to walk into any pharmacy, and buy anvil, ibuprophene or paracetamol without a prescription. And there are many drugs and medications you will not need a prescription in Spain. You can just walk also into the drugstore or pharmacy and tell them your symptoms and they will give me the most affordable medication, even a homeopathic remedy if you don't want the conventional medicine, which are legal to sell in pharmacies in Spain.

So much is accessible without a prescription; this is great because half the time we know our symptoms and have had this same problem before and know what we need without the hassle of going to the doctors. Of course it is always good to get checked out by a doctor first, but sometimes it is just a hassle to have to make an appointment with your doctor to get a routine prescription.

FOR GIRLS: You can also get the **morning-after-pills** (Sp-*la pildora del día después*) at the pharmacist cheaply, birth control pills cost between 2-12 euros just show them the brand you take in the US and they won't need a prescription. If you use an **inhaler** or puffer back home [this is known as **ventolín-salbutamol** o inhalador de asthma] and forgot it on your trip, no problem 3-6 euros. The list goes on, it is awesome.

And there are other natural health or homeopathic stores, which provide herbs, creams, pills and herbal extracts if you prefer that. But, if you are really sick- **GO TO THE EMERGENCY ROOM FIRST**- or DIAL 112 and request an AMBULANCE. Even if you get a bill later, the Insurance will cover all that. Carry your healthcare with you at all times like you do in the States and make sure to tell them your correct name and card number. Then go to the doctor and the pharmacist will probably tell you to go. And with the insurance that I provided above you are going to have here you'll never have to pay for anything at the doctors, dermatologist, dentist… no co-pays no surprise fees, this is the way it is in Spain.

HOSPITAL

Phrases:
- **Where is the nearest hospital?** -- ¿Dónde está el hospital más cercano?
- **We need a doctor.** -- Necesitamos a un médico.
- **We need help.** -- Necesitamos ayuda.
- **Can you help us?** -- ¿Puede ayudarnos?
- **Where is the nearest police station?** -- ¿Dónde está la estación de policia más cercana? or ¿Dónde está la comisaria más cercana?

Olivia Young (Travels Untranslated)

February 18, 2014 at 9:36 PM

While I was really happy to find out my placement earlier than I did through the Ministry, that is the only positive thing I feel I've gotten out of this program. CIEE might be helpful for people who have never been to Spain before, but if you have and/or feel comfortable with a slightly lower level of organization, I'd say just stick to the Ministry program.

First off, our **insurance** under CIEE is terrible. We were told we have complete coverage, etc. etc., but what they failed to make clear is that if you have primary **insurance** back home, any medical care we receive must be paid for UP-FRONT. We will supposedly get reimbursed later, but I don't think anyone has seen their reimbursements yet.

This bothers me for multiple reasons: We paid a hefty program fee and still, somehow, have to pay up-front for our medical care. This makes absolutely no sense to me, and besides none of us really has the money to do that without dipping into savings. In addition, the Ministry-provided **insurance** is great. My friend got her wisdom teeth removed, and it was all completely covered by CIGNA. I feel like we had the wool pulled over our eyes on this one, and it's left me both frustrated with CIEE AND afraid to get sick.

(The only positive is that our CIEE **insurance** is also travel **insurance**, so we're covered for flight cancellations, rebooking, and myriad other travel-related costs.)

Europe and United States have different names for paracetamol.

You can't use aspirin? Don't Worry!

No one knew what I was talking about when I was asking about a puffer, Advil, or Tylenol extra strength etc....

What are the European terms for US drugs? What are some of the brand names? Why aren't common drugs given the same English name worldwide?

Below is a list I gathered throughout the years and will get you by under minor injuries or maladies. All of these don't need prescription in Spain. They will sell it to you over the counter and cheap!

VENDAJES Y GASAS = Wound Care, Bandages & Supplies, Wound Treatment, Wound dressing

BÁLSAMO DE TIGRE= TYGER BALM (You must go to the super store Decathlon to buy it for 10 euros, also mercadona sells a rubbing light tiger balm for 3 euros)

ALCOHOL 96 = ISOPROPYL RUBBING ALCOHOL, VETERECYN

AGUA OXIGENADA= Hydrogen Peroxide

TIRITAS= band-aid, plasters, sports strips.

PARACETAMOL= Aceta; Aspirin-Free Pain Relief; Aspirin-Free Anacin Maximum Strength; Dapacin; Fem-Etts; Genapap; Genapap Extra Strength; Genebs; Genebs Extra Strength; Mapap Regular Strength; Mapap Extra Strength; Maranox; MedaCap; MedaTab; Panadol; Tapanol Regular Strength; Tapanol Extra Strength; Tylenol Caplets; Tylenol Tablets 325 mg; Tylenol Regular Strength; Tylenol Extra Strength.

ESPIDIFREN or IBUPROFENO= Motrin, Ibuprohm, EmuProfen, Ibuprofen, Advil, Motrin, Proprinal, IBU, Ibuprofen UK Anadin Joint Pain, UK Arthrofen, UK Artofen, Ebufac UK, Neobrufen.

FRENADOL= acetaminophen/salicylamide, CODEINE.

GAVISCON= pepto bismol

Aspirina® 500 mg comprimidos efervescentes para dolores de cabeza, musculares y de espalda= Alka-Seltzer (aspirin / citric acid / sodium bicarbonate)

OMEPRAZOL = PRILOSEC

BETADINE or Povidona yodada = Betadine

Lidocaína= XYLOCAINE

ASACOL MESALAMINA 800mg (in Spain comes in bigger tablets or doses. Don´t need a prescription either) = Asacol HD mesalamine 400mg tablets.

CITRATO DE POTASIO= potassium acetate/potassium bicarbonate/potassium citrate systemic [KIDNEY STONES , kidney colics, Nephrolithiasis Renal Tubular Acidosis...

Lexatín/ Tranquimazín/Stilnox (insomnia pills, sleeping related problems)= trazodone (Desyrel), emazepam (Restoril), triazolam (Halcion), Doxepine (Silenor), Eszopiclone (Lunesta).

AfterBite/RepelBite= Bens, Natrapel, Afterbite

Hansaplast/Beducen/ Furacín=AfterBurns

Spray nasales/ Colirios/Inhaladores (allergy related, hay fever etc...)

Alavert/Claritin/ Zyrtec/Allegra= Mucinex nasal spray (oxymetazoline) Nasacort (triamcinolone) Nasalcrom (cromolyn sodium) Nasalide (flunisolide) Nasonex (mometasone) Odactra Omnaris (ciclesonide), Beconase (beclomethasone) Benadryl (diphenhydramine) Clarinex (desloratadine) Claritin (loratadine) Claritin-D (loratadine/pseudoephedrine) Dexacort (dexamethasone) Dymista (fluticasone propionate/azelastine hydrochloride) Elestat (epinastine).

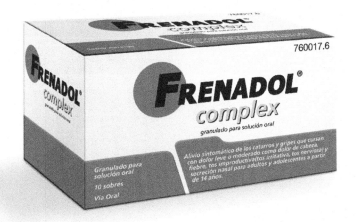

REFLEX SPRAY (ANALGESIC Spray for muscle strain, pains, bruised limbs etc) = Algipan, Algina, Algesal, Altridol, Gelol, Reumoflex, Voltarem.

I suggest, unless you know very well what medication you have to take, seeking doctor´s advice when feeling sick!

ALWAYS CALL 112 IN CASE OF EMERGENCY!!!

PART 2: MAKE A DECENT LIVING AND SETTLE DOWN IN SPAIN

CHAPTER 10
MAKE MONEY IN SPAIN
ACADEMIES VS PRIVATE TUITION

So, you just decided to take a leap forward and move to Spain for good!

It will be an unforgettable time, an experience that will change you for the better, a time you will remember for the rest of your life. And you will not regret it. I promise. But it won´t be easy? Nope. If it were, everyone would do it. But what is the one thing that causes the most stress among young expats?

Money. Money. Euros... Dinero. Pasta.

Whatever you want to call it; it's stressful having to think about money all the time. More than likely, if you are reading this you are coming to Spain as an English teacher whether it is through the Spanish ministry of education, the British council or as a Freelance teacher. For example, if you're an auxiliar from Britain or America or Australia you'll work 12-16 hours a week for 700-1000 euros a month.

If you are British or European, you can work legally in many sorts of jobs in Spain. If you are American, you are far less lucky. Spain's economy is not booming, but there's a great demand for English teachers in Spain right now. Most jobs you are going to find are related to teaching English. But there is good money to be made if you play your cards right.

Remember that employers here pay between 40 and 60 days after you start off working for them including the auxiliares or teaching assistant jobs. No-one is gonna pay you hourly more than 10 euros net. Teachers at schools or academies make between 5-10 euros per hour.

Clases particulares

This can be a huge source of income if you are motivated. Most people prefer you to come to their house to give a class, but I have had the occasional student who prefers to meet in their office, a café, or even at my house. The best way to find private classes is to put up an add on tusclasesparticulares.com. You'll get an average of 3 emails and phone calls from this site a day, and it can lead to a job at an academy since they advertise on the site, too. You ought to set this up as soon as you arrive in your destination city- if possible no later than mid-September to beat the rush of returning and new English teachers.

Another source of income can be online on websites like **http://lingobongo.com or VIPKid Teachers.**

How much to charge

You need to find out **what the average native speaker charges** for classes in your city in Spain. In Madrid, Barcelona, Vigo, Valencia or Bilbao it is about 20-30 euros per hour. In Orense or Zaragoza, for example it goes from only 12 to 20 per hour. It depends on where you are. Sometimes if I have students who want a lot of hours, like at least 6-8 a week, I give a discount. If you have groups charge per person at least 7 euros and you can make a lot.

Be **firm** on prices. There will be people who pay more. Having a native English teacher is far better than a non-native speaker. Most people usually have between 1 and 4 hours per week, usually 2 hours.

If you work at your school Monday through Thursday in the morning, and then you should pick up a few hours of classes in the afternoon. Logic says alone that if you work your ass off 4 days a week, make money and then have 3 day weekends for traveling and fun. You can usually earn **an extra 200-300 per week**. However, people are not very persistent with English classes and some of them will start dropping out or missing classes. Make clear to them, that if they miss a scheduled class, they must pay for your time unless they tell you well advance, they aint showing up for the class.

Academies

There are many English academies around Spain, all of whom want native English speakers. However, **you can't legally work there on a student visa** unless you get all sorts of permissions sorted out at the oficina de extranjeria and only a few academies can do the legal papers and understand the legalese [at the end of the book, I have enclosed a few academies that can help you out with this].

In Spain as an American, we cannot get work papers unless we have a contract. But not all is lost. A huge amount of money is moved under the table (*en negro*) in Spain. Many academies are willing to hire Americans and just pay cash to you every week or month. If you are lucky, you can try to get hired that way; it's probably your best bet for a larger, **steadier additional work and income**. And you don't have to waste time cancelling classes or traveling far between lessons. Academies pay less per hour [6-12 euros] than a private class but like I said they're set slots and classes don't get cancelled, plus you'll schedule wont change as much as teaching private lessons. Prepare a resumé-one page long- state where you have worked before and experience you have had teaching or even counseling at a summer camp. This is valuable experience that academies take into consideration.

Start looking up academies in your city just before you arrive. Send out emails and make some calls. Most schools start in September, and as you are in Spain, most academies will be hiring last minute in September. And they are always desperate for native speakers. The earlier you start looking the better.

Nannying, babysitting or au-pairing-Canguro (Spanish)

Babysitting is less prominent in Spain than in the US, because so many families live together or in the same city; there is always a cousin or a grandma around. Or they leave their kids at a cheap daycare or kindergarten (*guardería*).

Nevertheless, sometimes they do hourly babysitting in some regions or school English pickups. You go and pick up the children from school and talk and play with them in English. You can charge 10-15 euros an hour for this, and maybe it's close to your home. I would always get lots of calls from parents interested in having me watch their very young kids for a lot of hours, speaking only in English. Spanish parents have caught on the trend of **early childhood linguistic development**, the earlier you start teaching your kids a foreign language, the better. [I'll provide you with a list of au-pairing agencies at the end of the book]

Summer camps

A great deal of English teachers and auxiliares peace out of Spain as soon as their contracts end in May or June. English classes start waning down and maybe some stay for a few weeks to travel, but for the most part they head straight home for the summer, even if they are planning to come back in the fall. But for me, Spain is at its best in summer!

Most of the local fiestas are held in many Spanish towns and pueblos from May to September!

From my own experience, **it is much easier to find quick work in Spain over the summer** than to go back to the US for 3-4 months and expect to find a job then.

Baris · a year ago

Hi Jenny,

I just read about your writing, ' Cost of Living in Barcelona' and it helps me in many ways, thank you for that. I have some further questions, can I learn your e-mail so that ı can communicate you via there ?

Best Regards

Barış Özcan

∧ | ∨ · Reply · Share ›

Treavor Alvarado · a year ago

Wow, you buy one euro wine? I'm not saying, expesive is allways better. But try some finer wines and experince the real Barcelona. You sound like an expat That has not tallen fulls advantage of the cultural experiències of catalàn culture!

∧ | ∨ · Reply · Share ›

Besides, Spain rocks in the summer! You have the amazing beaches and a plethora of music and entertainment festivals like the bulls in Pamplona, San Isidro in Madrid, the *tomatina* in Buñol, batalla del vino in Haro or the fiesta del vino blanco in Cambados, just to name a few. Expect around 150-250 euros per week from a summer camp-counseling job. Many of the **summer jobs available and work agencies will be listed at the end of this book, too.** You should also get an extra summer insurance extension or a travel insurance with DKV in case you have an accident. [Your regular school or teachers health insurance will expire when your work is over]

CHAPTER 11
ALTERNATIVES TO THE
AUXILIAR PROGRAM-BEDA, CIEE,
FRANKLIN PROGRAM, MEDDEAS, UCETAM

There are many alternatives to the British Council teaching assistant program, the North American Language and Culture auxiliares Program with similar parameters and pay scales. However, when considering which program to choose from, it's important to account for factors beyond wages and teaching hours. If your goal is to live in a specific Spanish community, to get teacher training or even to improve your Spanish then there's a program out there for you.

What are the requirements and duties?

+You will be **acting as a cultural ambassador or teacher's assistant** sharing your experiences and knowledge of English.

+ You must have a **high school diploma or a bachelor´s degree**

+You will be **teaching students as young as 3 and up to 18 years**, but duties will vary depending on the needs of your assigned school.

+Participants in each program will be **asked to assist in curriculum planning and in the classroom.**

+Each program operates on a **student visa** and provides **health insurance** to participants

Meddeas

This program takes place at private schools around in Spain. **Meddeas** is a placement program that offers a bit more flexibility in placement options. Apart from having the company make every effort to try and accommodate your preference in placement ages and regions, Meddeas also allows you to choose whether or not you want to live with a host family.

You can also decide on a start date in January, in several cases, and you are welcome to renew at your center or another. Note that there's an age limit: you must be a college graduate from the last 4 years or be in your last year of study. You will be expected to work 20 hours a week, which allows you plenty of time for outdoors activities and teaching private classes. There is no cost to the program, though a deposit is required to hold your spot. This deposit ranges from 150 – 350€ and is returned to the candidate upon completion of the grant. This program will also assign you a tutor, who will clearly outline your job duties and hours, as well as supervise your work.

Meddeas could be the right program for you if you're looking to save on living costs by staying with a Spanish family, or if you'd like to know all of your job duties before signing your contract. To apply, you must send an interest form or letter to the Meddeas website and wait to get further information. Check it here
https://www.meddeas.com/teach-english-abroad

+ You´ll be working for 10 moths in a row

+ The pay scale monthly is about 900€ for 20-24 hours; with a host family, 450€.

+There's VISA support [student Visa]

 AL August 23, 2013 at 11:32 pm

What kind of teaching experience did you have before applying to UCETAM?

Reply

 amelie88 August 25, 2013 at 11:07 am

I actually didn't have any teaching experience, and they said that was fine. All you needed was a Bachelor's degree. Now on the website they recommend having teaching experience, but my guess is they will still hire you if you don't have any. Having teaching experience already would probably help with this program.

Reply

UCETAM

UCETAM stands for Unión Cooperativa de Enseñanza de Trabajo Asociado de Madrid—quite the mouthful! In essence, it is an initiative that was designed to create a bilingual/bicultural program in Spanish schools by increasing the hours of English language classes and having native English speakers lead these classes. In theory, the students who benefit from this kind of language instruction will come out with a better level of English at the end of their schooling. Auxiliares are only placed in colegios concertados, schools that are similar to US charter schools. These schools are based on a cooperative model—meaning that the schools are self-managed by teachers who are members of the cooperative (not all of them are).

UCETAM schools are concertados, half public – half private primary and secondary schools, that are not affiliated with any religious order but instead are part of a worker's union [*sindicato* in Spanish]. You may be expected to take on more of a role within the classroom, as UCETAM gives priority to those who hold education degrees from their home country. Apply here **http://colegiosbilinguescooperativos.com/auxiliares-conversacion/english-language-assistant**

You should apply to UCETAM if you're looking for a higher salary and to be placed in Madrid, or want to be 100% clear about what your job duties are. UCETAM has no age limit and is comes highly recommended by past participants.

Positions are either 18 or 26 hours and assigned randomly according to the needs of the center. To apply, you must send an email to the program directly at **julie@colegiosbilinguescooperativos.com**, which will then send you an informational packet with application materials and job responsibilities.

Your completed application, which consists of a questionnaire, letter of recommendation and current CV, must be received by late February. There is no cost to apply, but applicants are selected based on their application and an in-person or Skype interview. Candidates are selected and notified in late May.

"Not a bad post college gig, but weigh other options"

★★★ ▼ Current Employee · English Language Assistant in Madrid (Spain)

I have been working at UCETAM part-time (More than a year)

Pros

Really depends on where you are placed in Madrid but UCETAM schools tend to have better coordinators than other esl programs. Also there support getting legal status.

Cons

There are really pointless trainings that don't really help you teach. You can only do it for 2 years and you can't change schools. Unlike other programs there aren't 3 day weekends garenteed, and while lunch is free you take hike pay is only 900-2300€ which is less than other programs.

Advice to Management

Make the trainings more interesting and hands on, be more responsive to auxiliares complaints (not the case at my school but have heard of the coordinators consistently taking schools side in misunderstandings).

Helpful

+ Your is work here is 10 months

+Your regular schedule is 18 hours a week

+Your pay will be around 1,000€. 26 hours: 1441€. September and June are recalculated.

+Visa is provided as student or work VISA

+If you want to live in Madrid, this is the program for you. UCETAM only places its auxiliares in Madrid and the surrounding suburbs, so you are guaranteed a placement in Madrid if you are accepted. If you aren't interested in living in Madrid, then it's pretty simple— don't apply!

+Out of all the auxiliares programs that I know of in Spain, UCETAM pays the best. You have a choice of working 17 hours or 25 hours a week. I worked 25 hours and was paid just a little under 1500 euros a month. For 17 hours, the pay is around 800-1000 euros a month. You also get paid on time every month so you never have to worry if your paycheck will be arriving months late like with the Ministry program.

+For first-timers to the program, UCETAM will supply documents you can use to apply for your visa before leaving Spain. Once in Spain, UCETAM will help you apply for the NIE, the residency card, and a process that can be very lengthy and time-consuming.

+This job is going to look fantastic on a résumé. I didn't initially think about this when I applied to UCETAM, but living and working abroad in another country will definitely make your application pop out amongst other job candidates. My experiences living abroad in a foreign country strengthened my language skills, which in turn helped land me my current job (which has nothing to do with teaching languages).

+This one is obvious but I'll say it anyways because to me it represents the biggest pro: your Spanish will improve. I can't predict how much you will improve because everybody learns at a different rate. However, I can guarantee that you will be astonished at how much better a handle you will have on the language by the end of the year.

Your students will be your best teachers—trust me on this! I picked up on so much Spanish just by listening to my students interact and asking them questions when I didn't know what a new word meant. Students also loved the unexpected role reversal of having their teacher become the student.

This program is highly competitive!

+Work for over an academic year (September – September)

+Pay scale monthly is 580€ (18 hours) or 770€ (24 hours).

+Tuition costs are waived

+Provides a Student Visa and a full coverage insurance but check legalese just in case.

+The most common destination is Alcala de Henares in Madrid.

Rebe July 6, 2014 at 3:02 AM

Hi Cindy,
All of the application details are indeed on Instituto Franklin's website. Click on the Master program in the left-hand panel. Then, many bullet points will appear underneath that particular program in the same blue menu. Select "Application details".

It's mostly a difference in education styles between the US and Spain, which I experienced when attending the Complutense University in Madrid. Also, I think it's the type of program where you'll get out what you put in, so perhaps some of the mixed opinions came from people who didn't put in as much effort as I would have.

Best of luck! Which Master are you interested in?

Cindy Rojas July 9, 2014 at 4:44 PM

Hi Rebe,

Thanks for the help! I was able to find it :) I was thinking of doing the Masters in Bilingual and Multicultural Education. Now, I haven't got a good chance to look around your blog, but what was it you did in Madrid? Did you do the Auxiliares de Conversacion? I am trying to decide between these two programs.

Thanks!

Rebe July 9, 2014 at 11:56 PM

I was a student one year, and did auxiliares de conversación another year. Both programs (auxiliares and Instituto Franklin) will give you the opportunity to teach English... the big decision is if you want to be working towards a Master at the same time or not. Looks like a great program - where else can you get a FREE Master's degree and get paid for your "student teaching" time? Best!

Reply

The Franklin Program

The Franklin Program is a combination master's degree and internship that places applicants in schools either 18 or 24 hours a week in addition to offering classes in various disciplines. Participants choose to study a one-year Spanish Master's in Teaching Spanish as a Foreign Language, International Education or Bilingual and Multicultural Education through a blended degree that combines online and in-person learning on Friday evenings. Note that these MA programs have a tuition remission upon successful completion of the program with the exception of the straight MA in Teaching. All school placements, recognized as "internships" by the program within the Comunidad de Madrid, and Master's classes take place at the Universidad de Alcalá in Alcalá de Henares, a university city outside Madrid that is reachable by train. Classes are held in both English and Spanish. Much like college, early applications are open for the month of November; the process reopens January 16th through the end of February by web. The application includes filling out a basic web-based application and scanning the following documents onto the application form:

+**Placement Form:** Asks for your preferred age group for your practicum. Must write about your education background and experience working with children, and can be written in Spanish or English.

+**Health Questionnaire**

+**Color photocopy of your passport:** Passport must be valid for 12 months after the program's end date

+One passport-sized picture

+Xerox copy of your Bachelor's Degree diploma

+Official university transcripts copy

+Resumeé/CV

+Registration form document (**downloadable**)

+2 Recommendation Forms completed by your referees

+ Statement of purpose

You must also send a statement of purpose as a short video of yourself through WeTransfer to **admissions@institutofranklin.net** in place of essays. You can find more detailed information about what constitutes the required documentation on the Instituto's webpage here http://www.institutofranklin.net/ensenanza/teach-learn.

You'll be prompted to send hard copies to the Instituto Franklin for pre-admission review. Admission decisions will be made by late April via email. Accepted applicants must pay a 500€ program fee to the Universidad de Alcalá to guarantee their spot at the university and school placement, plus a $100 application fee via PayPal.

CIEE

The well-established study abroad program CIEE provides placements within the North American Language and Culture Assistant program in Madrid. The key to CIEE is support, choice and extras: participants can choose to do a Spanish language immersion course or earn a TEFL degree.

You can also request working in the professional program, teaching business English while making contacts in the bustling capital city. CIEE positions are located all around the autonomous community in both urban and rural settings, though you are able to request a specific city or age group when turning in your application. Note that applicants must be under the age of 35. **If you're gunning for a position in the Comunidad de Madrid, CIEE is the right choice for you**. Additionally, if you're uncertain about the transition to Spain CIEE makes your move easy with a four-day orientation and yearlong in-country support under their immersion program – you can also get a TEFL degree for an extra $1000.

However, there are extra costs to consider, as the program carries a $50 application fee along with hefty program fees upon acceptance: the ten-month program costs $2,200, or two months of your salary. That said, the programs are designed for newbies to TEFL teaching in Spain and offer 24-hour support. CIEE also offers a volunteer course of three months in Castilla y León and Castilla-La Mancha and has no age limit.

The application deadline varies depending on the program and community you choose, but aim to apply by March 1st of the school year in which you want to begin. Positions with CIEE cannot be renewed; however you can choose to renew with the Ministry of Education or any of the programs listed on this post as a second year applicant. CIEE also runs Teach Abroad programs in other countries, including Vietnam, Chile and Thailand. Check out their Teach in Spain specifics here **https://www.ciee.org/go-abroad/work/teach-english-abroad/programs/spain/teach-spain**

+10 months of work

+Pascale around 1,000-1,200 euros a month

+Student Visa and full coverage health insurance

+Madrid, Avila, Segovia and other central Spain Locations

What level of Spanish do you need to have to participate in this program? You really don't need to know any Spanish to be an auxiliar in the Spanish schools. Most of the teachers prefer that you only speak to the children in English. I have personally found my background in Spanish to be invaluable when speaking to the non English-speaking teachers at my school or answering the questions of my low-level kids. It is almost impossible to teach children who barely know English without being able to meet them halfway to the language barrier.

BEDA

BEDA employs more than 1,000 auxiliares de conversación each year from a multitude of countries, primarily in Catholic schools in the autonomous community of Madrid. While a vast majority of placements are in Madrid, BEDA is working to expand to other schools in other regions of the country such as the Canary Islands and Andalucía. Work duties are the same as in the Standard English auxiliar program, with a focus on oral language production and assistance with bilingual curriculum in addition to Cambridge exam preparation.

BEDA participants receive an orientation in early September and around 15 mandatory training sessions throughout the year in conjunction with the Universidad Pontífica de Comillas in Madrid. Private health insurance is also provided. Applicants are asked to fill out a questionnaire here
https://assistants.ecmadrid.org/language_assistants/enroll_info/1/0
And successful candidates are then interviewed via Skype or face2face. Upon acceptance into the program a 175€ enrollment fee must be paid. Applications open in late November and close in late January most years (2018-19 application dates are from November 28th, 2017 until January 31st, 2018). BEDA wages are calculated on a sliding scale, with the 2017-18 estimated pay beginning at 873€ a month for 18 hours of work. The maximum assistant hours top out at 24 a week, grossing a total of 1165€ before tax. The school placement you receive decides the number of hours they will need you.

2 advantages to the **BEDA** program: assistants can renew their positions up to three years (four years total) and training is provided to become official Cambridge English Examiners for those who qualify. Go here to download the application and for additional information and contacts. **http://www.ciee.org/teach/spain/**

+Nine months of work in different regions you can choose

+Graded scale based on the hours you teach example : 18 hours 900 euros... 24 hours 1,100 euros.

+Madrid has the most placements; Andalucía, Canary Islands, Castilla-La Mancha, Galicia, Aragón, Asturias, Valencia and Murcia also get a lot of these language assistants

+Health insurance with full coverage and student or work VISA

View More on Instagram

85 likes

imaniabroad_ I have fell in love with this city. Barcelona I will see you again soon! #soulsociety #travelnior #blackadventuristas #blackabroad #wegotoo #barcelona #Spain #Imaniabroad

view all comments

L: What about the mandatory class for all assistants, do you find it helpful, or a waste of time?

I: The mandatory classes are hit or miss. I would definitely not say they are useless. I have earned a lot from them and gained a

lot of resources for my private classes. They have also given me lots of ideas for games and activities to do with my classes. As a first time teacher I think I benefited a lot from the classes. However, after your first year I can see how the classes might become redundant and a waste of time. Of course some classes may have been a waste but as a whole I didn't mind them. The classes are also great for socializing and meeting new people. If you go to a BEDA class and don't meet one new person every time you are probably doing something wrong.

L: What is your favorite thing about working with BEDA?

I: My favorite thing about working for BEDA is feeling like I don't have to do everything myself. It is nice to know if I have any issues with my school or in general I can reach out to them and they will help.

L: What is your least favorite thing about working with BEDA?

I: My least favorite thing about BEDA is the pay.

L: Are you able to easily get in touch with coordinators with questions or concerns?

I: Yes, as a I have mentioned before the coordinators are very easy to contact. They respond quickly.

L: Do you have the option to renew for another year? If yes, will you be doing so?

I: Yes, with BEDA you can renew. Although, I have enjoyed my experience with BEDA working for such little money is just not okay with me. I am looking into more lucrative options in Asia for next year, if they don't work out then I will renew with BEDA

British Council Language Assistant

You can teach English on paid six-month or yearlong placements and experience another country. According to their website, the Brits, this is what they say...

What is it all about?

As an English language assistant, you can teach English on paid six-month or yearlong placements and experience another country, gain new skills and make your CV stand out. If you are from outside the UK and want to **teach your language here**
https://www.britishcouncil.org/language-assistants/la-in-uk
You can become a language assistant in England, Scotland, Wales or Northern Ireland.

Am I eligible?

For most destinations you must hold an EU passport, have completed at least two years of university, and be a native-level speaker of English. They have an info brochure here...
https://www.britishcouncil.org/study-work-abroad/english-language-assistants/eligibility

Why become an English language assistant?

The program gives you the opportunity to:

- Diversify your CV
- Hone your language skills
- Gain transferable skills, such as communication, presentation, time management, organization, team-work, independent work, and creative thinking / problem-solving
- Immerse yourself in another culture
- Gain cultural awareness
- Gain professional confidence.
- Spanish level must be an A2 (Understand some Spanish and Read some Spanish-Elementary Level)

All placements are paid around €700- €1K and teaching time is limited to between 12 and 20 hours a week, giving you plenty of time to pursue other interests. In previous years, British language assistants have used their time abroad to take part in a myriad of initiatives, from **starting a small business** to **appearing on TV**.

What will I be doing?

A language assistant's role typically includes:

- Supporting the teaching of English in an overseas school or university
- Planning activities and producing resources to help students improve their English
- Introducing UK contemporary culture through classroom and extra-curricular activities
- Supporting the running of international projects and activities.

When you arrive, you may also be invited to take part in an induction course. Language assistants will not be required to:

- Discipline pupils
- Cover for illness
- Mark/grade work regularly.

Any additional duties you may be asked to carry out should be agreed with you before your arrival at the host institution. You should also expect to receive further training upon arrival.

Language requirements

You do not need a formal language qualification to become a Language Assistant. These skills can be acquired through regular travel, private study or through a course at a university language center. We may test your language skills at a further assessment stage or telephone interview if necessary. It is in your own best interest to hold the required language level, as you will be expected to communicate and complete the necessary administration procedures in the target language upon arrival. You can self-assess your language level against the Common European Framework of Reference for Languages.

+China – No language skills required

+Spain – A2 Spanish

+All other countries – B1 in the target country's language

Passport

You must hold a UK, Irish or other European Union (EU) passport in order to be eligible for the Language Assistants Program in general. Please see the country pages linked below for more specific requirements. If you have a non-EU passport, then you are not eligible for the Language Assistants Program.

Secondary-school education

You should have completed the majority of your secondary-school education in the UK. This is because part of your role will be to share your knowledge of UK culture (including the different UK education systems) to the students you will be working with.

There are two exceptions to this:

+If you have an Irish passport and completed your secondary-school education in the Republic of Ireland, you are eligible to apply, so long as you are currently studying at a UK university.

+If you have a UK or Irish passport but completed your secondary education overseas, you are eligible to apply. Non-UK / Irish passport holders who were educated overseas for their secondary education, including in a British international school outside of the UK, are not eligible to apply for the program.

University

You must have passed two years of university-level education by the time you start your assistantship to be eligible to apply for the program. For China different criteria apply. Please see the China country page for more information on the website here
https://www.britishcouncil.org/study-work-abroad/english-language-assistants/eligibility

Preference of location

You must be flexible with regard to the location of your post and be willing to accept a post wherever you are allocated. For most countries, you will be able to select three area preferences, as well as preferences relating to the size of town you'd like to work in and the age group you'd like to teach.

However, the number of posts in each area is strictly limited and your preferences cannot be guaranteed. Please look at the preferences available for your country of application on the country pages and research the areas available thoroughly before applying at the website link that I´ve provided.

Background check You will need to apply for an International Child Protection Certificate (ICPC). The cost of applying for an ICPC will be approximately £60 and you should not apply for an ICPC until told to do so. In line with our Child Protection Policy and our approach to safeguarding children, they say, they cannot accept your application if you currently have any outstanding prosecutions or criminal proceedings for the offences outlined below or have ever been convicted of or received a caution, reprimand or warning for a sexual or violence-related offence or any offence involving any type of harm (physical, emotional or sexual abuse) to a child or children.

If you commit a criminal offence or are the subject of any criminal proceedings after you submit your application, you must inform the British Council in writing as soon as possible. Failure to do so may lead to your application being withdrawn.

Teaching qualifications You do not need a Teaching English certificate as a Foreign Language (TEFL) qualification to be able to apply.

Number of consecutive placements You can only be an English Language Assistant through our program four times, regardless of whether the posts were in the same or different countries. Both consecutive and non-consecutive years will be counted. Our partner organizations abroad will have their own eligibility criteria, so please check with us before applying if you would be able to stay for a consecutive year in that country. If you are applying for a consecutive year in Colombia, Mexico, Spain or Switzerland, please see the consecutive year application guidance notes below.

Graduates and university students in their last academic year in the following countries can apply to be a language assistant in Spain:

Germany, **Australia,** Austria, **Belgium** (French or English), **Bulgaria** (English), **Canada** (French or English), China, China-Hong Kong (English), **United States, Russian Federation, Philippines** (English), **Finland** (English), France, **Hungary** (English), **Ireland,** Italy (Italian), **Luxembourg** (English), Malta, Morocco (French), **Norway** (English), **New Zealand,** the **Netherlands** (English), **Portugal, the United Kingdom, the Republic of Fiji and Sweden (English)* Apply here**
http://www.mecd.gob.es/servicios-al-ciudadano-mecd/catalogo/educacion/profesorado/convocatorias-para-extranjeros/auxiliares-conversacion-extranjeros-espana.html

*All nationalities marked in bold are eligible for the auxiliares de conversacion in English program

Amber is doing Hispanic Studies at the University of Kent, and is spending her year abroad in Montilla, near Córdoba in Spain, working as a British Council **Language Assistant**. Here are her thoughts about her time in Spain...

Amber says: "In this video I delve into my main reasons for moving to **Spain** and what I have been getting up to so far. I hope that this video can inspire others to take language learning to the next level like I have :)"

Do you have questions for Amber about taking up a language at university or life in **Montilla**? Ask on her **Amora First YouTube channel**, email her on: amorafirst@gmail.com, or check out her instagram **@amorafirst** :)

CHAPTER 12
MONEY MONEY MONEY
MAKES THE WORLD GO ROUND

American Taxes: to File, or Not to File

American taxes for people living abroad can be pretty complex. In principle, all Americans must file taxes even if they reside or work abroad, however, there are exceptions. *Do I have to file?* If I don't, *what are the benefits of filing my American taxes when it's so much extra work?* The United States requires that you report here **https://www.irs.gov/businesses/income-from-abroad-is-taxable** for tax purposes. But, all of the *teacher assistant or auxiliar's jobs* overseas *income is a scholarship!* Yes, in Spain your stipend is classified as a scholarship. The US, however, classifies it as income. According the IRS, the penalties of not declaring foreign income can be considerable.

Consequences for Evading Taxes on Foreign Source Income

You will face serious consequences if the IRS finds you have unreported income or undisclosed foreign financial accounts. These consequences can include not only the additional taxes, but also substantial penalties, interest, fines and even imprisonment.

There are exceptions, however. Just like citizens living in the US, American citizens and resident aliens living abroad have a least filing threshold. For the tax year of 2018, that minimum is $10,400. Below, we're going to look closer at American taxes in different possible situations, and also where to put the income on your tax return (check here **https://www.irs.gov/individuals/international-taxpayers/us-citizens-and-resident-aliens-abroad-filing-requirements**).

American Taxes for First Year Auxiliares

If you're a first year auxiliar, whether or not you owe money to the IRS will depend on how much money you earned in 2018 before starting the Auxiliares de Conversacion program. A friend of mine was a graduating student who worked part time from April-August before moving to Spain in September of 2017; her first year income was under the least filing threshold. She filed anyway, and I recommend you do too, for two reasons:

+**You may get a Refund.** She got $718 back for filing her 2017 American taxes! That's a month's wages for many auxiliares.

+If you have federal student loans, you can use your tax return to renew **Income Based Repayment plans**. Without filing your American taxes, proving your income while living and working abroad will be harder.

If your earned income in 2018 is at or above the threshold of $10,400, you will not have a choice. You must file your American taxes.

If you know in advance that you're going to be an auxiliar in 2019, and that you'll have higher income for your first year filing American taxes abroad, you can adjust your withholdings before you go. You can do this by changing the personal allowances on your W-4 to zero, so that you'll be less likely to owe when your auxiliar income is eventually added on and not taxed as you're paid. Check here **https://www.bankrate.com/finance/taxes/adjust-withholding.aspx**

American Taxes for Second Year+ Auxiliares

Your American taxes won't get tricky until your second year in the auxiliar program. There are many variables that could affect what you may owe the IRS. Did you work for an academy? Or how about working for an online company? Did you go home for the summer, or Spend 330+ days outside of the US? Once you spend 183 days in Spain, you are considered a tax resident. Check here **https://www.expatica.com/es/finance/Taxation-in-Spain_471614.html** what does this mean? You may have to file taxes in Spain and the US. Spain has its own minimum filing thresholds, and you aren't likely to reach it as an auxiliar, unless you work for more than one employer in a calendar year. You can't start your Spanish tax process until April 8th this year, but Americans living abroad get an automatic two month extension on filing taxes, check here **https://www.irs.gov/individuals/international-taxpayers/us-citizens-and-resident-aliens-abroad** meaning that you won't have to file until June 15th. In the meantime, you can read more about Spanish taxes here https://www.rankia.com/blog/irpf-declaracion-renta/3779065-declaracion-renta-2017-irpf-campana-ano-2018-calendario-como-solicitar-borrador-tengo-que-declarar

My friend's second year in the program, not only was she a Spanish tax resident, but she was considered a resident of Spain for American tax purposes due to the **Physical Presence test** (Being outside of the US for 330+ days). Check the file here **https://www.irs.gov/individuals/international-taxpayers/foreign-earned-income-exclusion-can-i-claim-the-exclusion-or-deduction** This only happens if you do not go home over the summer. Like if at anytime of the year, you become, for example, a Bona Fide resident, with a residency card through Pareja de Hecho or marriage.

You should use **FileYourTaxes.com**, because they let you file for free without an American address. If you earn above the threshold for American taxes while being a tax resident in Spain, you can file the **Foreign Earned Income Exclusion**, check here **https://www.irs.gov/individuals/international-taxpayers/foreign-earned-income-exclusion**, which will make your first $100,000 untaxable in the US. This is a great option for people living in Spain long term and earning more than the auxiliares stipend.

Tax Resident in my Home State?

The following states wont let you off the hook easily,

+California

+South Carolina

+New Mexico

+Virginia

According to **Greenback Expat Tax Services**, these states will consider you a resident if they feel like you still have ties to the state, such as property ownership, a state driver's license, or even a mailing address at a relative's house. If you come from one of these states, you may be liable for state income tax on auxiliar income even if you live the entire calendar year in Spain. In that case, you will need to weigh the pros and cons of filing vs. not filing if you are below the threshold of $10,400. If the extra state tax is worth the benefit of transferring your tax info to your student loan IBR plan, then do it. For those who haven't got federal loans at all, and if you are below the filing threshold, there is no requirement. However, filing still may be a good idea in case of future audits.

Taxes Taxes and more taxes...

If you work at an academy or as an online English teacher while living abroad, this could also affect your American taxes (and maybe your Spanish taxes). If the extra income puts you above the threshold, you will likely owe taxes unless you qualify for the Foreign Earned Income Exclusion or the Foreign Tax Credit. The first one, as mentioned above will let you exclude approximately $100,000 of income per year, which is more than most of us will make while living in Spain. However, it's got one downfall. If you are planning to contribute to an **Individual Retirement Account** (IRA) at any point, you cannot use income that falls under this exclusion. The other option is to take the Foreign Tax Credit. You might end up owing some income tax, but it lets you take a deduction to account for foreign taxes. You can contribute to your IRA in this way.

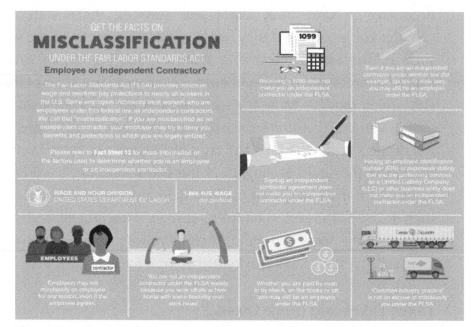

If you aren't planning to contribute to retirement while abroad, the FEIE is the best option. There can be some interesting tax implications if you work for an online English teaching company. Many of these companies were in their infancy over the past couple of years, and whether or not you were working as an employee or a contractor may have been unclear. Now that they're *"legitimizing"* themselves, many companies are giving out IRS 1099 forms, or classifying you as an independent contractor. If you work under these conditions, you will be considered self-employed by the IRS, and the minimum threshold for filing self-employment income is just $400! Independent Contractors must pay much more in taxes, because their employer is listed as themselves, rather than the company they work for. You will pay approximately 30%.

Where do you List your Auxiliar Income?

Now that you understand a bit more about American taxes for auxiliares or teacher assistants, *where do you put the income when you file*? If you are using TurboTax Freedom edition and are still a resident of the US, check the screenshots below,

*EDIT: TurboTax Freedom edition is different than TurboTax Federal Free edition. Freedom edition here

[**https://turbotax.intuit.com/taxfreedom**] is for low income ($33,000 Adjusted Gross Income or less).

Go to "Less Common Income." At the bottom, you will see "Miscellaneous Income". Click that.

Then, Choose the first option.

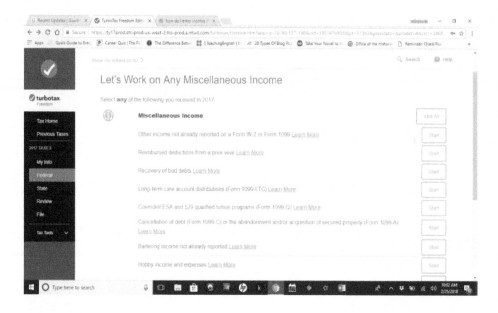

Click yes.

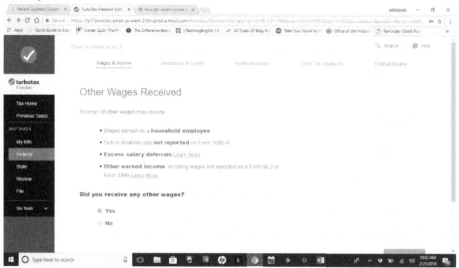

Then, Click yes again.

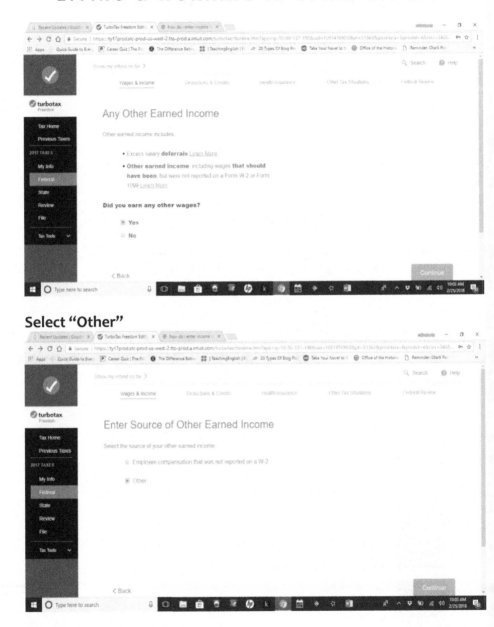

Select "Other"

Go on Google and Convert your earnings from euros to $ dollars. This is for a full year. Convert $2100 or $3000 for first year, depending on where you work.

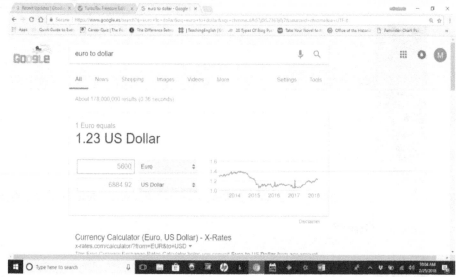

Now, Enter your converted income here.

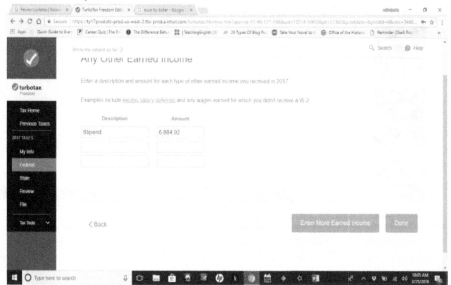

If you done it right, the total will appear in the column at the bottom.

Tell them about your bank account. You won't likely have enough ($10,000) for it to matter.

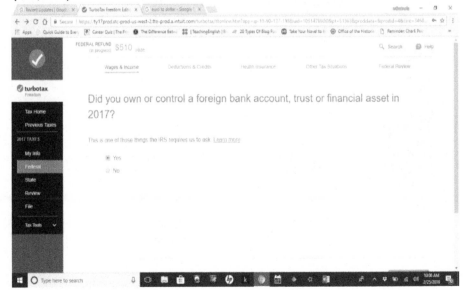

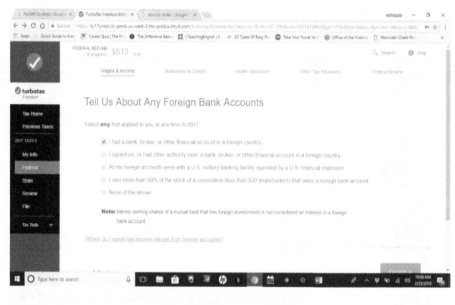

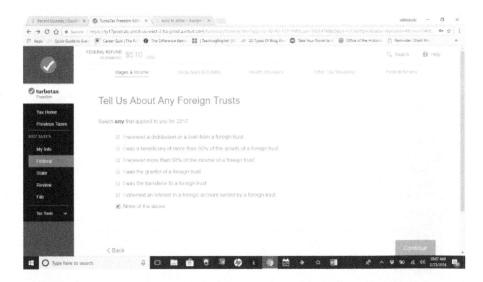

It will keep you asking more questions but follow my lead here

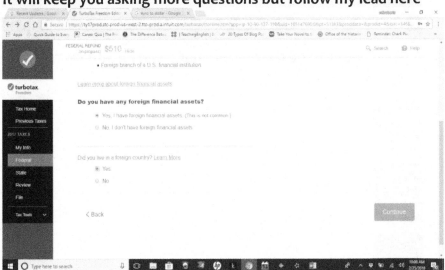

No extra info is required.

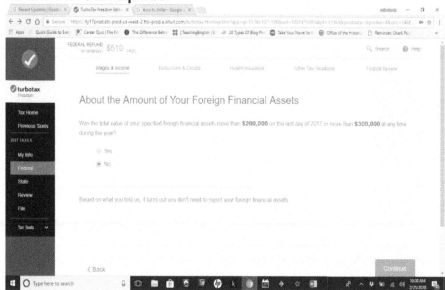

If you worked in the US, this number could be different.

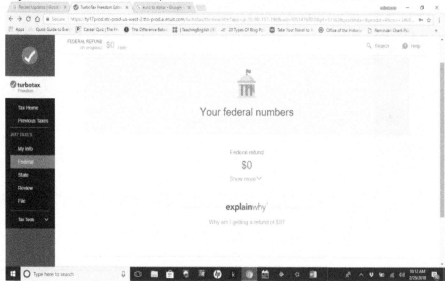

You must ignore the state tax at the top. Remember that this is only a test to show you step by step the screens, **THEY ARE NOT REAL NUMBERS**. This screen, however, shows that both Federal and State are free to file.

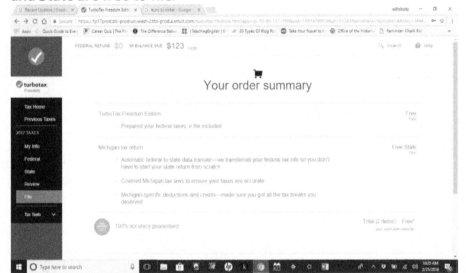

Please remember that this way is only free if you are still a US resident. Refer to the IRS website if you need recommendations for free filing for non-residents. As I suggested above, you can use **fileyourtaxes.com**. It´s free.

Average Income in Spain

This is the big Tamale!

According to many blogs including the Ministry of Education in Spain, the average income for an English teacher in Spain is between 700 and 1800 euros. As an auxiliar de conversacion or teachers assistant, you know that your income will be either 700 or 1200 euros a month, depending on the location where you have been assigned to teach.

What is more important than your actual wages, however, is how it compares to the average wages where you will live. This will determine how comfortably you will live compared to other people in your city. Madrid; Barcelona or Valencia [They pay here between 1000-1200 euros], almost for sure you will have to top it up with some little extra work. For other towns and cities around Spain, 700 euros is enough to live on. But let's see an example.

The average income in Vigo is 900 euros a month. The average in Madrid is 1600 euros. What this tells us is that, at about 78% of the average income in Vigo, compared to about 44% of the average income in Madrid, an auxiliar would live much more comfortably in Vigo on their auxiliar wages alone.

Note that I lived in both of these cities, and was able to get by perfectly fine on just the auxiliar income, even at 44% of the average. However, the closer you are to the average, the more money you will be able to save or spend on travel without having to do as much extra work on the side. Check my earlier chapters about cost of living and accommodation, food etc...

Final Thoughts On This...

From personal experience, I can tell you that Vigo, Marchena, Huelva, las Palmas de Gran Canaria, Valencia, Castellon and Alicante are the best ratio overall of auxiliar pay to average resident pay. In Alicante and Castellon, you would even be paid above average. Also, if you ended up yourself in one of these regions with a higher average income, it likely means you can charge more for private classes.

CHAPTER 13
HOW TO RENEW YOUR TIE SECOND YEAR IN ESPAÑA

+Current TIE plus two photocopies (front and back)
+Passport and two photocopies of each page
+Form EX-00 plus two photocopies here
http://www.ub.edu/uri/Documents/form_est.pdf
+*Carta de Nombramiento* plus two photocopies
+3 photo carnets (you won't need these right away when you hand in your paperwork but I'd have them just in case)
+Form 790 código 012 plus two photocopies here
http://www.exteriores.gob.es/Embajadas/CANBERRA/es/Documents/Modelo%20790%20Codigo%20012%20%28Solicitud%20de%20NIE%29.pdf
+Your current *health* card [generali, adeslas, asisa, dkv etc] plus two photocopies

One of the biggest headaches of the year comes always at the end, when you need to renew your TIE (your identity card/ visa) for the following year.

And if you don´t actually plan on coming back the following year, but you want to travel outside of Spain during the summer and then come back to Spain (when your current card is expired), then it´s probably a good idea to STILL apply for a renewal, so you can then get an *autorización de regreso* (authorization of return).

+ **Collect the following documents:**
- **Two completed and signed copies of the** *solicitud de autorización de estancia y prórrogas EX-00.* You can download the application here **http://extranjeros.empleo.gob.es/es/ModelosSolicitudes/Mod_solicitudes2/00-Formulario_estancia.pdf**
- If you want a complete list of other forms you may need, go here http://extranjeros.empleo.gob.es/es/ModelosSolicitudes/Mod_solicitudes2/index.html

WARNING: Print a couple copies, just in case. One copy will be returned to you with a stamp or another form of verification that it was handed in (and will be used for your regreso application, while the other will be submitted). **DON'T LOSE THE ONE THEY GIVE YOU!**

NOTE: Use an address you will have for the coming months, or the address of a trusty friend. Schools address is better.

- Photocopy (in color is better) of your **passport**
- Photocopy of your **original Visa** from your passport
- Letter of appointment (*Carta de nombramiento*) of the current year (ie 2017-2018)
- Letter of appointment (*Carta de nombramiento*) of the upcoming year (ie 2018-2019)
- Approval letter from your school (*certificada de aprovechamiento*) for the current year. Ask your school for this.
- Photocopy (**OF BOTH SIDES**) of your **current TIE card** (I was turned away because I only printed one side and had to beg people for 10 cents so I could copy the other side)
- **Bank draft 790/code 052.** (SEE DIRECTIONS BELOW)

1. Click that link, choose MADRID as the province, and then fill in your info in the document.

2. Choose box: 1.3 (*Prórroga de la autorización de estancia por estudios, movilidad de alumnos, prácticas no laborales o servicios de voluntariado (titular principal y sus familiares)*. By doing this, it should generate an amount of **16.98 Euros** (as of May 2018).

3. Leave the IBAN section empty.

4. When it is filled in, generate a PDF and print it (there will be 3 pages), take it to any bank and ask to pay the "tasa". You should pay 16,98 Euros, which is stated on the form. **BRING CASH TO DO THIS AND BE AWARE OF THE HOURS THE BANKS ALLOW YOU TO PAY TASAS!**

5. Don't lose the stamped copy they give you! This is worth money! The bank will keep one page, stamp one page, and give you another.

6. **Original passport**
7. Original **current TIE card**
8. **Bring EXTRA COPIES OF EVERYTHING**

+ Take all of the documents to be registered

- You can go to the registry office or to ANY public registry office. Last year and this year, I went to an office on **Gran Via, 3 in Madrid, for example.** And it was easy and painless.
- They will ask where to send the documents. You want to send to: **OFICINA DE EXTRANJERÍA DE Madrid, Vigo, Valencia etc...[Your Region]**
- Any additional documents that you hand in later should also be sent to the above address.
- They should give you your documents **AND A "RECEIPT" [resguardo] (instead of the stamp they used to use) THAT CONFIRMS THAT YOU HAVE, IN FACT, REGISTERED YOUR DOCUMENTS. YOU WILL NEED THIS RECEIPT (along with the EX-00) IN ORDER TO APPLY FOR THE REGRESO.**
- If you need to send additional documents, they can be taken to any public registry office and then sent to the SAME ADDRESS as above.

AUTORIZACIONES:

AUTORIZACIÓN PRÓRROGA DE ESTANCIA ☐
PRÓRROGA AUTORIZACIÓN ESTANCIA POR ESTUDIOS ☑
AUTORIZACIÓN RESIDENCIA (DA 1ª RD 2393/04) ☐
AUTORIZACIÓN RESIDENCIA CIRCUNSTANCIAS
EXCEPCIONALES (ART. 46.8.a RD 2393/04) ☐

EXPEDICIÓN TARJETA DE IDENTIDAD DE EXTRANJERO
POR AUTORIZACIONES DE:

RESIDENCIA TEMPORAL INICIAL / CIRCUNSTANCIAS
EXCEPCIONALES / TRABAJO TRANSFRONTERIZO
INICIAL / ESTUDIOS ☐
RENOVACIÓN RESIDENCIA TEMPORAL / TRABAJO
TRANSFRONTERIZO 2 AÑOS ☐
RESIDENCIA PERMANENTE / TRABAJO
TRANSFRONTERIZO 5 AÑOS ☐

RÉGIMEN COMUNITARIO:

CERTIFICADO DE REGISTRO / TARJETA RESIDENCIA
FAMILIAR CIUDADANO DE LA UNIÓN ☐

EXPEDICIÓN DOCUMENTOS DE IDENTIDAD:

AUTORIZACIÓN INSCRIPCIÓN INDOCUMENTADOS ☐
EXPEDICIÓN CÉDULA INSCRIPCIÓN ☐
DOCUMENTO IDENTIDAD REFUGIADO O APÁTRIDA ☐

EXPEDICIÓN DOCUMENTOS DE VIAJE:

TÍTULO DE VIAJE / DOCUMENTO DE VIAJE CONVENCIÓN
DE GINEBRA O APÁTRIDA ☐

OTROS DOCUMENTOS:

AUTORIZACIÓN DE REGRESO ☐
AUTORIZACIÓN EXCEPCIONAL ENTRADA O ESTANCIA ☐
ASIGNACIÓN DE NIE ☐
CERTIFICADOS / INFORMES ☐
AUTORIZACIÓN EXPEDICIÓN CARTA DE INVITACIÓN ☐
CARTA DE INVITACIÓN ☐
COMPULSA Y DESGLOSE POR CADA DOCUMENTO
RELATIVO A CARTA DE INVITACIÓN ☐

EXPEDICIÓN DE VISADO EN FRONTERA:

TRAMITACIÓN SOLICITUD AUTORIZACIÓN O VISADO DE
TRÁNSITO O VISADO DE ESTANCIA EN FRONTERA ☐

Ingreso efectuado a favor del Tesoro Público, cuenta restringida
de la A.E.A.T. para la Recaudación de TASAS.

Importe Euros ☐

Firma de pago: En efectivo ☐ E.C. Adeudo en cuenta ☐

Código cuenta cliente (C.C.C.)
Entidad   Oficina   D.C.   Núm. de cuenta

___ a ___ de _____ de _____

Firma:

+ Apply for Regreso

- Make an appointment. (Choose your region on the web or just go to the same place you went before for the NIE, Madrid, Vigo, Valencia etc... enter your information, choose an appointment. If there are no appointments before your intended travel dates, you should STILL choose a date and make an appointment and then you will be able to go to the office a few days before traveling and get your document. But keep checking back, as appointments will open up).

+ Check TIE status

- Two months after applying for reapplication, you will receive a letter (so make sure you use a good address when applying). This document is *resolución favorable que autoriza la prórroga*
- If your application is rejected, visit your local extranjeria police station or e-mail auxiliares.conversacion@ your region

+ Fingerprints

- Register your current address (empadronamiento) when you come back to Spain the following year (THIS IS IMPORTANT!)
- Book a digital fingerprint appointment.
- Bring the following to your appointment: Passport, three color photos (printed from the machines in metro stations), Application EX-17, go here

  http://extranjeros.empleo.gob.es/es/ModelosSolicitudes/Mod_solicitudes2/17-Formulario_TIE.pdf
- Bank draft modelo 790/012 that has been paid and stamped at a bank, your *certificado de empadronamiento*
- Go to your finger print appointment on your scheduled day with those documents and expect to wait....

+ TIE collection

ALL OF THE SPANISH REGIONS ARE PRETTY MUCH THE SAME WITH PAPERWORK AND PROCESS. JUST THE LOCATIONS AND APPOINTMENT ADRESSES AND OPENING TIMES MAY CHANGE THINGS TO REMEMBER

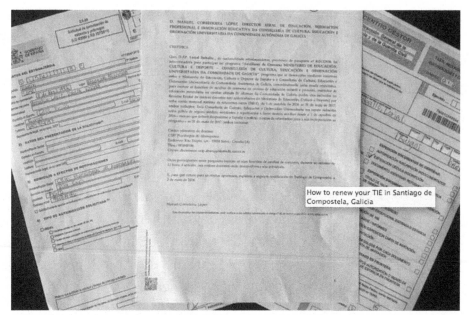

How to renew your TIE in Santiago de Compostela, Galicia

- 35 days after your fingerprint appointment, you can pick up your brand new, shiny TIE from: *Brigada Provincial de Extranjería y Fronteras from any Police Station of any region assigned to you.*

- **You cannot begin this process until you get your** *carta de* **nombramiento from your school again.** As soon as I got my placement in Vigo I emailed the coordinators there and asked them if I could get my carta ASAP since my TIE is expiring in May and I need to renew it. I got my carta a week later!

- If you are **switching regions** or provinces email your current and future coordinators to see where the best place for you to do your paperwork is. For example, you are currently in Madrid but since you're going to be working/living in Vigo you'll have to go to Pontevedra or Vigo.

- This could even affect you if you are living/working in Valladolid for example but then change to Salamanca. Ask the right people because it is better to place a safe bid here.
- If you go home for more than 90 days you may have to get a **whole new visa** so email your coordinator because it could be different for specific cases.
- Make sure your passport will be **valid** during the time of your stay

CHAPTER 14
HOW CAN I TRAVEL AROUND OR OUTSIDE OF SPAIN?

As an auxiliar, you get three day weekends every weekend (what???) longer weekends when there are bank holidays, and week+ long breaks for winter and Semana Santa. You'll probably end up traveling with other auxiliares, as they have the same schedules (just make sure you all want the same things out of your trip)! Transportation options depend the availability of the city you're placed in. If you're in Madrid, you're pretty much in the center of everything, so you can weigh your different transportation options. Most of these will be available in larger cities (except flying):

- Train – **Renfe;** AVE is the high speed one
- Bus – **Alsa** is a big one
- Plane – **Ryanair** is the go-to budget airline for auxiliares
- Car – Rideshare with **BlaBlaCar** or rent

Keep in mind that the **TIE card expires** when it says on your card, for most of people, surely May 31st or June 1st, but sometimes the TIE cards have expiry dates like September 12th. This isn't uncommon. If you're planning on getting a round-trip ticket to anywhere, and would be leaving the **Schengen Area** after an eight-month stay and returning a mere three weeks later.

Getting to know somebody

me llamo	my name is
¿cómo se llama Ud.?	what's your name?
soy de	I am from
vivo en	I live in
¿de donde es Ud.?	where are you from?
¿cómo está Ud.?	how are you?
¿cómo le va?	how is it going?
estoy bien	I am fine
¿que pasa?	what´s happenin'?
¡nos vemos!	be seein' you!
hasta luego	see you later
hasta pronto	see you soon

Tastes, preferences, needs

no me gusta	I don't like
me gusta	I like
me encanta	I love it!
prefiero	I prefer
me gustaría	I would like
no importa	it doesn't matter
es necesario	it's necessary
es importante	it's important

HELP words!

no hablo español	I don't speak Spanish
no entiendo	I don't understand
¿habla inglés?	do you speak English?
más despacio, por favor	speak slower please
¿me ayuda?	can you help me?
necesito un médico	I need a doctor
estoy perdido	I am lost
¡ayúdeme!	help me!
¡peligro!	danger!
¡cuidado!	careful!
¡llame al policia!	call the police!
¡ladrón!	thief!
¡para!	stop!

Non EU-resident tourists must leave the Schengen Area for 90 days after spending three months in the region. Many language assistants claim we get an "automatic tourist visa" once our TIE is up to travel freely, but don't buy into this, please. Get your TIE card renewed first (DO NOT risk getting deported or being blacklisted from returning into Spain.)

The Trains in Spain are best!

Riding the train around Spain is not only a great experience-you can meet lots of interesting new people- but also is very practical to reach out places. Although the network may not be nearly as comprehensive as France's, for example, it reaches nearly all corners of Spain, making it possible to explore Spain solely by public transportation.

Amelie Milet · 3 years ago

Oh I took the DELE when I came back from Spain back in 2012 at Instituto Cervantes in NYC. You could definitely do C1--I was only in Spain for two years and I passed it. If you do in the States, just know it will take them foorreeever to ship you your certificate which is proof you passed haha.

Also I've been to Provence a few times, including Avignon. If you can make it to Arles, definitely go. I'm not sure if you'll be there around the time they start up the open air Provencal markets for the summer but I think Arles is known to have the biggest one. I always ended up buying Provencal themed tablecloths for my mom. And this may be harder to get to via public transportation, but Les Baux de Provence is not to be missed (google image, you'll see what I mean). It can get very crowded, but we ended up going in the evening right before it closed. Bingo--NOBODY around and the views were amazing. Pont du Gard is also pretty cool--some cool Roman aqueducts which rival Segovia's but you may not have time. I covered a lot of these places on my blog (shameless plug) but I can't tell you how jealous I am that you are going to Provence. Love that region.

∧ | ∨ · Reply · Share ·

Types of Trains in Spain

Metro: The underground or Subway, most popularly known in Britain as the Tube. Runs in regions like Barcelona, Valencia, Madrid, Basque Country. Get a **carne joven** monthly card.

Cercanías: These are short distance or commuter rail that you can find in the biggest metropolitan areas like Madrid, Barcelona, Sevilla, and so on. They make few stops in the major city they're named for but they continue far out into distant suburbs and surrounding villages. You can distinguish them by their red and purple design scheme. Also called *Rodalies* in the Barcelona area.

Media Distancia: For regional "medium distance" trips you can take MD trains. Sometimes they travel within a single region (e.g., Galicia or Andalucía), but often they can go halfway across the country (e.g., from Madrid to Badajoz on the Portuguese border). Look for the orange and purple livery on the train cars.

Also called *Intercity* and *Regional* in certain areas. The high-speed variant of MD is called *Avant* and works as a regional train service that runs on the high-speed rails.

Larga Distancia: This is the "long distance," trains; these trains make cross-country hauls, often from Barcelona to Galicia or Alicante to Asturias. Spain's half dozen or so night trains (*trenhotel*) fall into this category, as do all AVE high-speed trains that depart from Madrid. The *Alvia* train is a hybrid of normal- and high-speed service, and can hop on and off the high-speed tracks if a section of the journey hasn't been completed yet. All long distance trains offer a cafeteria car for coffee, sandwiches, and snacks, and bear two purple stripes to distinguish them from MD or Cercanías trains.

Feve: A minor player in the Spanish train network, Feve is a system of narrow-gauge rail that runs along northern coast (and in Murcia). A series of mountainous routes connects eastern Galicia with Asturias, Cantabria, and the Basque Country. Feve's tiny train cars are usually painted blue and yellow.

Major stations and regional hubs

Madrid-Atocha: This is *the* major train station in Spain, a huge sprawling complex encompassing Metro, and Cercanías, regional, and high-speed services. It can be a little disorienting until you realize that the turn-of-the-century wrought-iron hall isn't actually a station but the *old* train platforms that were converted into a lobby and indoor garden. All the AVE trains depart from Atocha as well as all trains going to the south of the country (think Extremadura, Andalucía, etc.).

Madrid-Chamartín: Far to the north of Madrid's historic center is the Chamartín station, where you can catch the Metro, Cercanías trains, high-speed trains to <u>Segovia</u> and Valladolid, and long-haul trains to the north of the country. If Atocha mainly serves destinations in southern Spain, then Chamartín is its counterpart for the north.

Barcelona-Sants: The major terminal of the Catalan capital, Barcelona's Sants station receives AVE as well as Metro and Rodalies traffic. From Sants you can now ride the French TGV high-speed train all the way to <u>Paris'</u> Gare de Lyon thanks to the r line from Figueres to Perpignan.

Barcelona-França: Although not connected to the AVE network, Barcelona's other main train station is a grand Modernista structure covered by twin iron roofs, and historically sent off France-bound trains (hence the name).

Ourense & Monforte de Lemos: Here in Eastern Galicia these two stations are where the two halves of crazy-long trains meet up from A Coruña, Ferrol, or Vigo on their way to Madrid or Barcelona.

Palencia & Valladolid: In the center of Spain's sprawling north-central Castilla y León region, Venta de Baños (outside Palencia) is where most trains coming from Madrid-Chamartín branch off and continue on to Asturias, Cantabria, and the Basque Country. Near the regional capital of Valladolid at Medina del Campo, trains from Madrid head out to Galicia via Zamora.

Miranda de Ebro: On the border between Burgos province and the Basque Country, Miranda de Ebro serves as the gateway to the Basque counties as well as the crossing between the Madrid-Irún and Cantabrian-Mediterranean train lines.

Alcázar de San Juan: This anonymous town in La Mancha is a major juncture for trains coming from El Levante (Valencia, Murcia, Almería) going to places like Madrid, Sevilla, and Granada.

Linares-Baeza: Due to Andalucía's mountainous borders, historically the station of Linares-Baeza was the only way in or out of the region by train. While the AVE bypasses Linares on its way to Córdoba, the city is still a major hub for normal-speed rail today.

Border crossings

Figueres-Perpignan (France): You can take a high-speed train between Figueres in northern Catalunya to Perpignan in southern France.

Irún-Hendaye (France): These two Basque cities on the Bay of Biscay are separated by merely a river. So while it is possible to simply walk across the bridge, it's super easy to ride the train from Spain into France.

Tui-Valença (Portugal): The two historic border towns of Tui (southern Galicia) and Valença (northern Portugal) sit on either side of the Miño River. The Vigo-Porto express train passes through here. **Fuentes de Oroño-Vilar Formosa (Portugal):** The Madrid-Lisbon night train makes an awkward arc north from Madrid before heading back down south into Portugal, crossing the border in western Salamanca province in a town called Fuentes de Oroño.

Ultra Fast Trains (Ave)

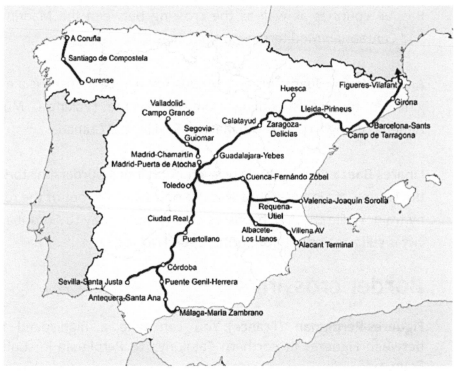

Madrid-Andalucía: Spain's AVE network was inaugurated in 1992 when the link between Madrid and Sevilla came on line. Today it also connects with Málaga (via Córdoba) on the Mediterranean coast.

Madrid-Barcelona: In 2008—a decade and a half after high-speed rail first came to Spain—the AVE finally arrived in Barcelona, passing through the Aragonese capital of Zaragoza as well as Lleida and Tarragona along the way. In Zaragoza a spur breaks off north to Huesca, and from Barcelona the line continues north to Girona, Figueres, and France.

Madrid-Valencia: Linking the Mediterranean coast with Madrid and the flat plains of La Mancha, this AVE route connects Madrid, Valencia, and Alicante. *Future expansion*: Murcia, Cartagena, and Almería.

Madrid-Castilla: Although it currently exists only in *Media Distancia* form, the high-speed service from Madrid-Chamartín heads north to Segovia and Valladolid in the center of the Castilian *meseta* or high plains. *Future expansion:* León and Asturias; Palencia, Burgos, and Cantabria.

Madrid-Toledo: It's nice that it only takes half an hour from Madrid-Atocha to get to the beautiful historic city of Toledo, but the only destination you can get to from Toledo's train station is... Madrid.

Madrid-Galicia: Somewhat awkwardly, the Madrid-Galicia high-speed link is partway done, but only in Galicia, which means the Galician section is somewhat stranded. Still, it does a fine job of bringing the far-flung cities of A Coruña, Santiago de Compostela, and Ourense together across extremely rugged terrain in a little over an hour.

How much does a Train Ticket cost?

The AVE tickets, some times from Madrid to Barcelona, you can buy them for as less as 20 euros and as much as 50-70 euros.

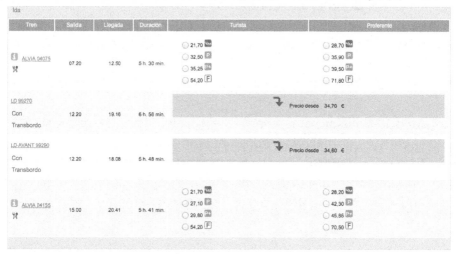

Flexibility: Although you have to pay for the full cost of the ticket, you also get flexibility as there's little to no cost to cancel or change your trip (and no problem if you happen to miss your train).

Preferente: Essentially first class, but you gotta pay 20-30% extra.

Ida y Vuelta: If you buy a round trip ticket you get 20% off your total fare. It's also possible to do a compra múltiple and still get the there-and-back discount on a circuit journey between three cities (A > B > C > A).

Promo: If you look online far enough in advance, you can find amazing steals with up to 70% discounts. I once took the train from Lugo in Galicia to Madrid for 16€, and from Santiago de Compostela to Barcelona for 20€. The risk with the Promo fare is that you can't cancel or change your ticket.

Promo+: Same as the Promo deal above, but it has up to a 65% discount off the standard fare and allows you to change or cancel your ticket for a small fee.

Mesa: If you have a group of four people, you can buy a "table" of four seats and get a steep 60% discount. Because of this great deal, Spanish websites like Compartetren.com and Compartemesa.com have sprung up to act as a virtual bulletin board to see who is riding the AVE at the same time and to see if a group of strangers can buy an entire mesa together and split the cost.

Carné Joven: If you have a European Youth Card (a.k.a., a carné joven) you can get an automatic discount of 20% regardless of the journey. Right On!

It's pretty simple. You can go **in person** to most any station in the country and pay with cash or credit card.

Useful Phrases

- **Quería un billete...** (I would like a ticket...)
- **para la próxima salida a...** (for the next departure to)
- **para el tren que sale a las...** (for the tren that leaves at...)
- **para el tren que vuelve a las**... (for the train that returns at...)
- **de ida y vuelta** (round trip)
- **con descuento carnét joven** (with youth card discount)
- **¿hay transbordo?** (is there a connection anywhere?)
- **¿puedo pagar con tarjeta/efectivo?** (can I pay with a card/cash?)

Are you a bit freaked out about trying Spanish? Then, you can usually pay at computerized machines available in a variety of languages. Be aware that only chip-and-pin cards will work at these kiosks. Another option is purchasing the tickets from the RENFE website online at

http://www.renfe.com/EN/viajeros/index.html

Filling out your personal and payment information is the hardest part; just try to accommodate your address into Spanish concepts of streets and residences, and cross your fingers that they'll accept your credit card—sometimes it works and sometimes it doesn't. If everything goes through, you can print your PDF ticket then and there, access it via your email, or have it sent to your iPhone's PassBook app, for example. Finally, you can also take your confirmation code and print a physical copy of your ticket at any train station.

+Check the SNFC for France
+ If you want to go from France to the United Kingdom, England etc… you can check the Eurostar train. You can purchase tickets starting at 35 euros. Check **goeuro.com**

Susan Beardar

I have abandoned any kind of belief in achieving my bookings by internet. Too many variables as well.…

Also one thing you have not included is the Dorada card.(I am officially resident here) And yep I am old officially. As such I pay (currently) 6 euros annually for a special card which then entitles me to very large discounts. Anything between 25 and 40 per cent. Variables like week days and weekends but worth checking up on as it only takes one medium journey to gain from it.

While I love the old part of Atocha station in Madrid it can be hell to find your way around as signing is poor if you are not a local. Knowing what "cercania" means will help though. Even spanish people find it difficult especially under stress of time, family , lots of luggage etc.

A little story: The AVE line has become a bit of a joke down in Murcia and Andalucia - bit like the airports that still havent been permitted to start trading.

There is 19 kms of train track including a very long tunnel near Mojacar which was to have been part of the AVE system which has been dropped. Another very big white elephant.indeed

1 ∧ ∨ · Reply · Share ›

Some of the places I strongly suggest traveling are the following,

France: Carcason, Cannes, Avignon, Azay-le-Rideau, Bayeux, Chinon, Mont-Saint-Michel, Nîmes, Paris, Pont du Gard, Saint-Malo, Versailles, Villeneuve-lès-Avignon.

Germany: Aachen, Cologne, Berlin, Black Forest- Bavaria.

Italy: Rimini, San Marino, Citá Vaticano, Bologna, Florence, Naples, Pompeii, Rome, Dolomite

Morocco: Chefchaouen, Fez, Meknes, Moulay Idriss, Volubilis

Portugal: Lisbon, Porto, Sintra, Aveiro, Algarve, Cascais, Viana Do catelo, Braga, Albufeira, Povoa de Varzim, Ofir, Valença do Minho.

United Kingdom: London, Wales, Cornwall, Scotland-Edinburg, Glasgow, Stonehenge, Winchester, Lake District, Brighton, Essex, and Gibraltar.

Spain Andalucía: Antequera, Almería, Carmona, Cazorla, Córdoba, **Granada**, Hornos de Segura, Iznatoraf, **Jaén**, Linares, **Málaga**, Marbella, Puerto Banus, Torremolinos, Fuengirola, Sabiote, Segura de la Sierra, Sevilla, Marchena, Úbeda, Villanueva del Arzobispo **Aragón:** Zaragoza-El pilar, Albarracín, **Huesca**, **Teruel**, **Asturias:** Gijón, Cangas de Onís, Covadonga, Lastres, Luanco, Llanes, Oviedo, Picos de Europa, Ribadesella **Basque Country:** Bilbao, San Sebastián, Vizcaya **Cantabria:** Comillas, Puente Viesgo, Santillana del Mar...

Castilla-La Mancha: Albacete, Alcázar de San Juan, Campo de Criptana, Toledo **Castilla y León:** Astorga, Ávila, Balboa, Burgos, Las Médulas, León, Ponferrada, **Salamanca**-cathedral y plaza mayor, **Segovia**-aqueduct, Toro, Zamora **Andorra:** Andorra la Vieja. **Catalunya:** Barcelona, Besalú, Figueres, Girona, Palafruguell, L'Escala, Reus, Santa Coloma de Cervelló **Extremadura:** Mérida **Galicia:** Sanxenxo, A lanzada, Grove, Cambados, Pontevedra, Vigo, Isla cies, Allariz, Betanzos, Boiro, Boqueixón, Combarro, A Coruña, Ézaro, Fisterra, A Guarda, Lugo, Mondoñedo, Muros, Cee, Muxía, Noia, Ons Island, Ordes, Ourense, Padrón-pimientos verdes, Ribadavia, Ribadeo, Ribeira Sacra, Santiago de Compostela- old town and cathedral, Tui, A guarda, **La Rioja:** Logroño, San Millán de la Cogolla **Madrid:** Alcalá de Henares, Aranjuez, Madrid, San Lorenzo de El Escorial **Navarra:** Pamplona Valencia: Castellon, Benicarlo, Vinaroz, Alicante, Jávea, Benidorm, **African territories of Spain:** Ceuta, Melilla. **Murcia:** la manga del mar menor

WARNING: Whenever I travel around big cities, I try to avoid large crowds and packed city centers at rush hour. The escalating Islamic terrorism in Europe has made me stay alert in all of European cities including Spain. Make sure you carry your ID´s and credit cards with you and if possible have always photocopies of the originals stashed away in a safe place.

CHAPTER 15
HOW TO DO PAREJA DE HECHO CIVIL UNION

Now that you know Spain pretty well, you have traveled around Spain and Europe... suddenly, you meet the love of your life!

Darn it! I wanna stay in Spain a little bit longer!

Well, then hold your horses and listen hard... because I'm enclosing a strategy, which can help you stay in Spain a little bit longer and happier.

IMPORTANTE: Nueva sede del Registro de Uniones de Hecho en la C/ Los Madrazo, 34 a partir del 02/02/18.

El registro permanecerá cerrado por traslado desde el 26/01/18 hasta el 02/02/18. Los citados mantienen sus fechas de inscripción en C/ Gran Vía, 18 hasta el 30/01/18 y en la C/ Los Madrazo, 34 desde el 31/01/18 en adelante

Apply for "pareja de hecho" (civil union) in Spain

If you're living in Spain (or thinking of moving here) and are in a relationship with a local, you've probably heard of "pareja de hecho." "Pareja de hecho" means something like "official couple" and is roughly the equivalent of a "civil union." It gives you many of the benefits of being married, without many of the obligations.

One of those benefits is being able to live and work in Spain if your "pareja" (partner) is a Spaniard or a European citizen. Once you have official pareja status, you'll be able to apply for a residency permit under the "reuniting with family" process, exactly as if you were married. Here are the steps you should follow:

Request an appointment

The first step is to go right now to **Consejeria Autonomica** (Junta de Andalucia, Xunta de Galicia, Generalitat in Catalunya, Xunta de Valencia and so forth) of your region to the **Registro de Pareja de Hecho** and make an appointment for the PdH Monday through Friday between 9:00 AM and 2:00 PM. The wait for an appointment can be up six months or more. This must be done in person but the process is simple and takes about 5 minutes. *Be sure to bring your TIE or passport with you.* You'll end up with a little piece of paper with your appointment date and a sheet of instructions...

Requirements

The requirements for PdH vary by community, so *verify what the requirements are in the area where you will be filing*. In Madrid, for example, the requirements are as follows:

+You must be over the age of 18.

+You must have lived together for 12 uninterrupted months. In Madrid, this is confirmed through the written statement signed by your witnesses.

+At least one member of the union must be "empadronado" in the Community of Madrid. You do not have to be "empadronados" together.

+You must be single, divorced, legally separated or widowed.

+You must not be related.

+You must not be already "pareja-ed" with someone else.

+You must be mentally capable of entering into the union.

Paperwork and Documents

One month before your appointment, you must show the following paperwork, *original and photocopy*, in person at the very same office where the appointment was made Monday through Friday between 9:00 AM and 2:00 PM. *These documents must all be a maximum of 3 months old at the time of your appointment*, so plan accordingly!

This only applies to Madrid, for example. If you want to become a pareja de hecho in Galicia, for example check here **https://www.mundojuridico.info/las-parejas-de-hecho-en-galicia/**

+A completed "solicitud" –
http://www.madrid.org/ICMdownload/JRVI.pdf

+Proof of the paid "tasa" – Modelo 030. You could wait and turn this in the day of your appointment. The cost is currently 82.12€.

+Valid NIF or NIE, passport or residency card for both members of the pareja and two witnesses. *For the witnesses, you can provide a photocopy of their IDs when you turn in your paperwork.* On the day of your appointment, your witnesses will need to come in person with the valid IDs.

+Certificate of Empadronamiento – Not a "volante". You can request this online and have it mailed to you at https://www-s.munimadrid.es/solicitudCertificadosPMHWeb/solicitudDocVolante.form

+Proof of marital status – Basically an official paper that says you are single. Spain regularly provides this to its citizens but there is no U.S. equivalent. Basically, get a birth certificate from your home state and a paper from a lawyer that says you are unmarried, divorced etc. Same applies to Aussies or non-EU members.   The American embassy won't give you a paper like this because they don't have it. It doesn't exist.

For Spaniards – All cities in Spain have a Registro Civil, -Juzgado De su Localidad- its free and its at the Spanish Courts. So go to the Registro Civil to ask for the rest of documents required. First Ask for The **FE de Vida y Estado** and **Partida de Nacimiento documents.** You don't need an appointment, just your Spanish ID- DNI español.

For Americans or non-EU-residents – You must make an appointment with your embassy, in this case, the U.S. Embassy for "notary services". The U.S. Embassy is located at Calle Serrano, 75, in Madrid, so whether you live in Alicante or Madrid, you'll have to do this. Appointments can be made via their website. At the appointment, you will sign a sworn statement, in Spanish, that you are single. The US general consul will then stamp the document. All you need to bring is your passport and 40-50€.

Because this document is from a foreign government, *it must be "legalized".* This means another appointment, which can be made **with a notary or the servicios consulares in Spain ,** at the office of legalizations.

Anonymous asked 3 years ago

0

I'm applying for a pareja de hecho but my partner gets paid under the table and doesn't use a bank account. We have also been living together for a year and a half but aren't empadronado at the same place. Have you heard of anyone having problems with these things? Thank you!!

1 Answers

Shaheen S. Staff answered 3 years ago

0

Hi there! I apologize for the delay, this question stumped me and it took me awhile to find the answer. At any rate, I came across someone in our Facebook group who was in a similar situation and was able to get it resolved.

"I just went through the pareja de hecho process and my boyfriend is also unemployed. They didn't require any work contract from him (though they did look at my pre-work contract). They asked him for a bank certificate of his account signed and stamped from his bank. they also said he has to have something like a minimum of 8,800 euros."

In short, he might need to open a bank account and put some money in there, at least temporarily.

As far as not being empadronado in the same place, I have heard of several people who managed to get pareja de hecho despite that. You apparently need to have two witnesses vouch that you did actually live together even though you weren't empadronado.

I hope that information is helpful!

Once you have your "pareja de hecho" status, then it's time to apply for residency, which will give you the right to live and work in Spain. The process for applying for residency, along with all the requirements, can be found on this **official information page (in Spanish)** here

http://extranjeros.empleo.gob.es/es/InformacionInteres/Informacio nProcedimientos/CiudadanosComunitarios/hoja103/index.html

One thing to remember is that, you shouldn't have any problem doing "pareja de hecho" with your partner; however if at least one of you is **not gainfully employed** you may have trouble being approved for residency. If neither of you are employed, it is possible to make up for that by showing funds in the bank (rule of thumb I've heard is around 10,000 euros at minimum).

Is There Another Simpler Way to Do Pareja de Hecho?

Yes. According to the ministerio de justicia and as of January 2018, **Notaries** can now do the same in their offices as what I have laid out above. You have to pay much more. However, notaries have now power of attorney to get people married in Spain. Ask or consult the local listings for a Notary Office- Notarios o Despacho de Notaria. I'm sure they'll explain the new process, no problem!

PART 3: Spain and Beyond

CHAPTER 16
SENDING/RECEIVING MAIL AND PACKAGES IN SPAIN

Information on sending packages and mail home, particularly to the USA and Canada. Shares the generally negative experiences with the postal service in Spain and how to avoid these problems in the future. Remember that stores with the big brown-and-yellow "tabaco" signs are estancos, and all estancos sell stamps (same price as the post office). *Los Correos* is the name for the Spanish mail system. USA: Mail from the USA generally takes about 7-10 days (although recently I received a package after only 4 days). For express delivery from the USA, don't use FedEx. They don't have offices here, so they pass it on to MRW, who can take 3 days just within Spain! Using the regular post office's Priority/Express mail is cheaper and faster. Another alternative is UPS (phone: 900 10 24 10)—they got a document from Sevilla to Manhattan (door-to-door) in 23 hours.

Canada: I've had few packages sent without problems. Customs have held packages for weeks, sometimes threatening to send it home or destroy it, only to complete the delivery later anyway. One of the packages sent to me was returned to the sender, utterly shredded and destroyed having fallen victim to customs' curiosity over one package of gummy bears. The contents were worth hundreds of dollars and there was ultimately no compensation. Also, do not send vitamins, although prescription drugs seem to cross the borders without difficulty. If you can buy it in Spain: do so. Shipping charges, at least across the Atlantic, can be horrific.

Ultimately, expect problems in either direction; if you're expecting a parcel from home, double or triple the normal expected time, although it should eventually arrive. Don't send anything important home using the regular Spanish mail system. Things seem to get lost quite often. If you do, ensure it's *certificado* for the extra 5€ or so. Try UPS or the Priority/Express mail.

17/Mar/2010:

Citibox **said:**

> Please understand that ordinary homeopathic medicines are treated as drugs coming into Spain and confiscated. Where possible, do not send anything direct to Spain from outside the EU. From 2 March 2010 there is a new customs law charging IVA (VAT)on anything over €22 and duty as well on anything over €150 coming into Spain see here http://www.citibox.es/blog/important-fedex-information-iva-imports-spain/

Fragiles and breakables: the Spanish Correos do not offer any type of fragile handling service, so you either package up your breakable materials to the nth degree and risk it, or send it via UPS or another private courier.

CHAPTER 17
GETTING PREGNANT IN SPAIN

This chapter covers the information about the pregnancy process in Spain, how to get health insurance, finding out your benefits and rights and help for getting the best pre natal and post natal care.

It might seem a bit daunting to get pregnant in Spain, especially if you're not from here, don't know the medical system or speak the language and on top of having to deal with the usual issues of being pregnant, having to sort out the legal and logistical ones as well. However, unlike many things in Spain, when it comes to being pregnant and having a child, things often run quite smoothly, especially if you've done your homework well ahead of time.

The first thing to make sure you have, once you find out you're pregnant, is health insurance. A European Health Insurance Card does not cover most maternity services, so check with your social security and/or health insurance to make sure you're fully covered. The Spanish Social Security system covers all Spanish nationals who reside and work in Spain, as well as foreigners with residence permits in Spain. Spanish nationals, who do not reside in Spain, are also covered under certain circumstances; protection also usually covers the entire family of the insured person.

As far as hospitals in Spain go, there are both state-owned social security hospitals and private clinics throughout the country. Someone who is not entitled to social health care has the option of getting private care, which requires paying a monthly fee for private coverage. It's a good idea, if you opt for the private health insurance and if you know you want to have a baby, to secure the insurance and have it in place at least ten months before becoming pregnant, just to simplify things.

There are a few places to look for private health insurance. For example check out:

- o **La Caixa**-One of Spain's most popular banks and it has quite an extensive private health insurance plan (many other banks have great programs as well) (lacaixa.es)
- o **Bupa International**-provides expats with private health care (http://www.bupa-intl.com)
- o **Sanitas**-The Spanish Arm of Bupa (http://www.sanitas.es)
- o **Asisa**-One of the largest private health insurance providers (http://www.asisa.es)

When it comes to finding a doctor in Spain, there are plenty of great obstetricians in Spain and the best way to find a reliable and credible one, is by word of mouth. Speak to people you trust, other mothers who have had children and ask them to recommend a doctor. You can also ask your General Doctor (GP) for some names. When the time comes to have the baby, if your Spanish isn't necessarily good, it's a great idea to bring someone with you to the hospital who speaks the language fluently, just in case.

Most regions in Spain however, do provide translation services in the hospitals and clinics.

What to do after the baby's Born-Registering a birth

Births must be registered within eight days (but up to 30 days is accepted) at the local civil registry office (Registro Civil). It is the parents' responsibility to ensure this is done and it must be carried out in person by a parent or direct family member. In some cases the hospital, clinic or midwife may register the birth.

Hijo/a

're ...... LENNON

dos ... KELLEHER .... TORRES

de ..BRENDA... y de ..MARIA..JOSÉ

el día 30... de ..JULIO........... de 2016

B.ENIDOLEIG

'o Civil de .... (provincia) Tomo ..9

'aciones Pág. ..47

' y fecha:

fica(h) y fir....

.... el día .... de ....

The birth registration includes:

- o   Name of the newborn
- o   Date, time and location of the birth. In the case of multiple births, when the exact time is unknown for each newborn, indication shall be given of the order in which they were born, or that this could not be determined
- o   Gender of the newborn
- o   The parents, when the relationship is legally recognized
- o   The number assigned to the birth or verification file
- o   The time of registration

Birth certificates must state whether a child is legitimate or illegitimate. Children born within 180 days of their parent's marriage or within 300 days of a divorce, a marriage annulment or the death of the father are considered legitimate.

How to register a child born within a marriage

A parent must take the following to the Civil Registry:
- o Medical delivery report (this yellow form is provided by the hospital where the delivery took place)
- o NIE (Foreigner's Identification Number) of the parents
- o Libro de Familia (Family Book, if available) or marriage certificate legalized and translated

How to register a child born outside of marriage

In this case, a declaration is required by both parents, with the father and the mother both registering the birth in person, providing the following documentation:
- o Medical delivery report (yellow form is provided by the hospital where the delivery took place)
- o The parents' NIEs
- o Indication of the mother's marital status
- o If a prior marriage existed, the legal presumption of paternity must be removed by providing a marriage certificate and a separation certificate or divorce decree (witnessed) In the case of separation, two witnesses must accompany the parent to the Civil Registry.

Spain has a pretty good system when it comes to Maternity leave, affording the mother 16 weeks of paid leave!!!

It's important to note that post natal care in most Spanish hospitals is limited and the mother is usually released about 48 hours after giving birth, unless there are complications. It's a good idea to secure some help at home for the first few weeks if possible, either by a registered nurse, a caretaker or even a friend or family member if possible.

Maternity & Paternity leave in Spain

Spain has a pretty good system when it comes to Maternity leave, affording the mother 16 weeks of paid leave. In cases of multiple births, this period is extended to 2 more weeks for every newborn child. The mother's position at work must be secured upon her return. Fathers are entitled to 15 days paternity leave (depending on their job). In 2015, however, this will be increased to 30 days. If there are complications for either the baby or the mother, the father is entitled to longer leave.

Financial assistance for parents in Spain

In order to encourage more mothers to have babies in Spain, the Spanish government adopted the 'Cheque bebe' program [around $3,000 worth of expenses for the baby]. Since 2008, if you are a legal resident in Spain (ie: pay your taxes) mothers are now entitled to a 2500 Euro check from the government for either the birth or adoption of every newborn baby. The 2,500 euros increases to 3,500 in the case of families with three or more children and single-parent families.

Possible resources and potential birthing services:

Check out a few sites that can help connect you with others who are pregnant and get some more feedback and advice:

- o Robyn, a registered nurse, certified doula and certified childbirth educator from the U.S. offers Pregnancy and Childbirth courses as well as Doula services (private labor preparation, post-natal home care and possible labor and delivery support) in and around Sevilla. Check out her site: www.luzyvida.eu
- o www.mybabyspain.com/healthcare-spain.php
- o www.midwiferytoday.com/international/Spain.asp
- o www.nacerencasa.org

For those of you who want assistance or a more organic birth for your baby you can check this out too. https://lianadoula.com

CHAPTER 18
EMPADRONAMIENTO IN SPAIN: REGISTERING IN YOUR COMMUNITY

Now, I'll explain in more depth about local registration in Spain (*empadronamiento*) and getting yourself registered with your city (*empadronado*). Discussion of the benefits of *empadronamiento* to you and the city in which you live in Spain, how and where to get *empadronado*, required documents, renewal, and moving.

- What is the *empadronamiento?*
- What benefits do YOU receive from getting *empadronado?*
- What benefits does the CITY receive when you're *empadronado?*
- Essential Spanish vocabulary: Navigating through all the *padrón*-type words
- How and where to get *empadronado*
- Required documents for getting *empadronado*
- Renewal, moving, and other concerns

What is *empadronamiento?*

Empadronamiento refers to the process of registering with your community's *padrón* (city roll), also called the *Padrón Municipal de Habitantes*. The municipal *padrón* is the official record of all the people who live in a particular community and is the official way to verify or accredit your stay in Spain. By law, everyone who resides in Spain should be registered in the community where they live.

In practice, city registration is your key to becoming a member of your Spanish community and you can apply as an individual or as a family. Whether you are here in Spain legally or not, you should register with your local *padrón*, as it provides innumerable benefits if you intend to live in Spain for any extended period of time.

What benefits do YOU receive from getting *empadronado?*

First, registration means that you're an official resident of your community. Consider this your first step to integration into Spanish life. Second, the *empadronamiento* is the way that your stay or residence in Spain is verified or accredited – a necessity for a variety of administrative procedures.

For example, you will generally need to prove your city registration to do the following things in your Spanish community:

- Enroll your children in local schools.
- Get married.
- Apply for a local health card (*carnet para la asistencia sanitaria*).
- Vote.
- Apply for certain visas.
- Apply for residency by way of a general amnesty or *arraigo*.

What benefits does the CITY receive when you're *empadronado?*

Based on the number of inhabitants, a city or town receives money from the government to provide services to those who live within its jurisdiction, which means that if you're registered or *empadronado*, then the city receives money to provide services on your behalf. It's therefore in the city's best interest (and yours too, for optimum service levels) to have an accurate count of who is really living in the community and using (or potentially using) the public services in question.

How and where to get *empadronado* in Spain

Registering with your city is a question of filling out a form and gathering together the required documents. Considering the amount of bureaucracy required for other official procedures, *empadronamiento* is pretty painless. Once I had the form filled out and the documents in hand, it took me only a half hour to: 1) wait in line at my local *junta* or regional government in this case Madrid, 2) have the application processed, and 3) receive confirmation.

CHAPTER 19
DRIVING IN SPAIN: LICENSES & REGULATIONS : INFORMATION ON DRIVER'S LICENSES & REGULATIONS IN SPAIN

There are few things in life as hard and intimidating as getting a Spanish driver's license...

Do you *really* need to go through all the trouble of getting a Spanish driver's license? Well, the answer is that it depends.

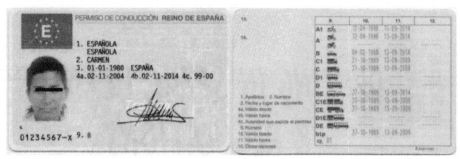

EU citizens are in luck and spared from having to go through the whole process. As a nonresident, an EU driver's license is valid in Spain, and vice-versa. If you are a resident, then you must alter your license. There are two options: either get your EU driver's license "stamped" or you exchange your license for a Spanish driver's license.

As a **non-EU citizen**, you have my condolences; you will need to get that Spanish driver's license after all. Depending on your nationality, non-EU driver's licenses may be valid for the first year after arrival in Spain. After that, you are officially required to have a Spanish driver's license. (Some expats, however, have been known to use their home-country license for years without problems. Not recommended, but possible.)

For **US drivers**, bear in mind that because each state has its own rules, foreign countries make agreements with individual states! That means that your California, Oregon or New York driver's license is valid (for the first 6 months only) in Spain, but your Massachusetts driver's license is not (whether the police know which states are valid is another question).

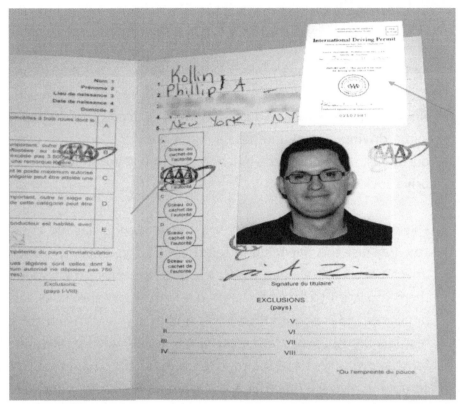

For **Canadian drivers,** you are currently required to have both your provincial driver's license and an International license, which are valid for up to a year of living in Spain. If and when you get your residence, these are valid for only six additional months at that point. You can get your International driver's license from many registry offices or CAA offices (or the provincial equivalents) by showing your valid provincial license, spending a half hour, and approximately CDN$30.

I suggest you bring your **Triple AAA driver´s booklet,** which is issued at any DMV for a $50-100 dollar fee. And you will be fit to drive in Spain and Europe for a year at least!

Now for the fun part... **To get a Spanish driver's license you must: join a driving school** and pass a medical exam, computer exam -40 questions, and behind-the-wheel test. **Choose automatic if you cant drive stick!**

The driving schools here or autoescuelas have a flat fee about 50-70$. Pay just the flat fee and tell them that you already have a US driver´s license but need to do the Spanish driving test ASAP. Tell them you want to do 3 on-the-road-lessons [cost about 25$ each] to familiarize yourself with the vehicle and that you just want to do the test in a month. Practice the computer tests [150-300 tops] and pay for the driving test and the road tax fee around 150$ tops. Go to the computer test at Trafico first and then a week later do the behind the wheel driving test. I suggest you down hit the gas a lot and make less than 50 km, keep the speed at 30-40 tops on the road test. If they take you to a highway then comply with the road signs. And don´t forget to practice parking backing up and on a very reduced limited parking spot.

Your autoescuela instructor and an official from the government will be with you in the car at the moment your driving is tested. DO NOT PANIC! Follow instructions always from the government official. And Watch out because they might try to trick you while doing the driving test!

While doing the test I was prompted by the government official to drive through a one-way street, which I didn't do, and of course, didn't comply with his instructions [sometimes they trick you so you fail the test! Watch Out!], and I pointed that I wasn't allowed to drive through there. Then, He took me to a residential area and prompted me to drive through a residential street that had a sign, which stated "RESIDENTS ONLY." So, obviously, I followed the sign not the official and made a U Turn, quickly. He said I passed with Flying Colors and I did it very well.

They gave me an **L (Conductor Nobel)**, which you should carry in your car for 6 months only since you already have a foreign driving license. **Is that all?** Yes, but going back to hard, it's not as easy as it sounds. It can be a long, treacherous road fraught with pitfalls, Keep in mind that newer driver's licenses are now of the plastic card variety and look similar to a DNI or Californian ID card.

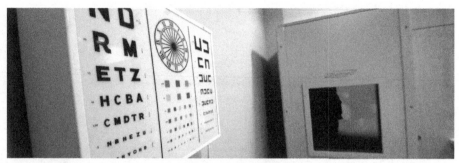

Speed limits have been lowered from 130km/h to 120km/h as of early 2017. So the top speed in Spain is 120km/h Autopistas and Autovias [freeways and Highways-toll charge]. You can do 130km however on some A roads. On city roads the speed limit is 30-50km/h.

Getting a Spanish driver's license can be expensive because you have to join a **driving school** and take classes [Take just 4 test drive lessons tops and do all the computer exams you can, I suggest doing 150-200 computer exams] The US contrary to Spain does not have the traffic road discs icons or signs They're called Señales *Obligatorias* or *de Obligacion*, so you have to study them all. They are usually triangular or round, and white and red! It doesn't matter how many years of experience you have driving in your own country. Driving in Spain is considered a different animal, and of course, you'll need the driving school's car to take the behind-the-wheel test. Then you'll need to pass a **Psicotécnico- medical and eye test, the cost is 30-50 euros tops**. [At that time, I lived in Vigo and I went to Centro medico Psicotecnico Zamora on Calle Principe] Fortunately, this part won't be too difficult. "The doctor certified me as fit because I was able to handle some computer game similar to Space Invaders,"

Next comes the **difficult computer test**. The good news is that it's multiple-choice test and you can choose to take the exam in English or watered-down Spanish if you don't feel up to the full-blown Spanish deal. The bad news is that the scope of the exam "goes well beyond the standard rules of the road," "Questions pertaining to car mechanics, first aid, and technical specifications for vehicles ranging from scooters to quads to automobiles to delivery trucks are not only fair game, but are fairly common. "Having taken both the State University of California Masters in Anthropology and the Spanish computer driver's test, I can say with certainty that I walked out of the former feeling much more confident that I had passed."

Finally, you must take a behind-the-wheel test. Your instructor will sit in the passenger seat and the examiner in the back. "The exam lasts for 30 minutes and takes place in live traffic," "Drivers can expect to face such delights as city streets, winding alleys, roundabouts-circles, construction zones, hills, and the universally-despised parallel parking maneuver. If you're unlucky (and many are), the latter two will be co-mingled." You'll receive your results from your instructor once the examiner-government official is gone. Like the computer exam, if you fail, you can take it again. And that's all there is to it, folks.

Then if you find yourself with a traffic violation, you might want to take a look at http://www.todomultas.com (in Spanish only) to appeal your fine.

Where are the cops?
In my 4 days of extensive driving, I swear I just saw one police car on the highway! That too was at a site of an accident. And yet, the speed limits enforcement and compliance is quite high. I guess they use cameras and technology a lot more in Europe, for traffic rules enforcement. If you are caught speeding, the ticket is mailed to you – complete with your picture driving the car, as proof.

Round-Abouts/Yield
When driving on city roads – a 'round-about' circle is something that might confuse an American driver! It's a different system of yielding – instead of a 4 way stop sign.

Gas/Petrol Stations

The first time you pull into a Gas Station – be prepared for a sticker shock! Gasoline is currently priced around 1.60 Euros/liter. At the present exchange rate, that roughly translates to USD 7.60/Gallon. Diesel is a little cheaper at around 1.40 Euros/liter (USD 5.80/Gallon). Add to this the price of a comparable car is approximately twice as much in the U.S. – and you will understand why driving is so expensive in Europe!

At Gas Stations in Europe you can literally fill 'Gas'…LPG (Liquefied Petroleum Gas), that is. Note in Germany and the Netherlands, they refer to Gasoline as 'Benzin'. Instead of 3 varieties of gasoline and 1 variety of diesels – at European filling stations, you will typically find 2 varieties of gasoline, 2 varieties of diesel and LPG. Initially, I was confused to note the significantly higher octane rating numbers in Europe.

However, that is apparently because of slightly different standards. (For more information,
checkout: http://en.wikipedia.org/wiki/Octane_rating)

Reliance on Diesel and LPG is part of the drive towards reducing cost / km. LPG is significantly cheaper than Gasoline. Diesel typically yields a much better fuel efficiency in terms of km / liter.

Driving in Spain Tips

- They **drive on the right**! This is a bonus for the American, as it is familiar and the same as the US! That said, they do drive pretty fast and typically only use the far left lane for passing. If you find yourself sightseeing in the left lane, scoot on over and drive in the right lane.

- Are you planning on a **Car Rental**? Most car rentals will be manual transmission you will need to specify automatic and it will typically cost quite a bit more. Unless you are staying in a city environment, we do recommend renting a car. This will allow you to explore off the beaten track and make some amazing discoveries. Just make sure you have a map of Spain or some sort of navigation in the car, on your smart phone or other electronic device.

- Do not use a **cell phone** while driving because it is against the law, unless it is hands-free. The Guardia Civil has fined many motorists for using their cell phones and often set up checkpoint at on/off ramps near the highway. I was pulled over once, accused of using a cell phone. I was only adjusting my sunglasses and it took some convincing to prove I was not using my phone.

- Slam on your brakes for **pedestrians**. Spaniards (in Southern Spain and most places we have visited) are very courteous to pedestrians and you better stop if you see someone in the cross walk / Zebra crossing. Many pedestrians don't even look before crossing, because they know vehicles are supposed to stop.

- The pedestrian crossings or cross walks are marked with black and white wide striped lines. If there is no traffic light at the crossing, the pedestrian has the right of way. Always expect the unexpected, as you can see in the comments below, someone has had a different experience in Barcelona.

- Your car is meant to be scratched, dinged and loved.

What are the best tips to find deals for a rental car in Spain?

To get the best deals on a rental car, there isn't just one way to find the deals. I usually search many ways and compare and play with the dates and times for the car rental. We usually search a few ways:

1. **Directly with a car rental company.**
   - We have rented via **Gold Car** many times from the Malaga Airport. This summer I rented with my wife in June, July and September and paid from €93 to €300 for each 28 day rental from them. This was the price only for the rental, excluding the fuel policy or insurance. We needed to return the car and rent another every 28 days. We find if you are in their loyalty program they email you great deals. We have also used many others visa the aggregate option.
   - **Sixt** we've used them 2 times in Spain and they are pretty popular.
   - **AutoEurope** is another
   - **Hertz** is also readily available in Spain

2. Through a **search aggregate**: These are search engines which compile many car rental companies and provide a nice matrix or comparison chart, so you can find the best deal possible. This is usually how we rent our cars and believe me I search them all for the best deals.

   - We almost always compare prices from all major car hire companies with**Skyscanner**.
   - There are also the biggie vacation bookers with car rental deals like **Expedia** and of course you can also look for great prices with **Priceline** too.
   - There are also some good deals with **Holiday Autos** available and you can almost always find a good offer with **RentalCars.com** too.
   - Some friends of ours like to you DoYouSpain, or you can check prices for a Car rental in Spain with **Easy Car**. You may search for a rental now in the box below.

3. You really need to **check all of your options** and all of the details. On the surface something may appear less expensive or more expensive, but check to see what is included. Often with the aggregate searches, they will include a free additional driver and perhaps fuel, so that could save you quite a bit of money.

Ride Shares In Spain

Just in case you don't want to do the driving, here are some sites, which offer **ride sharing in Spain!**

- Blabla Car
- Amovens

Discover Spain:

- Costa Tropical Spain is a world of its own.
- Things to do in Barcelona, Spain with kids.
- Just north of Barcelona, discover Girona key attractions.
- Merida, Spain is a place to discover with the Roman Ruins as a top attraction.
- Spend Spring in Seville and experience the Feria.
- Cordoba is divine, check out our 1 day guide to Cordoba, Spain
- There are plenty of things to do in Madrid, and it is an all time favorite of ours.
- Malaga is the hub of Costa del Sol and is special.
- Valencia is modern and full of history.
- Take a mud bath in Murcia, Lo Pagan

Should you need further info get this great book of an American family driving in Spain at https://gumroad.com/l/driving-in-spain

By the way, if you're crossing a road on foot without following the traffic lights or just crossing in the middle of the road not via the walkway or similar, keep in mind you can get fined and given a violation slip for jaywalking in Spain. It is quite common in Madrid and Barcelona.

CHAPTER 20
BUYING AND SELLING A SECOND HAND CAR IN SPAIN.

Well, now that you have a driver's license, you rented a car, you know the Spanish roads and traffic pretty well, and you need a motor to cruise around like in that Christian Slater´s movie -True Romance?

If you're looking for a second hand car in Spain you must follow the following steps,

Every car needs to have the following documents up to date to start the buy / sell process:

- o *Permiso De Circulación* - In England you would call this the Log Book. It gives the car details, number plate, chassis number, make and model, year of first registration, and most importantly the name and address of the current owner.
- o *Inspección Técnica* - Also called the **ITV**. In England you would call this the **MOT**. It gives the car details, the amount of gases spewing from the muffler, and is stamped and dated with the last ITV inspection passed and stating for how many years (1 or 2) this is valid. In California, for example, would be the **Smog check** but an extended Euro version.
- o *Impuesto Sobre Vehiculos* - This is equivalent to a road license fee. It is payable yearly to the *Ayuntamiento* where the owner is registered. In the states you deal with the DMV and get a sticker. It's more or less this, but more complex here in Spain.

So one of the first things to check, whether buying or selling, is that these are all in order for the car in question. Ask to see the original of all these documents before going any further.

Let's assume you've found a second hand Spanish car you would like to buy. Ask the seller to **show you the originals** of these three documents. Check that the names correspond between them. Check the seller's **ID** too. If the person selling is not the owner for any reason, such as family member, or second hand car dealer, then you need to make sure that they are allowed to sell the car. This is particularly important in the case of a private sale.

The *Permiso De Circulación* is valid if the name and address are correct and the details correspond to the second hand car you are trying to buy.

The ITV could be out of date, or nearing it's renewal date. If this were the case, then you would be well advised to ask the owner to pass the ITV before you continue.

The car might be for sale because the owner knows about an ITV problem that is not obvious to a prospective buyer without actually testing. Would you know if the car would pass the environmental checks for gas emissions or noise?

The *Impuesto Sobre Vehiculos* could easily be out of date by one or more years. Once you have bought a second hand car in Spain, you would be liable to pay the back dated taxes before you could register the car in your local *Ayuntamiento*.

The bureaucratic process

If you are buying through a second hand car dealership, then they will take care of all this part. If not, then go to another dealer for your car. They will ask you for your official identification, Passport, *Residencia,* and anything else they could require for the processing of the transfer of ownership.

If you are buying privately you will need to make sure you have a full day free to go to your local *Jefatura De Tráfico*. It is a huge advantage for both you and the seller if you can both go. That way, any little details that could cause a hiccup in the process can usually be sorted out on the spot. If he/she cannot be there, you will need copies of all the car documents, his/her documents, and a signed declaration allowing you to make the transfer in his/her name. It is unlikely that the seller will refuse to go with you though, as he will want to keep the documents in his possession until paid, and you will not want to pay until you know the car can be transferred.

20/Jan/2011:

dgb380 said:

To let you know some background on me: I speak Spanish and have lived in Spain for 26 years:

Now let me tell you my experience.

1. Make sure your NIE card has not expired before going to Trafico (my 1st mistake)

2. Pay the "Impuestos" - Taxes before you go to Trafico (my 2nd mistake)

3. It's not cheap (you might as well pay a Gestor to do the work since they do it in bulk and charge more or less what it cost the average person to do it by himself)

If you want any advise or a motor insurance quote: please see bloomfieldsure.es

Regards
David Bloomfield

Take plenty of CASH with you, and **take plenty of PHOTOCOPIES with you of all your own documents.** Take documents that are not apparently required, such as your _Empadronamiento_ and your driving license. If you get a '_Jobsworth_' then you will need these things. On the other hand, a 'Jobsworth' is your biggest protection against a fraud, as he will be double-checking the details of the car being sold. And **take a BLACK PEN** with you. It is no joke if you need to fill in a section you missed on the form, or anything like that, as you can lose your turn trying to borrow a pen, and so have to wait the full queue again.

1. You need to get the _Solicitud._ This is the official form to request the transfer of ownership. You can get this before the day and fill it out at ease, preferably with the seller, as you both need to enter details. You can print a copy from here **http://www.dgt.es/es/hojas-informativas/index.shtml**

2. At the _Jefatura De Tráfico_ you will have to queue up for a long time at the _Caja_ to make the payment of (currently) 43.40€, which is the cost of the transfer. Cash is the best way to pay, as it avoids any problems of cards not working. Make sure you are in the correct queue. There is nothing worse than queuing for an hour or more only to be told that you should be in the even longer queue at the next window! They will give you a receipt and either a number, or you will be directed to another queue, depending on the _Jefatura._

3. At the next window, when your number is called, or you reach the head of the queue, you and the seller will produce all the documents listed above for the car, the *Solicitud* filled and signed, the receipt for the payment you just made, your ID documents, the sellers ID documents (which is why he should be there with you) and any photocopies of these documents that the guy behind the desk asks for.

4. He might well ask you to pay the *Impuesto Sobre Vehiculos* for the coming year. If so, this is for the buyer to pay. Keep the receipt for this to show at the *Ayuntamiento* later when you register the car there. It is worth mentioning here that if the guy behind the desk is skimping things, he could easily pass over any unpaid road tax by stating something like "You do realize the *Impuesto Sobre Vehiculos* is outstanding?" and move on to complete the transfer. This is where you could find yourself landed with the seller's back-tax. Another good reason for checking it is up to date before you start.

5. You might find that there is another payment to make for transfer from one community to another, or because there is a deferred *Impuesto de Matriculación* or registration tax. If this occurs, you need to agree with the seller which of you is responsible for that payment. A deferred tax would normally be the seller. Change of community tax would normally be the buyer. Whatever it might be, sort it out quickly so you don't lose your turn. You will be glad you brought real cash with you at this point.

6. Extra payments are sometimes taken at this desk, or sometimes you are sent around the queues again. Patience is required!

All being well, the worst part is over. The car is in your name. Now you can go to your *Ayuntamiento* to make sure the road tax is in their system and paid up. There is no rush about this, but depending on where you live, it could mean another morning in a queue.

A side issue worth mentioning is that you can also ask the seller if he could transfer the insurance to you. You could find it beneficial and it is easy to arrange. It means you can drive the car away same day with insurance included.

What can go wrong at the *jefatura*?

o The local tax is not paid up to date. They insist you go to the *Ayuntamiento* to sort this out and return. Solution: This is a real pain. But you have no option. The seller has to do this and the time all this can take might well mean you have to return to the *Jefatura* the next day.

o Documents are not in order. Solution: Find out what needs to be done to put things straight, and do it. It will probably be something silly and simple, but time consuming. If it is an inconsistency in the car documents, you might have to forget the deal. Usually though, it is just that they need another photocopy of your documents because you are not Spanish.

- o There is an embargo or other financial lien on the car. Solution: If this shows up on the computer at the *Jefatura* then the deal falls through. The seller cannot sell the car until he clears this problem, which will take a long time. Get back any money you have paid to the seller. Kiss goodbye to the 43.40 Euros. Go look for another car.
- o There is an unpaid traffic fine. Solution: Arm lock the seller and take him to the office where fines are paid. It is usually in the same building. If it is an old fine, then it could now be lodged at SUMA. Whatever the case, the seller must pay these fines. Again it might mean using up so much time that you will have to complete the transfer the following day.

What else could go wrong?

Apart from the usual difficulties associated with second hand car purchase in any country, the Spanish system opens up a number of extra pitfalls. This is because of the possibility of the transfer process not being completed.

The seller will want some sort of down payment before going into the transfer process. Once completed, he will expect to be paid the balance before handing over the new car documents in your name and the car keys.

- o You need to be able to reclaim that down payment if the deal falls through at the *Jefatura*.
- o If the seller has to go to his *Ayuntamiento* to pay back-taxes, it is a good idea to accompany him. You don't want him to disappear with your down payment and not return to complete the transfer. The same goes for fine payments. But don't get pulled into paying his fines for him, unless it is taken off the outstanding payment due.
- o Don't accept the seller's word that the transfer has been completed until you see the new *Permiso De Circulación* in your name. How could this happen? Example: the transfer process is held up because the back-taxes are not paid. Seller says he will deal with it all tomorrow and call you. He calls you to say everything is done and dusted, so you can collect the keys and pay him the balance. You get the keys, the documents except for the *Permiso De Circulación* the seller tells you it will be sent to you. It's all LIES!! He will steal the car back at the earliest opportunity, and you won't have a legal leg to stand on.

Generally speaking, if, at the start, you have checked that the original documents for the car seem to be in ok, and correspond to the ID of the seller, you can assume that the sale is being made in good faith. Just doing that will detect the majority of the con tricks. **If a seller cannot produce all of those original documents in his own name, then be very careful!! Maybe better to look elsewhere!**

CHAPTER 21
HOW TO GET A JOB IN SPAIN: EXPLAINED

Are you having a hard time to get a job in Spain?

Don't you have all the necessary documents with you?

No pain no gain!

Even though, you don't hold a EU passport, things can get complicated but isn't impossible to land you a job!

The market is opening to people like you! Trust me I been there I done it!

It's a common misconception that **teaching English is the only job you can get in Spain**. While it is for sure a way to make a paycheck, there are other jobs available in Spain for the ambitious expat in the files of IT, customer care, marketing and social media, and even health care. Follow the next steps if you´re hunting for a job in Spain:

Speako Españolo

You get freaked out about talking in Spanish? Don't be embarrassed? if you're going to work in Spain, you should know Spanish. Even an intermediate level will take you far in understanding company culture, your boss or internal company communication. While English is becoming a business or vehicular language in some of Spain's larger cities, it's still got a long way to go in the South, North and pueblos. You definitely need español, so brush up on it and don't be shy when you move to Spain. **Go for it señorita!!!**

Do Some Networking

You might have to get together with people, go to coffee houses, local parties, festival and events where you meet people. The first time I got a job other than teaching English was when I met some realtors from Madrid in a Galician pueblo. The net day, I was literally flying to Madrid arranging meetings and briefings with high executives from America. Organize or have someone organize a Spanish networking group to help you find jobs in Spain.

Spain is regretfully rather infamous for hiring candidates based on their professional connections and word-of-mouth, rather than on merit. Get an edge in by amping up your LinkedIn game – join in on professional discussions in your field, following businesses with a strong presence in Spain and ask people to endorse you. Posting on facebook groups or Instagram is a good idea. Spamming here and there stating your expertise and how you can help people find solutions will be a great start. And don't be afraid to network face-to-face. There are many expat groups active around Spain, from professional women's networking to social outings to business people think tanks. Join, get active, and mention that you have expertise in this and that.

Consider Moving To Larger Cities

While living next to the beach in Albufeira or joining the expat community near Benidorm might sound appealing, consider heading to a larger city to work. Many international companies like Aon, Citroen, Ernst & Young, Accenture or GE have international hubs in Madrid, Vigo, Bilbao, Valencia and Barcelona.

I recently got a job with Citroen training them in English to take on some major cities in Iran and China. This also helped me get in touch and meet with new executives that offered me a job in Madrid.

Costco and Loyola University have set up foot in Sevilla. Bilbao is also a heavy industrial city, and Malaga's expat community is buzzing with jobs in tourism, catering and sports. If your current company has offices in Spain, start learning *español* and talking to your *jefes*.

Prepare a European CV and Have Some Info on Social Media

You'll need to adjust your expertise and add any pertinent courses or even if you hold a driver's permit, please put it down on to your Euro-style CV. If you're looking for examples for formatting or word-choice check out the Euro pass template by googling it. Simply input your personal information and work history. Try to have the file on pdf format and hope for no longer than a page. Most recruitment officers don´t read past the first page.

Most people from RRHH [recursos humanos-human resources in Spanish] after checking your email or name on your CV, start off by searching you on LinkdIn, Google, Facebook and even Instagram. Don´t have any private info, crazy pictures or a strange criminal profile on the Internet. Have a serious profile stating your qualities and expertise on the Internet. Don't use your name for an Instagram Personal Party Page!

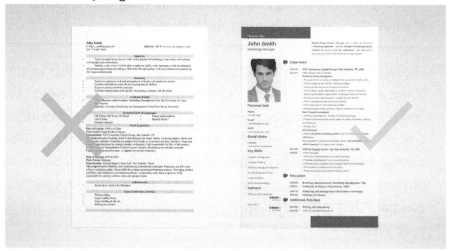

Use a Color Picture On Your CV

Another thing that is striking about European resumes is that they often ask for a color photo to be stuck to the top right-hand corner. Awkward, sure, but if you don't attach it right away, you'll be asked to send one to HR anyway. These pics should be ID size (European standard passport size) of your face and shoulders with a white background.

Be a Jack of all trades and master of none

Spaniards love multifaceted persons, I always thought I could only teach English, but needed something else to supplement my income in Spain. So, I started marketing myself as a freelance writer, a translator, and an interpreter and at one time as a voice over and anchor for a popular English speaking station in Spain. And I tell ya fellas! It really worked out for me!

So, consider yourself marketing a skill or skills you possess for some extra bucks. You could freelance write or translate, tutor, give yoga classes, conversations for 5 euros at a coffeehouse, maybe you are a good guitar or saxophone player and gig the night pubs for money, show people from the States or Canada around El Camino de Santiago, the Sights in Andalusia or become a tour guide. I can't really help you much on this one. It has to come from within you. Whatever you believe you're good at, you should exploit it and market it to people in Spain. Spain's black market is alive and kicking, and though it won't give you health benefits or social security, you can support your bad habit with a bit of creativity. In fact, it's common for Spaniards (and expats) to do more than one thing to make it to the end of the month. This may mean less *siesta*, but more cash. You can have a legal job at daytime and an under-the-table job at nighttime.

Highly Skilled Workers and Business People Are Wanted in Spain

Believe it or not, Spain is one of the leading countries in medicine, solar and wind power, wine and olive oil. That's good news for highly skilled workers who have more of a chance of a visa and gainful (**if not lucrative**) employment. The company, that wants to hire you, must have at least 250 employees and jump through a number of hoops on your behalf, though if it's a large enterprise, chances are they've got the infrastructure in place and have sponsored other foreign nationals in the past.

Entrepreneurship is a hot topic in Spain, with nearly 100,000 new businesses registered in 2016. The federal government enacted a special **work permit visa** in early 2014 for those looking to create a business to spark employment and revenue. The biggest catch to the 'Ley del Emprendedor,' under which the aforementioned workers fall, is that you have to have been living in Spain for at least a year and register your business plan with the local trade union [sindicato].

Applying For A Non-Lucrative Visa

You are ready to move but you don't want to leave that fantastic American job behind. It brings you 50 thousand dollars a year and your superior gives you 40 days sick pay and a holiday package you cant refuse. If you're concerned about taking a sabbatical, why not apply for a non-lucrative visa to live in Spain, but telecommuting to your current job? If your work does not need a specific location, then Spain is made for you! You get the best of both worlds – an awesome wage with the Spanish lifestyle.

CHAPTER 22
MISTAKES TEACHERS IN SPAIN MAKE OVER AND OVER AGAIN

So you're moving to Spain soon, what now?

Now that mid-August has arrived in full-force, the inevitable panic that accompanies an impending move overseas has slowly begun to sink its claws in. This is nowhere near as evident as in my inbox, where I receive a daily barrage of emails from future English teaching assistants in Spain asking me questions ranging from how to apply for the visa to what kind of electric razor works best with Spanish outlets.

Before, I used to comment in the plethora of Facebook groups and blogs dedicated to the Auxiliares de Conversación program in Spain. However, I notice after I posted something that there were a few hundred people refuting some of the facts that I knew were true about the VISA, NIe and other parts of the teaching assistant programs. After that I stopped commenting except for a random post here and there in an effort to help people but needless to say it was futile. auxiliar's mistakes in Spain on Facebook seem to post the same questions over and over and over again. I know Google exists. But not many lazy people coming to Spain seem to use it.

Since I started working in Spain many moons ago, I made many mistakes. I WISH I had a book like this when I moved down to Spain; I wasn't even in any groups till the end of the first year. Everything I learned was through trial and error.

So I thought I'd go ahead and compile a little list of the most common mistakes, fuck-ups, which not only Americans make but also British teachers and people alike when they come to Spain in the hopes of making a year go by a little smoother.

+ Bring Enough $$$$$$$

I don't know how much the government tells you to bring to Spain now, but my first year they suggested $800. Ha.Ha.Ha. Depending where you live, that won't get you very far.

While I don't believe you need to have 10K stocked away in the bank to become an auxiliary or a teacher, the more cushion you have, the better. Of course a budget for Madrid is not the same as a budget for a village in Extremadura, so it's important to research a little about where you're going. Factoring in the fact that many regions in Spain don't pay their auxiliares on time or until November or even Christmas, off the top of my head, I would say $2,000 to $2,500 is a good start. Of course, you can definitely come with less and make do. I definitely recommend coming a little earlier and setting up some afternoon private classes [I would suggest 1-2 private classes a day, at least, charging an average 15-20 euros an hour would suffice] so you can make extra money on the side right away.

+ Agreeing to a place before checking it out DON´T BE STUPID! Why would you EVER agree to an apartment before seeing it, let alone in a foreign country???? DON´T DO IT! My suggestion is to get a cheap hostel or an AirBNB apartment first and go check out places in the meantime and get your paperwork sorted out first. You won't know the city well until you come here, the proximity to your schools, bus routes, and most importantly, the bars and discotecas.

+Don´t settle for a shithole because you didn't have enough time
This was a big mistake I made my first year and got it sorted out in my second year. While I'm sure many people had a lot of luck finding a place a few days before their first day of work, but not me. I´m a dude and most managers or owners in Spain prefer ladys. Where I lived my first year was a large university town, and classes started mid-September, which means by the time I arrived at the end of the month, shared apartments were out and I ended up in a shithole.

I'm a big advocate of arriving early so that you can get to know your city better, go introduce yourself to your school and negotiate a better schedule and also grab some private classes and work without fighting all of the other teachers for classes. I figure if you can get to Spain by September 7-15th is probably perfect.

+Opening a bank account with Santander
Check with other teachers or auxiliares, which banks perform better for them. Their reputation with auxiliares and foreign teachers from taking forever to send you a card, charging you all kinds of fees and causing all kinds of problems when you want to close the account at the end of the year. My favorite banks are BBVA, Abanca and La Caixa, the blue one from Cataluña. BBVA and La Caixa are everywhere, but if you settle in the North of Spain ABanca is pretty good, too. They all have afternoon hours, online banking AND free checking accounts. Can't beat that.

+ Overpacking- A backpack or rucksack is enough. Trust me on this one!
Don't overpack, don't do it! Leave those high heels, winter clothes and trimmers at home, don't give in! This is a mistake I always make. I always overpack and regret it immediately. Spain has great, cheap shopping and you will collect many an odd knick-knack on your adventures around Europe. With baggage fees as high as they are, don't throw your money away early. Try to fit all your stuff into one suitcase, a big carry-on and personal item.

For dudes, if you can bring just a backpack that will be perfect. You can always pick up a cheap second bag in Spain to bring your stuff home. It's just not worth the weight and fees for the journey there.

+Blend in

Why would you move to Spain for a year and only hang out with people from where you're from? Of course when you first get here to Spain, it's important to feel comfortable and make friends with everyone. Some of my best friends in Spain are not Americans, and I don't know what I would have done without them. They, Spaniards, actually helped me out to set up my bank account, to get my NIE, to open a freelance company in Spain... and believe it or not, all of this for free. I had to give some of my time back to them instead. But no hardwork!

In fact, wherever I go to I always made the effort to go out often and meet as many locals as I could. Living with Spaniards will help you out a lot. Whether I was grabbing drinks with co-workers, going for walks with my students (usually adults) or chatting with the regulars at my favorite coffee houses, I forced myself to be as outgoing as possible and get to know the real Spain. I can't recommend enough taking that step outside of your comfort zone and trying to blend in as much as possible.

+ Do Not Trust Public Officials Unless They resolve the problem for you there and then!

If you haven't already figured out from the visa process, the paperwork associated with moving to Spain for a year can be long painstakingly process. Some people have luck on their side and go through the whole process of the visa application at home and the applying for a NIE (residency card) in Spain fine. While others aren't so lucky. I´m sure if you follow the steps I provide in this book, you will be successful in Spain. I can't even begin to tell you how many times I would talk with someone in the *extranjería* (Foreigner's Office) and get one answer then talk with someone else and get a different answer, then talk with some higher official in Madrid and get a totally different answer! It's a waste of time sometimes and your time is money. Your best bet is to talk to a lawyer friend if you have it or meet one and if not, I have provided a list at the end of the book, which I have used before and thanks to it I have been able to resolve the situation.

So take what you hear with a pinch of salt, ask around, post in the auxiliar groups, scan the online forums, and then if you're still dazed and confused, talk to a Spanish lawyer first... Usually, they give free and informative consultations in Spain. If not offer them some free English classes instead. I´m sure they´ll help you.

And don't hold back. This is your year!

CHAPTER 23
AROUND SPAIN IN 18 FOODS

I am a big fan of Spanish food. Italian and Spanish are my 2 favorite foods in the world. Trust me! If you stay in Spain or Italy you won't miss those Californian burritos, spicy cheesy chili fries or Venice Beach smoothies at all!

Spain has great food!

And now, I would like to take you on a journey around the regions of Spain and how they are known for each and specific type of food. Like Flamenco is only exclusive to Andalusia, Pulpo is only exclusive to Galicia not to the whole of Spain. There are 17 autonomous communities and two autonomous cities that are collectively known as **"autonomies"**.

Spain regions are like little countries inside a larger country. They have their own culture and gastronomy, too. If Extremadura is known for having great meat, Galicia is famous for having great fish and so on.

Here are 18 most famous dishes and foods from different Spanish regions,

This is by no means an exhaustive list, there are so many amazing foods to try that Spain is an endless discovery for foodies and gourmands, with prime high quality ingredients and regional specialties. Even if you're a vegan, there are a lot of veggies and fruits to choose from in Spain.

Warning: there are a lot of meat dishes and some of them may not be for the faint of heart!

!Que Aproveche!

+ Paella in Valencia
One of my personal favorites, this is a dish traditionally made with rabbit in Valencia but the most popular version is with seafood. However, there are many other rice dishes that can't technically be classified as paella but are cooked in the same paella pan in the same manner such as black rice with squid (arroz negro con chipirones)

+Ensaimada in Mallorca

Ensaimada, is the most famous Mallorcan pastry. It is a spiral-shaped pastry made from flour, eggs, water, sugar, dough and 'saim' (pork lard). Often eaten for breakfast or as an afternoon snack or 'merienda'. Ensaimadas can also be filled with 'cabell d'angel' (a very sweet pumpkin filling), cream or chocolate. During Carnival, it is typically eaten with sobrasada-is a raw, cured sausage from the Balearic Islands made with ground pork, paprika and salt and other spices. At the airport you can see many hexagonal ensaimada boxes, it is one of the most popular souvenirs to take home from the island.

+ Escargots in Catalonia

Although the most famous dish in Catalonia is the **Calçot**, which is a type of scallion or green onion in the Catalan language, I'm going to venture into the slimy world of snails as a food specialty, the mind often goes to France. However, Catalonia is famed for its escargot, so much so that they have an annual gastronomic snail festival in May, which takes place in Lleida where over 200,000 people take part and consume a total of 12 tones of snails!

The most popular method of cooking snails is "a la llauna", which translates loosely as "with a can". The llauna is a flat, shallow roasting tray of thin steel in which snails are arranged before the entire tray is placed on a hot grill. The snails are eaten with a toothpick and a side dish of allioli [garlic mayonnaise] is a required accompaniment. It's cooked a la llauna or stewed a la gormanta, with parsley and bacon and thickened with cornstarch, and in samfaina, a classic Catalan tomato sauce very similar to ratatouille.

+ Patatas a la Riojana in La Rioja

A smoky potato, served with chorizo, is the perfect pairing for the excellent wines in the La Rioja region, especially with a good crianza. This simple and homely peasant dish consists of potatoes, onion, garlic, sliced chorizo and paprika.

+ Pinchos in Basque Country

One thing you notice about the Basque country is the sheer quantity of pinchos in all the bars. Pincho, which in Basque means "spike", is the answer to Spain's tapas. The small pieces of bread topped with delicious bite sized toppings and held together with a wooden cocktail stick evolved from the Spanish tradition of Tapas and reached the Basque Country in the 1930s, in San Sebastian.

Not happy with ordinary tapas, bars created their dishes in miniature and displayed them along the bar, so that customers could help themselves. One of the best and legendary pincho bars I have been to is called *Bar Sport* in San Sebastian. They even have an amazing txangurru, which is a mouthwatering baked dish of shredded king crabmeat cooked in its shell in the oven.

+ Fabada in Asturias

Fabada is very similar to the British baked beans or the Mexican Menudo with frijoles but tastier. The secret is down to the quality of the beans or *"fabes"*, they can cost up to 20 euros for a packet depending on the quality. Other ingredients include morcilla, chorizo, pork shoulder and saffron. This tasty Asturian dish is one you must try if you make it to the North of Spain.

+ Cochinillo in Segovia, Castilla y Leon

This is awesome local dish of suckling pig baked to perfection with crispy crackling skin from Segovia is a must to try. Cooked in a clay oven over a few hours this dish is tender and savory. Usually they cut it with a plate to show you how tender the meat is and how it falls away from the bone. Ernest Hemingway wrote about Casa Botin's cochinillo in *The Sun Also Rises*. The American writer loved the dish and had his very own table at the restaurant in Madrid.

+ Cocido In Madrid

This is the most typical Madrileño dish, loved by Spanish people on the wintertime. It is a warm, hearty stew made with chickpeas, pork belly, chorizo and morcilla as well as some vegetables. Though the origins are undetermined, many people believe this dish was an evolution of a Sephardic-jewish dish called adafina, the first versions being kosher and not containing eggs or pork. Some of the most popular restaurants serving cocido are *Malacatin or La Bola*.

+Cecina in León

Leon has a few famous dishes but the most well known is Cecina, this is served at for free with your drink at various tapas bars in the old quarter. There are different types of cecina, from venison to beef to donkey and at various degrees of spiciness. The meat is salted and air dried and served in thin slices, best accompanied with a rich, red wine or a cold local beer Mahou o Estrella.

+ Migas from Extremadura

Migas is a traditional dish all across Spain and was originally a breakfast dish that made use of leftover bread. In Extremadura, this dish is made of day-old bread soaked in water, garlic, paprika and olive oil and is served with spinach or alfalfa and maybe some pork.

This dish is a typical Spanish comfort food dish and is not often found in restaurants. If you go to Extremadura or Salamanca ask also for Jamon Serrano or Jamon de Pata Negra.

+ Prawns in Andalusia, Huelva

White prawns also known as '*Gambas Blancas de Huelva*', this crustacean has a long and well-developed body, which is larger than the head. Captured on the Atlantic coast of Andalusia, in the Gulf of Cadiz, 95% the prawns are caught entirely by hand. This delicious and flavorful prawn is highly prized. The most common way of eating them is simply stir fried or char-grilled, sprinkled with coarse sea salt. Awesomely Delicious!

+ Octopus in Galicia

Galicia is a region that provides some of the best fish and seafood in Spain, one of the most popular ingredients is octopus. *Pulpo a feira*, as it is known in Galician, is alternatively known as *pulpo estilo feira* in Spanish.

+Pescaito in Andalusia, Malaga

Now from Southern Spain, delicious fried fish called pescaito! Another dish said to have originated from 16th century Jews in Andalusia and Portugal, this was a favorite for late breakfast or lunch after synagogue services on Saturday mornings. There is also a common belief that pescaito frito was inspiration **for British fish and chips** and brought to England by Sephardic Jews.

Tuna in Andalusia, Cadiz

In early January 2012, Tokyo restaurateur Kiyoshi Kimura paid Y56.5m for a 269kg Bluefin tuna at the Tjsukiji fish auction. This single fish would provide him with up to 10,000 pieces of sushi, the tuna was from Barbate, near Cadiz, southwest Spain, where tuna has been caught for more than 3,000 years. Tuna from Barbate is world famous, they are not harvested by huge fishing vessels but herded by small boats and caught by hand. This tuna is so popular with the Japanese that they travel to Barbate to select tuna straight off the fishing boats, vacuum pack and freeze them and send them by plane to Japan. The tuna is most famously served as Mojama, wind-dried tuna cured in salt and served in this slices like Carpaccio.

+ Arroz Meloso in Murcia

A strong contender with Paella, the rice dishes of Murcia are delicious and full of seafood, cooked to the point of not being too soupy or too dry, similar to a risotto. Aside from rice and seafood, Murcia is also known as the greenhouse of Spain and famed for their flavorful tomatoes and watermelons.

+ Morcilla de Burgos in Castilla y León

Morcilla is the Spanish version of a blood sausage, similar to the British black pudding but with more spice. It originates in the region of Castile and Leon and has a dry firm texture, due to the inclusion of rice, and retains its Moorish influence in the use of cumin as a seasoning.

+ Percebes in Galicia

This is my favorite dish from Spain. A kilo of these cost over $200 dollars.

They're scientifically classed as Pollicipes cornucopia, more commonly known as goose barnacles. Far from it — they're delicious, with the flavor of sweet lobster and the texture of an oyster washed over with a tang of sea spray. Ask gourmet Spaniards about this star of the cocina and they will dissolve into lip-licking rapture. Barnacles are not the only delicacy on offer in food-loving Galicia. With a little planning, it is possible to eat your way through the calendar on a gastro-tour of saints' days, each celebrating a particular homegrown specialty. Highlights of the year include: Pigs' ears festival at Sales-Vedra , in March; oysters at Arcade-Soutomaior in April; trout and kid at Pontecaldelas in May; peppers from Padrón (a national favorite) in August; cockles from Cabana y Ponteceso in September; and the big seafood festival in October at O Grove.

Head down the coast to the gastronomic wonderland of the Galician sea estuaries, Spanish fjords or rias. There are lots of tempting eateries on the way south, but try to hold on until you get to the seafood capital of O Grove near Pontevedra . Choose a restaurant, check that it's serving the barnacles, and then sit yourself down for a steaming treat.

CHAPTER 24
LEGALLY WORKING IN SPAIN

This, friends, is the million dollar question!

I hear this question often, and many times it's proceeded by: I can't move abroad, if I can't legally work!

I understand the need for income stability, and personal growth so I'd like to breakdown the question with more detail.

Although this chapter has been researched thoroughly, it's time-sensitive, as the laws in Spain change pretty often. So, I encourage you to research and ask questions. Also, if you know something that I don't, which, believe me, is entirely possible, please shoot me an email!

Do you have a European passport?

Then yes, you are legally able to live and work in Spain and are entitled to use of the public health care system. All you need to apply for is a N.I.E., which is a free, and easy step that simply gives you an identification number. I covered this issue thoroughly in Part 1 of this eBook.

Do you have dual citizenship, one of which is European?

Yes, it's the same deal as above; however, when entering Spain and handling any legal matters, use the European passport instead of the other one.

I'm American but my parents / grandparents are European. Can I apply for a European passport and then work in Spain?

I've met several people who have obtained legal work rights this way. An Argentine who was granted Italian citizenship, an Australian English citizenship, a Jamaican British citizenship, an American Polish citizenship, and another American Irish or British citizenship. Each country has its own hoops to leap through in order to fulfill these requirements and they're very different.

They more often than not, require birth certificates, death certificates, translations, etc. It's a long, expensive and exhausting process. It's possible, but, if it's July, and your goal is to live in Spain by September or Christmas, as the latest, you will most definitely need more time. Read one success story here from Dan Catalan of the Expatriate Adventures here http://expatadventuresofdanman.blogspot.com.es/2016/03/i-was-granted-polish-citizenship-and.html

I'm a citizen of Andorra, the Philippines, Puerto Rico, Equatorial Guinea, or (any) Latin American country. Am I eligible?

Yes... but only after 2 years of living in Spain. After 2 years, you're eligible to apply for Spanish nationality, which would then guarantee your right to live and work in Spain. Apparently, there are also talks of granting nationality to those individuals who can prove that their Jewish ancestors were of **Spanish descent**!

I'm American, do I need a visa to come to Spain?

There is an agreement between the United States and Spain. As American citizens you're able to enter the country and stay for up to 90 days without a visa. This, however, does not grant you the right to work, own property, or start a business. You can travel, eat, party, take a few photos, and then head home.

Can Americans get work visas in Spain?

Absolutely; I have covered this earlier. However, they can only be obtained from the Consulate in your home state / city. **You cannot come to Spain for 90 days, and on day 91 "apply" for a work visa.** It doesn't work like that. You need a job offer from a Spanish company, or a company based in Spain with a contract, medical certificate, valid passport, criminal background check, proof of income, etc. Then, the Consulate will either approve or deny the application. This process can take up to a year in total between finding the job, securing the offer, translations and acquiring the documents. Plan ahead!

Then why are there so many English teachers in Spain? Isn't teaching a job?

Yes, it is in fact a job; I have been covering this and it is the purpose of this book and the easiest way to get your golden ticket to reside in Spain. But, the way these laws are set up... If you've been hired through the Auxiliares de Conversación program, or BEDA, or UCETAM or CIEE or Meddeas it's technically a stipend, a grant not a salary.

Excluding Beda, you don't even pay taxes on your salary but you have to file though, and many programs require that you also study at the same time just to make sure you're complying with the whole Student Visa thing.

But, I heard you can work an extra 20 hours even on a student visa as a non-EU national!

Again, yes, the perfect example is myself, but there's still the catch that it has to be in the same field (teaching) and you need your employer to offer you a part-time contract and vouch for you (read: pay your social security). You can't say, work as an English teacher then work an extra 20 hours as an architect or a waiter. You can apply, but unfortunately, there's no guarantee you will be approved, and it can take up to 1-3 months to process. In my case, it took me a month from extranjeria and my employers had powerful lawyers. Some were academies in different regions of Spain, which I have listed at the end of this eBook.

How do I make money then?

If you can't get a legal job? Many people work under the table by teaching private lessons. Most academies do not want to hire someone without legal working rights because if caught, the fines are up to 30,000 euros.

I've lived in Spain for 3 years, can I modify my student visa for a work visa?

Yes, you can! You may be eligible for *arraigo social por cuenta ajena* or *cuenta propia*. They'll break down exactly what you need!

Can I just become a freelancer if I live in Spain?

You can apply for an entrepreneurship visa *before* moving to Spain. Or, if you have: a bank account, a NIE and a social security number, you can apply to be a freelancer! It's very straightforward. Get to talk to a lawyer first.

My boyfriend / girlfriend is Spanish / European

Can I work then? If you're not ready to put a ring on it, and you've been living together for at least 1 year (Requirements vary by region) then you can apply for *Pareja de Hecho* , which is a civil union. [I covered this in the second part of this eBook chapter 15] You'll need to be of age, prove that you're both single, living together, and have a valid passport and/ or NIE. This will make you eligible to apply for the "family member of the EU" residency card. You can live and work in Spain for 5 years! Yay! It is not valid in other EU countries, as each place has its own rules regarding civil unions. Boo! For that, you'll need a ring!

My husband / wife is Spanish Can I live and work in Spain?

After one year of marriage (and I'm assuming living in Spain) you're eligible to apply! Although it's not guaranteed, it's almost always approved. Family is family! If you live in another country, and your Spanish husband or wife lives in Spain and works for one year, you can apply for a visa that will "reunite" the family. Then you can also live and work legally!

There's hope! There are options, but the best piece of advice I can give you is plan ahead. Things move much slower in Spain, and when dealing with international laws and regulations. My advice is to get a lawyer and follow the rules because the last thing you want is to get deported and banned for a few years, or even fined!

CHAPTER 25
FALSE FRIENDS: WHAT TO SAY OR NOT TO SAY IN SPANISH

1. Bigote

Meaning:
Bigote does not mean bigot. If you meet someone who is intolerant and unreasonable, you'll just have to find another name to call them because the Spanish word **bigote** means <u>moustache</u>!

The best way to learn a language is to go and live (even for a short while) in the country where they speak it. For me and for you, that would be Spain.

Spain Spanish is nothing like the Tex-Mex Spanish they teach Americans in the States. We don't say *ándale* here and I can't remember the last time I used the formal "you" *usted* or *ustedes*. People eat *tortilla de patata* here, not corn tortillas [tortas in Castillian] or tacos. *Burritos* are small donkeys, not a tasty budget dinner option from **Taco Bell or El Pollo Loco.**

But don't worry, younglings. It won't happen overnight but if you make a conscious effort to hang out with locals, get to know your teachers, and force yourself to speak as much Spanish as possible, you'll improve. Accept that you will make mistakes and move on. Accept you will say at least one truly embarrassing thing, and learn from it.

And don't get obsessed about finding a Spanish lover to help you improve your Spanish either. My wife is Spanish and her English is almost perfect since he lived in the UK for many years. And most of the time, we speak in English. So, my Spanish language skills come from my Spanish friends and from conducting business in Spanish, not from my Spanish ex-girlfriends or my wife.

So, if you want to learn Spanish or any language my advice is you should go out and meet people, try to conduct your business in Spanish and also talk a lot and make mistakes. Making mistakes isn't bad. In fact, when you make mistakes, even if people laugh at you, is most surely when you are going to learn the most Spanish. Trust me!

Beginning high school and college Spanish classes, as well as most self-study Spanish courses start off by teaching vocabulary and verb conjugations. You practice speaking, but the focus is on the individual word or phrase. Lists of words are memorized and tests are given on verb conjugation. So when it comes time to speak, the words and phrases are separate in your mind. It becomes a matter of trying to pull all the pieces together and form them all into a sensible sentence, not just speaking. The key to becoming more comfortable in speaking situations is to practice and learn the phrases as a whole, not in separate pieces. Like when you were a baby and repeat it many times, once you have repeated the Spanish phrase around 1,000 times in your head, you'll be like a native. This way when you are trying to remember what to say you recall more than just a word - the whole sentence pops into your mind.

So, the first golden rule to speak good Spanish is to talk a lot and not feel embarrassed even if you say something like pussy, pregnant or dick by mistake in Spanish. Don't worry even if your Spanish friends laugh at you. Laugh along with them at yourself! Then ask them how to say it well and that's it. Its great therapy, too!

As time goes by, you'll feel talking like a Spanish native and even correcting them. Yeah! Spanish people do make mistakes, too when talking in Spanish. Same mistakes we make when we write or speak English, because we don't think grammar or rules, we think phrases to communicate a thought or an image in our heads.

+Preservativo

I remember going to an Eroski the first time and asking one of the girls at the cash box if the pumpkin can I was buying had *preservatives [condoms in Spanish]*- in Spanish you translate preservatives as *conservantes*. The girls´ reaction was to laugh out loud and proceeded to ask me what part of England I was from. The situation was funny and fortunately, I bonded with the girls and that very same Friday night I was hanging out with them at the local club and learning more Spanish fast. This one is a false friend in Spanish. It does NOT mean preservatives, like in food.

So, *Preservativos* are condoms. That's right, condoms, rubbers, and a raincoat. Remember the next time you go to a market or a grocery store in Spain trying to find out about your food having certain preservatives in it, say *conservantes* and don't say conservativos either- that means in physics something related to particles, too.

+Pollo/Polla

Ok, your are one of those Americans with a thick accent in Spanish?

Careful with this one!!!

In Spanish you have 5-vowel sounds period.

There are 20 vowel sounds in English. Yeah! A lot!

Most of the time, Spanish people will understand you. However there are a few instances where you really need to polish your accent. And this is one of those instances. We know *Pollo* is chicken, however, *polla* is something entirely different. A lot of Americans have an open "O" which means that O sounds like an A in Spanish. Thus **Pollo** becomes **Polla...**

Yeah! you guessed that, **right**!

Polla is dick, penis, cock ... OMG! ☹

Don´t feel embarrassed! Spaniards will know you're foreign so after a while they´ll take it in as normal! Besides Spaniards use a lot of swear words!

So, watch out next time your are ordering a roasted chicken with *partitas* in Spain, otherwise it can lead you to some pretty embarrassing moment.

+ Embarazada

What do you think this word means at first glance? Here's a hint; it's NOT embarrassed. This is probably the classic mistake English speakers make in Spanish. *Embarazada* means "pregnant." If you want to say **you're embarrassed** or something embarrassing you in Spain, you say *me da vergüenza o es embarazoso o embarazosa*.

Ex 1 I'm embarrassed = me da verguenza/tengo verguenza o es una situacion embarazosa

Ex 2 That's so embarrassing = Eso da verguenza, vaya bacile, eso es embarazoso.

NOT TO BE CONFUSED WITH => I am embarrassed = ~~Estoy Embarazada/o~~ => I am pregnant

Got It? :-]

+Molestar

This one does take a while to get used to actually saying out loud, but it's important to know. You don't want to get the wrong impression from someone complaining that their boss *"molested"* them all day in the office. You might want to know that the true translation of *"molest"* in **Spanish is To Disturb** and your boss wont be **molesting** you but **disturbing** you. Yeah!

+Constipada

Something wrong with your tummy? Do you have a cold then?

Actually this is usually the other way around, when Spanish speakers learn English. *Estoy constipada* in Spanish means I have a cold or I am stuffed up (runny nose, too). However, if you have problems with discharging... you should say to the pharmacist or the doctor, *tengo estreñimiento=I am constipated.* **Out of the way this one too! Alright??**

+Zorro/Zorra

Again like pollo, native speakers of English we tend to say the O´s like A´s in Spanish. So, if you say that someone is a zorro- someone is clever or just the animal: fox. But if you say the last O like in Pollo and make it into an A. that will sound to the Spanish ears like ZORRA.

Careful! Zorra in Spanish means "bitch," " prostitute," or "whore."

+Club

We all surely like that Madonna´s tune *"going to the Club…"*

When Americans come to Spain, one of the first things they do is to hit the club scene and the Spanish nightlife here. Thousands of bars and clubs where you can drink and dance till dawn, Spain has a plethora of nightspots to choose from. However, once you have finished at the bars and you want to go get your dance on and burn some calories, you head out to the club.

Except dance clubs in Spain are called *discotecas* or *discos*. To put it layman´s terms, a **club** in Spain is oftentimes a **whorehouse** on the side of the national roads or highways aka *barra americana* or *puti club*.

+Estoy caliente

One of the biggest problems where Spanish and English diverge is when you cannot translate word for word. Many times you can get pretty close, but a lot of words in English that use the verb **"to be"**-*ser* or *estar* in Spanish use "to have."

Here is a perfect example. **Dude, it's really hot outside!** (This, obviously, happens a lot in Spain), and you want to say, "damn, I'm hot, I want to cool down." In Spanish, we say j*oder,* **tengo calor,** *and quiero refrescarme.* Literally we say in Spanish "**I have heat.**" If you translate it literally, it's **estoy caliente,** and well, that's referring to *I´m a horny as hell...* hahahaha!

+Éxito

Looking for the metro exit at the Cuatro Caminos station in Madrid? Suddenly, you ask someone ¿*Donde está el éxito?*

If you were to ask someone where you could find the **éxito** you might be in for a bit of a philosophical reply. Instead, look for the signs marked **salida,** and get on with your day. To make things even more confusing, the word *suceso* in Spanish means "event" or "something that happens." **Exit=Salida =>Success=éxito**

CHAPTER 26
SOCIAL SECURITY NUMBER IN SPAIN

Any foreigner working or studying in Spain is entitled to a Spanish Social Security number, necessary for tax purposes as well as contracting and all procedures related to labor and work. Petitions are made at the *Instituto Nacional de Seguridad Social,* which also handles pensions, disability, motherhood and fatherhood, death and survival and public health care.

The Spanish Social Security system benefits all workers who are active within it. Each calendar day *cotizado [taxes paid into the system],* that a worker has been employed, counts towards your Spanish pension and unemployment benefits, so make sure to check that your place of work has given you the activation, called an *alta.*

Why do I need it?

Every person who works for a registered company in Spain is required to have a Social Security Number, called a *número de afiliación de la Seguridad Social*. An employer generally pays for Social Security. This number also helps track pensions, unemployment and sick days, as well as maternity or paternity leave. A new law, passed in late February 2014, has drastically cut fees for employers who wish to register new employees in social security to help promote growth and job creation. Fees range from 50€ to 100€, but are only available to those who are not already registered.

The vast majority of workers fall under the regimen general, or general scheme, which includes employees who work under another person, working partners of capitalist companies, civil servants and military personnel and foreign-born residents who work in Spain. Once a citizen is made active in the system, they are covered for life and their number will not change. For members of the European Union states, and spouses or family of Spanish citizens, affiliation with the Social Security system is as simple as presenting a valid ID.

However, North Americans will need to hand in a valid work permit in order to gain access to their number. The system also covers self-employed workers, called autónomos, who pay their own social security and are not eligible for unemployment, as well as students from foreign countries.

Where do I get a social security card? What do I need to bring?

Each capital city and the larger provincial towns have Social Security offices, typically open Monday through Friday from 9 in the morning until 2 in the afternoon.

To find your local office, use the office locater tool from the Social Security's website. You can search by autonomous region, or zip code. Some offices require appointments while others do not.

You will need the following paperwork:

+Passport or Foreign Resident Card

+A copy of Passport or Foreign Resident Card

+Form TA-1

The TA-1 is not available in English, though it is available in the co-languages of Basque, Gallego, Valencian and Catalan. You can download it, fill it out and print it here http://www.seg-social.es/Internet_1/Trabajadores/Afiliacion/Servicios%20/Modelosde solicitude31190/ModeloTA1Solicitudd572/index.htm

Help! How do I fill out the form?

Here's the important information you'll have to fill out:

Section 1: Personal data

1.1 : First Surname / Second Surname (if applicable) / First name

1.2 : Gender (M for mujer or female, V for varón or male)

1.3 : Type of ID (mark with an X):

Spanish DNI number / Foreigner's Card / Passport

1.4 : Number on your identification document

1.5 : Social Security number (if applicable)

Date of birth / father's full name / mother's full name

Place of birth / province of birth / country of birth

1.6 Disability (if applicable) / nationality /maiden name (if applicable)

1.8 Street Address

1.9 Email address /option to have information sent by text message / Mobile-cell phone number

Section 2: Relevant Social Security Data Mark with an X:
Activation of Social Security / Number Assignment for Social Security / Change in data
2.1: Cause for data change (if marked X)
2.2 Listing of any accompanying documentation Section
3: Option to have data sent to a second address added for communication purposes

At the bottom left, the solicitor/lawyer and his or her employer must, write the place and date, then sign in this format:

En Bilbao, el 5 de mayo de 2018
By filling out a form and handing in your original and a photocopy of a passport or another form of ID, you will be given a *número de afiliación* de la seguridad social. Keep in mind that you won't be given an actual card like you might have in your home country, so be sure to keep the official form with your number for tax purposes.

While this number is active for health care immediately, you will not start earning days towards unemployment or your pension until you are employed and a lawyer has activated your work contract. This number is recognized throughout Spain and its autonomous cities in Africa.

What's covered under Social Security?

Health and some Medicare is one of the biggest assets of being in the social security system, and your employer covers the necessary fee for your basic care. In most regions, general doctor visits and emergency care are free at public clinics and hospitals.

Some prescriptions and surgeries are not covered under the social security umbrella and must be paid for after care has been administered, though often at a reduced cost. Note that dental care is not part of the social security system and must therefore be paid out of pocket. Except for dental work for children under 12 and tooth extractions for adults, which are free of charge. For more information, contact a social security office in your region. Every autonomous region has its own regulations for the administration and compensation, as well as rules related to the type of contract you possess, so visit your nearest office or ask a lawyer.

CHAPTER 27
QUESTIONS TO ASK YOUR APARTMENT OWNER/ LANDLORD/MANAGER

When moving to Spain, often your priority would be to find a place to call *hogar, dulce hogar*-**Home Sweet Home**. And, like many things in Spain, it's an exercise in patience! **Renting an apartment/flat in Spain** is far from a simple task.

After you've found a few *pisos* you're interested in viewing and have made appointments to see them, be prepared to ask your landlord /manager- *casero/a* tough questions.

While this may cancel out a few accommodations early on, you'll end up saving yourself a lot of tome and money. Not sure what to ask? – Try these questions:

+How much is rent and how will you be expected to pay? Rent will take up a sizable chunk of your income, most financial experts say up to 1/3 of your salary. Typically, renting in a city center or in newer developments will cost more, as will choosing to live alone. Make sure to ask your future landlord about how to make payments. Some *caseros* may ask you to pay them cash-in-hand, while others will expect a bank deposit to be made during the first few days of each month. And some even an *abal* or bank guarantor.

+What utilities are included in the price of rent and what utilities are paid separately? Typical utilities include water, phone + internet and electricity, though unexpected costs like building maintenance fees, called comunidad, or propane tanks to heat water could hike up your monthly outgoings. Ask potential landlords which utilities or gastos are included, and which are not. Some homes even have orange canisters, which must be purchased from a gas station-gasolinera or a *butanero*-butane authorized sellers.

+How often does each bill come, how will you be notified and how will you be expected to pay? Oftentimes landlords will contract all of the utilities in their name and tell you how much you owe each month or quarterly. Sometimes, they'll want you to put the bills in your own name, which means the amount will be automatically deducted from your bank account and usually before the physical bills arrive in the mail.

Ask beforehand about which system your *casero* prefers and how much the monthly bills typically account for. If the bills remain in your casero's name, make sure to see a copy (a scan or screenshot sent via cell phone will suffice) before paying. Note that not all bills are monthly: some bills come bimonthly or even quarterly! Also keep in mind that in shared flats bills may be split between roommates evenly or at a percentage based on room size or usage. I am going to go out on a limb here and say – ask!

+What is the length of the contract and what down payment or fianza is expected? Will you be staying for a full calendar year or just the school year? Note that most caseros – though not all – will expect a one-month security deposit upon signing the lease in addition to the first month's rent. The deposit-*fianza* should be returned in full to you, the tenant-*inquilino*, when you move out, unless you've broken lots of things and left the place a mess! Make this clear so that there are no surprises at the end of the year.

If you found your *piso* through an inmobiliaria or rental or real estate agency, make sure you don´t pay a fee in advance or pay for a listing of properties. Usually, landlords pay the agents a commission. Most inmobiliarias don't charge you when finding you accommodation. Landlords may take care of this cost for you.

+ What is the policy on guests, pets, family and friends? Will visiting friends and family be charged for crashing on your couch? If you're renting an whole piso, having guests around shouldn't be a problem, but in a shared piso space, you might encounter some logistic problems. If you have family and friends visiting you in Spain, make sure to talk over the details and logistics first.

Where will guests sleep, whose bathroom will they use, will the living room be overrun with suitcases and souvenirs? You have a cat, Are pets allowed in the premises? If you need to pay a little extra to have your pet or friends around, find out first!

+ Who will you contact and how if there is a problem with the apartment? Issues with mold, faulty appliances and broken furniture are just a few of the typical problems you might run into in your new Spanish home. Make sure to ask who you can call or email, in case of an emergency, flooded bathroom, electric outage, etc.– be it in the middle of the night, a weekend or a holiday – so that someone will come running. Spanish landlords are notorious for being careless, after all, they don't have to live with you, so be persistent! Remember, it's their job to keep the property up to perfection, especially if they expect timely rental payments.

+When sharing: are you responsible for only your room or the whole apartment? If a roommate moves out mid-contract, who must pay? You'll find 3 types of rental situations in Spain: A. renting an entire piso yourself, B. renting a piso with a group of people or C. renting a single room or bedsit. If, you and a group of people are planning to rent a whole piso, a single or multiple names must go down on the contract and those people are then legally responsible for paying rent regardless of who else comes and goes. Make sure it's clear what expectations there are regarding what you owe, especially should a roomie decide to pack up and take off.

+ Does your casero/a live in the house? Watch Out!

It's a bit strange to ask, but we promise you won't regret it, because where your landlord stays will undoubtedly affect potential social gatherings, whether or not guests are welcome and how comfortable you feel in your own apartment. Besides make sure the casero doesn't come in the house often without your permission or in case of an emergency. My landlord in my second apartment would come around without telling me and as I was arriving home, he would be siting on the couch watching football games and shows without my permission. Let alone, if I had money and some money was missing, this situation was pretty awkward to deal with accusing the person directly renting me the house. Also agree on a public place and a time at which the casero can collect rent from you. With *caseros*, I usually agree to meet at the local coffee house. Just walk down the stairs and voilà 2 yards from my place; grab a coffee that he often times pays for and I hand in the rent where everyone is watching. Just in case, there is any mix-up in the near future.

+Can your casero kick you out of your place in a blink of an eye? What are the tenant's rights in Spain?

Well, for those of you who have watched *Pacific Heights* with Michael Keaton, Mathew Modine and Melanie Griffith, it does not happen like that in Spain either. You ain´t that lucky yet! By the way, it's a great movie. I suggest you watch it with friends!

Under the **Ley de Arrendamientos Urbanos** (better known as the *Ley de Alquiler-Law of Renting Properties*), you cannot be kicked out of your apartment without a timely notice-usually between 30-45 days. Caseros must give tenants sometimes in some regions at least 2-months-notice.

Should you be the one who decides to move out early, remember that you are legally bound to notify your casero at least 28-30 days before hand. However, this is only true for tenants who have a legal contract, known as a *contrato* (*de arrendimiento-a lease* in plain English).

Also have in mind, that Spaniards DO NOT pay the last months rent that is common practice among Spaniards renting in Spain, so that the owner of the place does have to return your deposit. I personally and always do it. Sub letting or sub renting pisos is not allowed in Spain by law and if I were you, ask them to show you a contract or papers. If the **piso is very nice and cozy** and the casero is asking you to come up with an ***abal***- a local guarantor or bank guarantee pre-paid amount. Turn the piso down and find another one. Foreign people are not entitled to get abal except that you have 1 million in the bank. It does work for Ronaldo and Messi but you aint neither one of them. The best thing about **central heating** is just that, that you have real central heating. It´s a bad idea to have electric heating in your piso, overall in the north of Spain since electricity in Spain is very expensive. Buildings in Spain, which have central heating, turn it on in October and it gets turned off by mid April. If you live in the north of Spain, you will need it.

CHAPTER 28
PROS AND CONS ABOUT BEING A TEACHER ASSISTANT IN SPAIN

Lets start with the Cons

+Some Program You Don´t Get Help To Get Settled

All you get from, for example, the Ministry of Education auxiliary program is a few documents to help you get your TIE and the promise of a monthly paycheck. The first paycheck doesn't come for at least a month after you start work, which means you have to pay for all your start-up costs. Bring some savings, at least 2 thousand dollars or pounds.

With some programs you're on your own to:
- Buy your plane ticket to Spain
- Find a place to live
- Open your own bank account
- Get a mobile phone
- Find transportation to and from your school (many auxiliares are placed in two schools in two different towns)

Some people get lucky and have helpful teachers at their schools and manage to get help with accommodation, carpooling and doing even the paperwork. Others arrive in Spain with no one and have to do everything themselves.

+ Not being able to Legally Work as A Student

700-800€/month (up to 800-1200€ /month in Valencia-Madrid-Barcelona) is enough to survive on, but it's not a lot to live on. Some of the job is technically a grant and auxiliares are issued student visas. Fortunately that means not paying taxes and not paying into social security. But unfortunately, you can't legally work always on a student visa. [Check the chapter where I talk how you can legally work on a student VISA]

Many teacher assistants get hired as off-the-books employees at places like language schools or tour guide organizations. And that means no legal rights to things like minimum wage, fair working conditions, and employers who won't take advantage of you or fire you on the spot for no reason. [get a contract from an academy or at least a paper or a schedule signed by the head of studies of the academy]

Not to mention that if you renew for a second year, you have 1-2 months without a paycheck and it's up to you to find a way to pay the bills. [this is due to the change of location sometimes; so get the director de escuela-school principal to get the local regional coordinator to assign you the same school, unless you are unwanted by the school a second time around]

+Working with English Teachers Who Have Less Than Perfect English and Don't Want You There

During my first day in my school's plastica -**arts and crafts** class, the teacher handed me a list of questions she'd written about the day's lesson and asked me to read them aloud to the class, I barely recall the drill and the exact words, but...

it was something like this...

Male Teacher: "Write a circle in the paper if any? Which were represent the round?" ?????????????????????

In principle, I figure he meant to say :

"Draw a circle on any piece of paper! Tell me if a circle represents the same as a 360 circumference and if it is round!"

That's what I gathered once he explained it in Spanish to the class.

I kinda paused for a minute and asked to myself whether I should correct the teacher I'd just met in front of his class or simply read the sentence aloud like He'd asked me to.

It's awkward to be in a classroom when, for example, the official English teacher cant speak English at all and says things like, "Explain me the sentence" or mistakes "his" for "her" or "He" for "She" many times in a row despite the fact that you've been talking to them about it for weeks.

+ Not Being able to Choose where you Work

Like I have been saying previously most auxiliares programs, You can request your top three regions and type of city you want to work in (ciudad vs pueblo), but they end up placing you wherever they need you. It's **completely hit or miss**. Even if you're placed in the region you wanted, there's no guarantee that you'll be placed in the city you want, or that you'll end up in a good school.

You may get lucky with an amazing school with engaged kids and caring teachers, or you may draw the short straw and end up at a terrible school with problem students in an awful town.

+ Dealing with Spanish Bureaucracy

As much as I hate standing in line at the DMV back home, it doesn't even come close to the frustration I feel with every single encounter with a Spanish funcionario. Spain is notorious for long, complicated, unnecessary procedures to complete even the simplest of tasks.

+ Being told Everything at the Last Minute and in Spanish

The application for the auxiliares programs open in December, or maybe it'll open up in January, or maybe you'll have to wait until February to start applying. And it's anyone's guess as to when the assignments will start rolling out, when the first paycheck will come, whether or not you'll be able to decipher the last minute urgent emails that the government will hopefully remember to send you.

Accepting this auxiliares´ job means accepting the Spanish tradition of taking a long time to do everything and waiting around for things with crossed fingers.

+Teaching English with no training in Teaching or English

Apparently being a native English speaker qualifies you to work with children. If you didn't study English or Education in college, and very few other auxiliares that I've met did either. Being an auxiliar means being asked things like:
- What is the difference between "manage" and "direct"?
- Can you explain what a "trowl" is?
- Should I use the second or third conditional tense for this sentence?
- How come everyone laughs when I say the word "beach"?
- How do you spell "miscellaneous" and what does it mean?
- Can you write a list of regular verbs on the board?
- What does "might as well" mean?

That´s why I suggest you check some videos on how to teach children and please check the ESL resources at the end of this book. Not planning your lessons means not knowing what's coming either. Some teachers let you know before class what the lesson will be about or what you'll be discussing, but others toss you in and open the floor for difficult questions. Please talk to schoolteachers before and after the class about lesson and action planning...

I'd estimate roughly that 20% of your time in the classroom is spent thinking hard about a question and saying "Uhhh. Ummm. Well..."

Now Lets check the Pros

I have to admit that my job as an auxiliar de conversacion (aka "Language and Culture Assistant") in Spain has been one of the most amazing experiences of my life. It's an incredibly rewarding job, you meet many different people, and can be a lot of fun. Not to mention that this is probably the easiest job you'll ever have, unless your next career move is housesitting.

+ A Lot of Free Time

This job is 12-14 hours a week (16 hours in Madrid). And it's not 12 hours of manual labor in the sun. It's not 12 hours of challenging work that pushes you to your cognitive capacity. It's not 12 hours of university lectures that require lots of outside reading and studying and paper writing.

It really depends on the program you choose, but regularly, It's 12 hours of reading paragraphs, singing songs, writing words on the board, and talking about how many inhabitants your hometown has. For many auxiliares that means sleeping in late, ending the workday at 3:00PM, and having a 3-day weekend every single weekend.

On the other hand, if you are heading for a job at an academy, then you may have to work 20-30 hours a week, but also most of the times you'll be working will be mostly from 4pm to 800-900pm, Monday-Friday.

+ Easy to get accepted

Jobs, on most of the Spanish teaching assistant programs, are granted on a first come, first serve basis. There's no intense vetting process to determine your qualifications, there's no interview, and I'm pretty sure they'll never notice your "official transcripts" which some times people just I copy and paste into a word document.

The requirements, for example to be a "Language and Culture Assistant in Spain" for most of the programs or even jobs at academies or schools are:

- Be a native or bilingual speaker of English (or French, German, Italian, Portuguese, or Chinese)
- Hold a US, Canadian, Australian, New Zealand, or EU passport
- Either Be a junior or senior in university, or have completed a university degree
- Or have a TEFL or ESL qualification
- Have Elementary Spanish skills

There's not even a test or course requirement to determine your Spanish level, the test is whether or not you can make it through the application.

So basically if you're an English-speaking college kid, you're in.

+ Easiest way to Live Legally in Europe

A few auxiliares that I've met signed up for this job because they had a passion for the English language or teaching. Most usually sign up because they wanted to live in Spain or travel Europe.

These teaching assistant programs are a (relatively) simple way for non-Europeans to land a legal position in Spain, rather than trying to make it as illegal, Spanish-speaking immigrant.

+ Being the Good Cop in the Classroom

The auxiliar job is light on lecturing about grammar, giving exams, assigning homework, and disciplining the students. And it's very heavy on singing songs, doing crafts, discussing holidays. You get to be the fun teacher. Sometimes, you'll feel like a special guest on a movie that drops into the classroom once a week, bringing tales of Halloween, Thanksgiving and peanut butter sandwiches with jelly.
Being young and from another country makes you kind of a novelty, the children will love you, because being a guiri in Spain is considered cool to them.

+ No Lesson, Action Planning, Paper Grading or Marking

Most of the programs just required you to be in the class talking to students or take children out of the class and tutor their reading and speaking skills. You don't have to do much work outside the classroom at all.

You don't have to be that teacher complaining to your students *"Oh God I was up so late last night grading your multiple choice exam."* You don't have to spend your lunch hour drawing up seating charts and checking off homework assignments. You don't have to stress about putting together the year's curriculum.

Occasionally you will be asked to prepare an activity for the class or put together a power point presentation or an oral one with some visuals about something British, American or from your home country. But for the most part, your free time is yours. You can spend your days learning Spanish, giving private lessons, traveling around Spain and Europe.

+ Lots of Extra Work and Money

If you are smart and witty like me and have some good speech prepared before hand. You can get a lot of Spanish to pay you to learn English. The best clients are adults. Children, often times, out of the classroom and in their own home environment, are hard to teach and keep them well behaved. You are going to spend more time trying to discipline them than teaching them basic English skills. It's a no-go unless you're quite desperate or extremely tactful with kids.

+ You Learn A Second Language

The main goal of moving to Spain, I guess, has to be learning Spanish like if it were your own. So get out there and be ready to handle business and night outings in Spanish. It´s the best chance you're going to have of learning a second language like your own.

CHAPTER 29
HOW TO WRITE LETTERS TO SCHOOLS, ACADEMIES AND OTHERS IN SPANISH

REDACTAR	Mensaje nuevo
Recibidos	Destinatarios juanmiguel@gmail.com
Destacados	
Importantes	Asunto Solicitud para el puesto: Profesor de Inglés
Enviados	
Borradores (5)	**Estimado Señor** Miguel,
▸ Círculos	He visto su anuncio en el que solicitan un profesor de inglés.

Soy de Inglaterra y tengo siete años de experiencia trabajando de profesor de inglés, tanto con niños como con adultos.

Le envío en **adjunto** mi curriculo, donde puede ver todos los datalles sobr mi educación y experiencia profesional.

Me gustaría tener la oportunidad de tener una entrevista con ustedes en la que podamos conocernos y comentar las condiciones de una posibe colaboración.

Aquí les dejo **mi número de contacto**: 00 34 555 666 777

Quedo a su disposición para cualquier aclaración.

Saludos cordiales.

Lara Hansen

Enviar

How to Write an Email in Spanish

Nowadays, writing letters is not as common as it once was, but knowing how to properly write a letter is still a valuable skill in any language.

Since youre gonna be writing to your director de escuela, your regional coordinator and perhaps to banks and others around via email, I suggest writing short and simple. Don't write more than 3 or 4 lines to anyone including your escuela or instituto once you want to touch base with them in Spain.

The guidelines below will help you write informal or formal letters to people in Spain, and many of them can be used to write professional emails in Spanish as well.

Writing Formal Emails in Spanish

Most of the emails you will need to write will probably be formal texts addressed to companies, schools, universities or government agencies. Customs with regards to formal emails may vary from region to region in Spain, but the following guidelines should cover the basics no matter which your recipient may be.

As with any formal text, remember to avoid slang or other informal language, and always address your audience using **usted,** unless you already know the person and he/she has allowed you to use the informal **tu**. Or you feel confident enough to **tutearla/lo** [talking informally to her/him]

Format

To start a formal letter in Spanish, you need to state the city you are writing from and the date in long format. but the end result will look something like this:

Madrid, 12 de septiembre de 2018 = Madrid, September 12, 2018

Notice how this part is aligned to the left, and keep in mind that months and days of the week are not capitalized in Spanish.

After you've written down the date, you will want to address the person you are writing to. A common way to do this is by using the word *estimado*:

- *Estimado Sr. Gómez:* - Dear Mr. Gómez,
- *Estimada Sra. Ríos:* - Dear Ms. Ríos,
- *Estimada Directora/Administradora/Profesora: -*
- Dear Principal/Admin/Teacher

Keep in mind that Spanish speakers often mention their college degree or position before their name, for example:

- *Ing. Julio Pérez* - Julio Pérez, Engineer
- *Prof. Nuria Lamas* - Professor Nuria Lamas
- *Dr. Mauricio Benitez* - Dr. Mauricio Benitez or Mauricio Benitez, PhD

In more formal emails, just mentioning the addressee may not be enough, and you will need to include more information about them, following the format below:

Sr./Sra. Name and Last Name
Position
Company or Institution

If this format is used, the *estimado* section may be omitted. In some cases, it is added right after the addressee's name, position and company have been mentioned.

If you don't know who will receive the letter, you can use expressions like the ones below:

- *A la Attención de/A quien corresponda:* - To whom it may concern,
- *Estimados señores:* - Dear Sirs,

Once you have established whom you are writing to, you can start the letter by explaining your reason for writing with phrases like the following:

- *Me comunico con usted para...* - I write to you in order to...
- *El motivo de mi carta es...* - The aim of this letter is to...
- *Por la presente solicito...* - I hereby request...
- *Me dirijo a usted en ocasión de...* - I write to you in order to...

After you have stated the reason for writing, you can use the next paragraphs to expand your ideas. Once you have made your case, you can use one of the following phrases as a closing line:

- *Saludos/Cordialmente, y a la espera de una respuesta, me despido.* - Cordially, and awaiting an answer, I send my regards.
- *Esperando una pronta respuesta, me despido.* - I await a rapid answer and send my regards.
- *Sin otro particular, lo saludo.* - Having nothing further to add, I send my regards.

- *Desde ya, agradezco el recibimiento de mi solicitud y aguardo su respuesta.* - I thank you for receiving my request and await your reply.

A short ending, like the ones below, follows this short closing line:

- *Atentamente,* - Sincerely,
- *Cordialmente,* - Cordially,
- *Un cordial saludo,* - Best regards,

To finish off, sign your name and below write your name in print and add any relevant information, such as your own position and company.

Example: Email you should write to school before you start the program.

Let's put all of these pieces together into a sample formal email:

Londres, 10 de febrero de 2017

Dra. Maria Rivas [or A la atención del director/directora del centro]

Directora Colegio del Amor de Dios CEIP

Estimada Dra. Sánchez,

Me comunico con usted para solicitarle información detallada sobre el programa de auxiliares del cual participo este próximo septiembre y para el que estaré trabajando en su colegio.

Más específicamente, me interesaría conocer los horarios de auxiliary, el email o contacto o el nombre del auxiliary del año pasado, y los profesores a los que me asignarán y si los puedo contactar para comentar con ellos sobre las lecciones, la planificacion y estructura de las clases. También me gustaria que me informase sobre el dia en que tengo que estaren el colegio y si existe alojamiento cerca y si hay profesores que me puedan llevar en caso de que tenga que vivir a más de 10-15 km del centro escolar.

Sin más dilación, la saludo.

Atentamente,

[Signature]

Sean Dykes

Santa Monica, February 10, 2018

On the email subject you should write something like:

Nuevo Auxiliar de Conversación

The guidelines for casual emails are much more relaxed than the ones explained above. You will be able to include more casual language, and you can use the informal *tú* instead of the more formal *usted*.

Cómo escribir un email formal en español

1 El asunto ➜	**2** El comienzo ➜	**3** El cuerpo ➜	**4** El cierre
● Frase corta	● Saludo + nombre	● Preséntate	● Despídete
● El asunto queda claro	● Estimado/a+ señor/a + nombre	● Motivo del email	● Ejemplo:
● Ejemplo:	● Uso de dos puntos :	● Usa "usted"	**Saludos cordiales**
Reunión para dudas	● Ejemplo:	● Ejemplo:	**Atentamente**
	Estimada señora Ramírez:	**Mi nombre es Sara y me pongo en contacto con usted porque...**	

Format

When it comes to format, casual emails are also more relaxed. The date is sometimes added in short form but, like in formal letters, it is also aligned at the top right of the page.

If you are writing to a friend, close acquaintance or family member, *estimado* will probably sound too formal, and you definitely won't need to list their position. Instead, you can use the friendlier *querido* and the addressee's first name:

- *Hola/Querido Juan:* - Dear Juan,
- *Hola/Querida Marina:* - Dear Marina,

The body of the email will follow a structure similar to the one you would use in English, starting by greeting the addressee and stating your reason for writing, and moving on to expand that reason in the following paragraphs.

How you end your letter will depend on how close you are to the person you are writing to, but here are some options:

- *Saludos* - Regards
- *Un abrazo* - Hugs
- *Un fuerte abrazo* - Big hugs
- *Besos* – Kisses

Keep in mind that you can use these opening and closing phrases, as well as the ones listed in the formal letters section, when writing emails in Spanish.

If you are writing to a school or the government, they sometimes offer samples of the email formats they prefer. If you are replying to an email someone else has sent you, pay close attention to the format they followed. It will help you to know the appropriate format for your response. Like the saying goes: *a donde fueres, haz lo que vieres* (when in Rome...).

This is an informal email to one of the teachers I was assisting at the time

Madrid, 12 de octubre de 2018
A la atención de Blanca Guedes
Profesora de Inglés de 4 y 5 de primaria
Colegio Amor de Dios

Hola Blanca:

¿Cómo estás? Espero que hayas pasado un buen finde. Ahora llevo unos días enfermo/a. Y te escribo para decirte que este lunes no podré asistir a clase. Te enviaré pronto un certificado o un volante del médico con el diagnostico y porque tengo gripe. No quiero contagiar a nadie en la escuela con la gripe y causar una epidemia.

Espero que no me echeis en falta estos días,
Muchos abrazos y sobre todo a los niños,
Atentamente,
Sean Dykes.

Part 4: Appendix
Interesting Links-Websites & Glossary

CHAPTER 30
USEFUL PHRASES, USEFUL SCREENSHOTS & LINKS
YOU SHOULD CHECK WHILE IN SPAIN

Profex

Renewal Application

LIVING & WORKING IN SPAIN 2.0

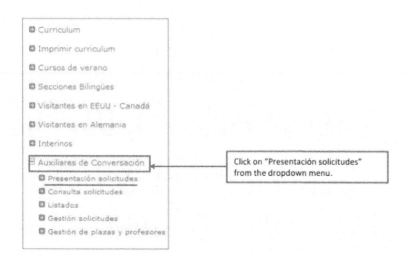

Most Current Year

Mensajes producidos por la última operación:

> Operación no efectuada: no se han encontrado registros que cumplan las condiciones de búsqueda

Pulse el botón "Ayuda" situa[...]   [...]na descripción completa del proceso de

> Make sure you select this option:
> **"2017 – Auxiliares de conversación extranjeros en España".**

Convocatoria: 2017 · Auxiliares de conversación extranjeros en España ▾   *click to renew*

| Actualizar | Nueva solicitud | Renovación solicitud |

Upload Documents

Choose Country and Region

Destino	Preferencia	Situación de destinos	
España	1	▬▬▬▬▬	✓
Andorra			

Remember that as a second year (first time renewal) you're likely to get anywhere that you want in Spain!

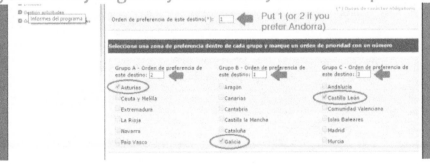

Complete Application and Specify City/School Preferences

Datos de interés
A. ¿Qué idioma desea enseñar? (*) ✓
a. Inglés ✓
b. Francés ☐
c. Chino ☐
d. Alemán ☐
e. Portugués ☐

Is this your first time renewing?

B. ¿Solicita la renovación por primera vez? (*) ✓
a.- Sí. ✓
b.-No ☐

Is this your first, second, third, fourth, or fifth time renewing?

C. Indique el tipo de renovación que solicita para el curso 2017-2018. (*) ✓

a.- Primera renovación

b.- Segunda renovación

c.- Tercera renovación ✓

d.- Cuarta renovación

d.- Cuarta renovación

e.- Quinta renovación

e.- Quinta renovación

Do you want to stay at the same school?

D. ¿Desea permanecer en el mismo centro el próximo curso? (*) ✓

a.- Sí ✓

b.- No

Do you want to stay in the same city or region but not necessarily the same school?

E. ¿Desea permanecer en la misma ciudad o comunidad autónoma pero no necesariamente en el mismo centro? En el caso de que desee cambiar de provincia, localidad o centro, indique sus preferencias en el apartado H. (*)

a. Sí

b. No

What is your current school, city, and region?

F. Reseñar centro, localidad y comunidad autónoma de destino actual. (*)

Type current school, city, and region

Do you want to change your region?

G. ¿Desea cambiar de comunidad autónoma? (*)

A.-Sí

B.-No

Add additional relevant information or personal necessities you have here

H. Información adicional que pueda ser relevante para la adjudicación de destino o el desempeño de sus funciones (ej. problemas de movilidad, discapacidades, problemas físicos o psicológicos, enfermedades crónicas, etc.)

Add what school, city, or area you want to go to and any additional relevant information, including disabilities, mobility issues, physical problems, or chronic illnesses.

Submit Application and Mail Signed PDF to Regional Coordinator

Do you still need to add your PDF documents to your application?

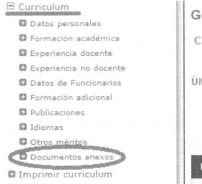

Latest update: May 23, 2018. 2018-2019 school year.

(Updated May 15, 2018). SCHOOL ASSIGNMENTS HAVE STARTED AS OF MAY 14, 2018.- Please check you email regularly (including spam folder) for assignment notifications.

Language assistants assigned to any school in the Murcia region ("Comunidad Autónoma de la Región de Murcia") for the 2018-19 school year will be assigned a monthly stipend of EUR 875 for 15 periods of weekly teaching schedule.

The whole process will be carried out on line (no need to post mail documentation). Once you submit your application and obtain an application number, for all further email communications with your Spanish Education Office contact in the US you are requested to include in the "Subject" field of the email: *18_2AX* plus the last four digits of your application number, plus your name and first name as in the example: *18_ 2AX 1234 Sample, John*. Please review the documentation below under the heading "General information" before applying.

Assignments will be given on a first-come, first-serve basis according to application number as long as the PROFEX system shows that you have also uploaded the necessary documents within a reasonable period of time after having signed up onto the PROFEX system and been given an application number. After submitting your application, please check your mail regularly for updates on the need to complete/change it (if applicable) and access your PROFEX account to track changes in the status of your application.

Once you application has the status of "admitida" no further action is required from you until the end of the application period (for more information see pages 6 , 7 and 9 from the "Application Guidelines").

Important notice for applicants who hold a US and a European Union passport or a Canadian and a European Union passport simultaneously.- please note that prior to arriving in Spain you must obtain a police background check and have it accompanied by a The Hague Apostille (US citizens) or a legalization (Canadian citizens).

What´s a Funcionario in Spain?

A funcionario is a civil servant or public official. They usually take a long government exam and can study for up to 8 years before they start working for the government. Then, they have a job forever. They simply are government employees in Spain, and they basically make a lot of money and can never be fired unless they do something really really wrong. They are probably so unhelpful because they are ill-informed themselves.

Here is a short video called **PUSH UP** https://www.youtube.com/watch?v=ZI5qo2Ad-Hg that explains them very well. Ok, this is how Spaniards feel about these guys. And that´s why Spaniards want to become *funcionarios* in Spain rather than set up their own freelance business.

ALI SON

October 31, 2017

REPLY

Hi! I'm doing a master's degree, and the end date of the program is September 30th, 2017. I was just issued a TIE with an expiration date of June 30th, and at the extranjería office in Valencia they told me it's because I can be in the country 3 more months after the date expires... but this seems wrong? Wouldn't I be illegal? Do you know anything about this?

Thanks!

~~You can, in fact, stay in Spain/Schengen Zone for 90 days after your TIE expires. It's because when your student visa expires, your status automatically changes to that of a visitor. Non-EU nationals from visa exempt countries (e.g. Canada) can be in the Schengen Zone for 90 days out of 180.~~

What's the Spanish NIE and TIE?

NIE is an identification number for foreign nationals who are going to reside in Spain. It comes with a resguardo – pink slip. The number will be assigned and printed to your TIE card later on.

what are the schengen-area countries? where is the schengen visa valid?

For the purposes of the Schengen tourist visa, the current Schengen area is composed of 26 countries. That's 22 European Union countries – Austria, Belgium, the Czech Republic, Denmark, Estonia, Finland, France, Germany, Greece, Hungary, Italy, Latvia, Lithuania, Luxembourg, Malta, Netherlands, Poland, Portugal, Slovakia, Slovenia, Spain, and Sweden – in addition to two associated countries, Norway and Iceland.

The Azores and Madeira, as part of Portugal, and the Canary Islands and Balearic Islands, as part of Spain, are included in the Schengen area. Ceuta and Melilla – Spain's autonomous cities in northern Africa – are a special case: they are part of the Schengen area, but border control is still in force there. France's overseas possessions, on the other hand, are considered to be outside of the area.

TIE is an identification card, which indicates that its owner has the legal right to reside in Spain for a period longer than six months.

Carta de nombramiento (language assistants) or acceptance letter from your university stating how long you will be studying there. Usually, sent to the applicant by email.

volante de empadronamiento is a temporary or informal certificate of your registration as a member of the community. For most of your local needs, this should be sufficient.

certificado de empadronamiento is the official certificate of your registration as a member of the community. You may need it for certain legal procedures with national or foreign bodies. **Hoja de empadronamiento** is the application form you'll need to register with your community.

Empadronado (for men)/**empadronada** (for women) (it's used as an adjective) is Registered with your community.

Ayuntamiento is the City or town hall.

Junta/Junta Municipal de Distrito is a city's neighborhood administrative office. For example, Madrid has 21 neighborhood administrative offices, which among other duties, process *empadronamiento* applications from neighborhood residents.

Empadronamiento (proof of address) refers to the process of registering with your community's padrón (city roll), also called the Padrón Municipal de Habitantes.

The municipal padrón is the official record of all the people who live in a particular community and is the official way to verify or accredit your stay in Spain. By law, everyone who resides in Spain should be registered in the community where they live. Some municipalities are not required to be *empadronada* in order to receive your NIE and then TIE

DNI (*Documento Nacional de Identidad*): This is the ID number for Spanish citizens. The same number is used for one's driver's license.

Alicia Foster · 2 years ago

I realize this is late, but I'm currently trying to navigate the NIE/TIE renewal process while changing programs, and I have some info that might help others. I emailed the Oficina de Extranjeria here in Barcelona and their reply (which I pasted part of below) explains that they make exceptions to the go-back-to-your-country policy if your studies are complimentary to those you've just completed. I plan to do like you did (I don't think I'll have every single paper ready either, but I'm going right when my card expires and taking all the paperwork I can) and I hope it works out! But I'm also kind of a weird case, coming from a sketchy, not-well-known program and changing to either being directly contracted by a school, doing a master's, or maybe taking a spot in a more well-established teaching assistant program. Wish me luck!

"En caso de desear cambiar de estudios, con carácter general, sería necesario volver a su país de origen, y tramitar nuevamente un visado de estudios adecuado a los estudios que pretenda realizar.

Sin embargo, cuando queda suficientemente probado que los "nuevos estudios" que se van a realizar, complementan los ya realizados, que se trata de materias de la misma naturaleza, o directamente relacionadas, así como que el segundo curso no sea de un nivel inferior al primero, se podrá solicitar la prórroga de la autorización de estancia, que ha de presentarse en los 60 días anteriores a la caducidad de su tarjeta.

En caso de producirse un cambio de estudios, la concesión de la renovación de la autorización de estancia por estudios se valorará por el instructor del expediente, a posteriori de su presentación ante esta Oficina. A estos efectos, la persona interesada deberá aportar, además de la documentación genérica indicada en la hoja informativa número 08 del Ministerio de Trabajo, la documentación que acredite que:
- En relación al centro de estudios anterior: que ha aprovechado los estudios durante el curso anterior.
- En relación al nuevo centro de estudios: acreditar haber sido reglamentariamente admitido en cualesquiera centros docentes o científicos españoles, públicos o privados, oficialmente reconocidos, para cursar o ampliar estudios o realizar trabajos de investigación o formación, no remunerados laboralmente, con indicación, según corresponda, de un horario que implique asistencia y/o de un plan de estudios, investigación o formación aprobado."

∧ | ∨ · Reply · Share ›

NIF (*Número de Identificación Fiscal*): This is the tax ID number for all individuals. For Spaniards, it's the DNI plus one letter; for foreigners, it's the same number as your NIE. Once you have an NIE, you do not need to re-apply for an NIF; if and when you have to pay taxes, use your NIE number. If you're a nonresident who has to pay taxes in Spain, you may get an NIF issued to you without having an NIE. This, of course, does not mean you get automatic residency in Spain, nor will it make it any easier to get residency.

CIF (*Certificado de Identificación Fiscal*): This is the same as the NIF, but for companies.

Social Security Number: Your employer applies for this number when you start your first job in Spain. This number then stays with you for all subsequent jobs. If you are self-employed, you apply for this number yourself.

Elevator is ascensor **Light** is luces o luminoso **central heating** is calefacción de gas o electrica **Furnished** means amueblado. **Alquiler** is for rent **Sin Amueblar** Unfurnished **Escaleras** Stairwell and landing **Con Portero** With a receptionist **Señora de la limpieza** Cleaning Service **Con Balcon** Balcony **1/2/3 habitacion/es** 1/2/3 bedroom apartment/flat **Mattress** Colchón Lobby **Portal**

Móvil is a cell phone/ mobile phone **internet WIFI("wee-fee")** **Llamadas** are calls **SMS o mensaje de texto** is   text messages **Establecimiento de llamada** is a call connection **tarifa** is a rate/fee/price **IVA** is the European sales tax.

Pregnancy
Midwife: matrona / comadrona **Epidural:** epidural (stress on "al")
Scan: ecografía **Maternity scan dept in hospital:** tocología **To give birth:** dar a luz (literally "to give light") **Birth:** el parto
To be x months pregnant: estar embarazada de x méses
To breastfeed: dar el pecho
At The Bank

banco – **Bank** La cuenta – **Account** La caja/cuenta de ahorros - **Savings** account La cuenta corriente - **Checking account**-el estado/estrato (de cuenta) - **(Account) statement** El saldo (de cuenta) - **(Account)** balance intereses – **Interests** cajero automático - **ATM** cheque – **Check** chequera – **Checkbook** débito – **Debit** pasta/dinero – **Money** crédito – **Credit** efectivo - **Cash**

-Quiero... - **I want to...**

+Retirar dinero - **Withdraw money**

+Hacer un depósito - **Make a deposit**

+Transferir dinero - **Transfer money**

Sell/Buy Cars in Spain

www.wallapop.es

A second hand car dealer in Spain (some nice cars)

Loquo (Barcelona) used cars - check around the other Loquo cities (on the left) for more.

CraigsList's Barcelona second hand cars - again, check around the other craigslist sites too

Apartment or Flat hunting sites

http://www.moveandstay.com

http://couchsurfing.com

https://www.fotocasa.es

https://erasmusu.com/es/alquiler-estudiantes-erasmus

https://www.enalquiler.com/

School directories

Spanish Ministry of Education [Spanish] Complete list of public and private schools. https://www.educacion.gob.es/centros

USA Embassy's list of English-speaking schools

https://photos.state.gov/libraries/spain/164311/education/american_schools_in_spain_september15.pdf

International Baccalaureate Organization Click on Services - IB world **schools** for a listing https://www.ibo.org/

European Council of International Schools

https://www.cois.org/index.cfm

The National Association of British Schools in Spain
http://www.nabss.org/colegios/
International-based directory of Spanish schools for expats
http://spain.english-schools.org/

List of some of popular universities in Spain

Les Roches School of Hotel Management – Marbella Location: Ctra. de Istán, Km.1. Urb. Las Lomas del Río Verde E, Marbella, Málaga, 29600, Spain Tel.: +34 95 276 44 37 This university in Spain is located in the Costa del Sol on the coast of the Mediterranean. Les Roches Marbella offers a unique learning experience as it was founded as a sister school to the main Les Roches campus in Crans-Montana, Switzerland. This is a private university focusing on hospitality management, however it offers a range of other degree programs as well. **For more information check out:** www.lesroches.net

European University Center for Management Studies, Barcelona Tel.: + 34 93 201 81 71 European University (EU) is one of the world's top business schools attracting students from around the world including countries such as Spain, Switzerland, Germany, The Netherlands, Portugal, Greece, Malta, Kazakhstan and Singapore. This University in Spain offers both traditional programs of Bachelor and Master of Business Administration (BBA & MBA). **For more information check out:** www.euruni.edu **Email:**info.bcn@euruni.edu

Schiller International University, Madrid Location: San Bernardo, 97-99, Edificio Colomina, Madrid, 28015, Spain Tel.: +34 91 448 24 88 Schiller International University is an American university with its main campus in Florida and seven other campuses based throughout Europe. Schiller's Madrid Campus gives students the opportunity to complete an American MBA degree in International Business. **For more information check out:** www.schillermadrid.edu **Email:** admissions schillermadrid.edu

Valencia International Business School Location: Paseo San Gervasio 71, pral 1a (International Admissions Department), Barcelona, 08022, Spain Tel.: +34934186282 Valencia International Business School offers both business and management education at the undergraduate and graduate levels. This university in Spain has specializations in: Business Administration, Business Communication, Public Relations and Sports Management. **For More information check out:** http://www.valencia.uibs.org **Email:** info valencia.uibs.org

Universidad Pablo De Olavide - Centro de Estudios para Extranjeros Location: Carretera de Utrera, km. 1, Sevilla, 41013, Spain Tel.: +34 95 434 90 95 This university in Spain is an accredited public university located on a 345 acre campus, 5 miles from Seville's city center. It has a center for International Students that offers the semester/year long Hispanic Studies Program along with many other degree programs. **For more information check out:** http://www.upo.es/intl **Email:** intl upo.es

Alicante University This university in Spain is a public university owned by the Spanish State. Alicante University has more than 33,000 students and is one of the fastest growing universities in Spain. It is located only 5min from the center of Alicante. **For More information check out:** http://www.ua.es/en/index.html

Granada University This university in Spain caters specifically to foreigners and is located in the Realejo district (central Granada) in the historic palace of Santa Cruz from the 16th century. This is a public university and is owned by the Spanish State. There are more than 60,000 students and it's known to be one of the most important universities in Spain. **For more information check out:** http://www.ugr.es/university.htm

Salamanca University This university in Spain is a public university owned by the Spanish State and is the third oldest university in Europe. Salamanca University is recognized as one of the best Spanish language schools in Spain and is also responsible for setting and correcting the two yearly DELE exams papers, the only officially recognized certificate by the Spanish government and Instituto Cervantes.

This university in Spain is not only very well known but is situated in one of the liveliest cities in Spain with students coming to study from all over the world. **For more information check out:** http://www.usal.es/webusal/Ingles/index.html

Available TV channels

http://www.uktelevision.info/stuff/frequencies.htm

http://www.lyngsat.com/astra2d.html

BBC Prime

http://www.bbcprime.com

BBC Prime is available on a number of satellites. Not just Astra 2.

Intelsat 904 – Katelco Plus

Hellas Sat 2

Eurobird 2 Orbit Network

Astra 3A Kabel Deutschland

Astra 1KR UPC Direct, Canal Digitaal Satelliet

Eutelsat W2 Toal TV

Hotbird 6, 7A, 8 TPS, Cyfra +, SKY Italia

Eutelsat W3A Diti Turk

Thor 2 Canal Digital

Hispasat 1C TV Cabo

Bars and Restaurants Where They Serve Free Tapas

It might seem the stuff of dreams, but it's true: there are plenty of bars in Spain where you can get free tapas when you order a drink or a beer. Follow our list to visit some of these very special establishments where food's included with your drink order. Note down the addresses and get ready to fill your boots for very few euros.

Barcelona

Raspall

Cal Chusco

La Xula Taperia

Gata Mala

La Bocatería de Mitre

O'Retorno

El Moll d'en Rebaix

Cecconi's

> **The famous Spanish tapa most likely has its origins in grocery stores of Andalusia the end of the 19th century**

Madrid

Ask for a beer and they give you a free tapa that's good-sized and flavourful. Think this happens only in Andalusia? Think again. In Madrid, there are lots of bars where every drink ordered comes accompanied by a portion of potato omelette, some cured meats, and even sandwiches or mini-burgers. Forget about the typical crisps or olives – here you can drink cheaply and eat well.

Petisqueira

La Blanca Paloma

Indalo Tapas

El Tigre

Entre Caceres y Badajoz

El Rincon Abulense

Los Amigos

El Respiro

La Pequeña Graná

Tapería Manxega

Taberna Mozárabe

Venta Matadero

La Peña Atlética de Legazpi

Check more free tapas and cheap food bars here

http://www.cervezamastapapormadrid.com/bares-madrid/

Andalucia

Granada

El Tablón

El Arenal

Aliatar

Los Arcos

Taberna de Kafka

Picoteca 3Maneras

Terra Bar

Las Niñas

Los Altramuces

Rossini

Jaraiz

Potemkin

Santo Domingo

La Borraja

Casa Lopez Correa

Papaupa

La Antigualla II

Damasqueros

El Pesaor

Seville

La Grande

Bodeguita Casablanca

Bar el Baratillo

Cervecería Abacería Alboreá

Cerro del Aguila

Jaen

El abuelo

El Gorrión

El Tito Nono

El perol de la abuela

taberna La Manchega

El Gordito

El Santuario

El Sanatorio

La Barra

La Quintana

Bomborombillos

Panaceite

Malaga

La Brocheteria

La Tranca

El Tapy

La Campana

Viva Maria

Mafalda

El Pimpi Florida

Huelva

Bar Pappis

Noviembre Tapas y Vinos

Los Cuartelillos

La Bodega

La tasquita

Almeria
La Bambalina
La Mala
El Bonillo
Tío Tom
Bella Ciao
Córdoba
El Burrito Cordobes
La Favorita
El Alpiste
Taberna Entrecalles
Pizzaiolo
Los Moriles
Cadiz
Taberna Casa Manteca
Virgen de la Palma
Mercado Central
DKY Gastronomia Gaditana de Abastos
Freiduría Las Flores
Cafe Royalty
At Horno al Gloria
Taberna La Manzanilla
Quilla
El Faro

Galicia

If you're visiting Spain, you may have heard that some restaurants offer free tapas with a drink. Well, that sure does not happen very often in Madrid or Barcelona. Luckily, I lived with a family in Moaña (region in Galicia) so I got a chance to experience the local tradition there. We used to go and have a drink out around 3x – 4x/week. You're definitely in free tapas country! It's nice to take a break from the city and eat tons of seafood, especially mussels, oysters, and the famous Galician octopus. People speak Galician, which sounds more like Portuguese but their tapas are great and delicious and most importantly you won't have to spend a dime on food when ordering a beer... Yeah! You heard right! They're always free when you order a drink!

A Coruña

La Bombilla

Pepa A Loba

Onda Sempre

Bistrot Ratatouille

Casa Ponte

A Taberna de Cunqueiro

Tatone

Casa Encarna

Zero Café

Cervezoteca Malte

Bar Reino

O Atallo

Buena Sombra

A Mundiña

The origins of the Spanish '*tapa*' are steeped in myth and explained by a number of anecdotes, some more credible than others. It is said, for example, that one particular tavern offered the king – exactly *which* king, depends on who is telling the tale – a glass of wine and fearing that a fly – or a speck of dust – might fall into the royal refreshment, placed a slice of ham on top. The king, a jovial sort, then asked for another drink with the same "tapa" – from 'tapar' meaning to cover.

Santiago

O Cabalo Branco

La Tita and the Moha

El Avión

Casa Pepe

Restaurante Orella

Tapas Petiscos Do Cardeal

Cafe Venecia

Angel

Café-Bar Croques

Café de Altamira

Kunsthalle

Lugo

Las Cinco Vigas

Paprica

Restaurante Bar Anda

Cervecería Cafetería Millenivm

La Fabrica

El Museo

Ave Cesar

Croquetas as tapas. LAS CROQUETAS DEL REBOTE

Two beers and this tapa will cost you €2 at O Cabalo Branco in Santiago de Compostela.

Vigo

La Taberna de Toni

Café Bar Saratoga

A Mina

Patouro

La imperial

Gran Cerveceria El Puerto

Café Bar Berdiales

El Escorial

La Porchaba

Meson Orensano

Bar Aldeana

La Varona

O Taller Tapas e Bocatas, Moaña

Ovella Negra, Moaña

Pósito, Moaña

Ponte de Japas
3ª Edición

DE TAPAS POR PONTEVEDRA!

FREE TAPAS PARTY NOV 25

Do 25 de novembro ao 8 de decembro

Pontevedra

El Pitillo

A Pousada do Pincho

Tabula Rasa Taberna

Chiruca

Capri Pasteleria

La Devesa

Casa Fernandez

Orense

bar Orellas

Taberna do Meigallo

el Duque

Pingallo

Casa de María Andrea

Casa Toñita

Mesón do Queixo

Trangallán

Taberna O Enxebre

El París

A Nosa Taberna

While most Portuguese people boast that their national cuisine is superior to Spanish food, they readily admit that the Spanish are the winners when it comes to tapas. At Badajoz, which is near the border with Portugal, you can feast on fried potatoes, chicken wings, liver on skewers and empanadillas – small savoury pasties filled with meat or fish. And at around €1.20 for a small beer, the drinks are great value too. No wonder Badajoz is considered to be one of Spain's tapas capitals!

el Pérez

A Baiuca

Atarazana s

O Arco da Vella

Rodolfiño

Bar del Samuel

León

LAS CROQUETAS DEL REBOTE

Flechazo

La Competencia

Camarote Madrid

Pajarín

La Piconera

Prieto Picudo

El Butano

Monalisa

Rioja

Logroño

Calle Laurel packs over 30 tapas bars into a two-block stretch

Bar Jubera

El Soriano

⊙⊙⊙⊙⊙ Reviewed August 23, 2017

The best free tapas (pinchos)

This was my favourite place for free tapas. For tips on ordering free tapas, see my review of Meson Cervantes.

Not only were these the tastiest tapas I had during my stay, they were also the biggest. Moreover, the location is perfect - just next to the famous Casa de las Conchas, literally one door down.

The free tapas are eaten inside in the proximity of the tapas counter, but you can then have your coffee at a table outside and admire the view.

 Ask X1_G8 about El Bardo

Salamanca

El Bardo

Ciudad Rodrigo

Van Dyck

Café Real

Mesón

Bambú

Ávila

Barbacana

El Rincón

Gredos

Don Camilo

El Rincón de Jabugo

Las Cancelas

What is a pintxo?

First of all, what in the world is a pintxo? Pronounced "peen-cho," it's essentially Basque for tapas, which are small plates (there's no such thing as San Sebastian tapas really. In Spanish, pintxos is spelled pinchos). Fun fact: two languages are spoken in Northeastern Spain – Spanish and Basque. While in some parts of Spain, you'll get a free tapa when you order a drink, you'll never get a free pintxo in the Basque region. San Sebastian pintxos are especially high quality and more gourmet – frankly, they're worth paying for. In San Sebastian, they typically range between €2 – €6 per plate.

Extremadura

Badajoz

Valdepasillas

San Roque

Santa María de la Cabeza

La Roca

La Corchuela

Bar Manolo

Mehtura

Segovia

San Miguel

Los Tarines

Duque

Euskadi – Basque Country

San Sebastian

Pasteleria Oiartzun

Gandarias

Zeruko

Borda Berri

Txondorra

Nestor

Txeptxa

Bilbao

La **Tapa** de **Bilbao**

Café Bar Bilbao

el Figón

Piparras

bar EME

Murcia

La Tapadera

Bodegón Los Toneles

Los Zagales

La Tienda de Susano

Pasteleria Zaher

El Sitico

Valencia

El Rincón De Las Tapas Gratis

Bar De Los Montaditos Gratis

La Consentida

Bar Ché- Taberna Vasca

El quinto pino

Bar Alhambra

Babalú

La Pilareta

Bodega La Pascuala

Sumptuous Paella

Most restaurants in Valencia serve paella all day, although real Spaniards eat it only as lunch. This time, we ate the most mouth-watering paella at home, made by my stepmother. According to a classic Valencian recipe, our paella included rabbit meat. Other valid options are chicken and duck. In the city of Valencia paella is not supposed to have any seafood whatsoever, but as we ate ours in Torrevieja, we followed their tradition and added shrimps. Saffron, garlic, sweet pepper and lemon are the key elements. But you'll need a special pan called paellera to get it right!

Mallorca

La Bodeguita

Ca'n Joan De s'Aigo

Cafe 1916

Wok Vs Sushi

Los 100 Montaditos Palma de Mallorca

Pop & Eat

Pintxo Pintxo Gorgorito

Bar España

Teaching sites online

http://lingobongo.com/
https://www.udemy.com
https://www.lynda.com
https://t.vipkid.com.cn

Resources ESL

https://ell.brainpop.com (great for kids and teens)
https://lyricstraining.com
https://busyteacher.org.
https://grupovaughan.com/vaughan-radio
https://breakingnewsenglish.com/

Important Shops/Stores

Ikea Clothes/furniture
Zara Clothes/furniture
Carrefour Grocery shopping /Clothes
Alcampo Grocery shopping
El Corte Inglés Grocery shopping/foreign foods/Clothes
Gadys Grocery shopping
Froiz Grocery shopping
Mercadona Grocery shopping
Eroski Grocery shopping
Lidl Grocery shopping/foreign foods/Clothes
http://www.madaboutfurniture.com/
http://www.perspectivelivingspain.com/
http://www.furnitureexpressspain.com/
http://www.citrus-iberia.com/furniture-packs-spain.html

Important Holidays

+Semana Santa (Easter/Lent)

Date: April 1-8th

City : Sevilla

+San fermin

(Running Of The Bulls... One of Spain's most famous, if not the most famous Spanish Fiesta)

Date: Early July (one week long)

City: Pamplona, capital of the Navarra region near the Basque Country (Northern Spain).

+La Tomatina tomato fight

Date: Fourth Wednesday in August

City: The small town of Buñol an hour outside Valencia.

+Las Fallas

Date: A five-day event leading up to Saint Joseph's Day on March 19th

City Valencia on the Costa Blanca

+Feria de Sevilla

Date: Two weeks after Semana Santa (towards the end of April).

City: Sevilla

+Carnival
Date: February 14th-20th
City: Tenerife-Cadiz-Galicia-Sitges-Barcelona

+Festa Major de Gracia (feast of the assumption)
Date: August 15th-21st
City: Barcelona

+ Moros y Cristianos (Moors and Christians)
Date: The specific dates for this Spanish fiesta depend on the particular city it is being celebrated in as it is held at various times of the year.
City: Alicante-Granada

+Semana Grande (big week)
Date: Third Week in August
City: Bilbao

+ Tamborrada
Date: 24 hours beginning at midnight on January 19th
City: San Sebastian

Other festivals that take place in Spain are the **Sonar Festival of Advanced Music and Multimedia Art,** the **Barcelona International Jazz Festival,** the **Festival of World Music, Fib** (Benicassim Music Festival – good times, but bring sun protection for you and your tent) and many more.

+Cabalgata de Reyes – Wisemen Parade
Date: Jan 5th at 18:00 pm
City: Vigo

Buy and Sell

https://es.wallapop.com

Cheap Flights

Ryanair
Vueling
EasyJet
Spanair
Transavia

Legal Aid Spain

https://www.atlanticoasesores.es
https://www.mylawyerinspain.com
https://www.citizensadvice.org.es/legal-aid-spain
http://www.spanishlegal.com
javierrial@atlanticoasesores.es
martaoubina@atlanticoasesores.es

Academies in Spain [The following businesses can provide you with a legal contract or prorroga even if your on a student or auxiliares VISA]
https://grupovaughan.com Vigo and Madrid
http://www.hollywoodenglish.es Vigo, Madrid, Pontevedra
https://www.ihmadrid.com/es Madrid
https://www.wallstreetenglish.com many regions
https://four-ways.com Coruña and Madrid
escuela official de idiomas in each region

Blogs Cited

https://www.mecd.gob.es/eeuu/convocatorias-programas/convocatorias-eeuu/auxiliares-conversacion-eeuu.html
https://www.americantravelblogger.com
http://artoftravelblogging.com
https://luxeadventuretraveler.com/
http://artofbackpacking.com/
http://www.willpeach.com
http://nocheckedbags.com/category/europe/spain
https://www.facebook.com/groups/151855544966473
www.barcelonesjove.net/
https://blogextranjeriaprogestion.org
https://www.spaniards.es/foros/profesoresvisitantes
https://photos.state.gov/libraries/spain/164311/citizen-services/auxiliares.pdf
https://www.youtube.com/channel/UCUkLbyQChmhLJEvt1n3LQSg
https://www.glassdoor.com/Reviews/Employee-Review-Ministerio-de-Educacion-RVW6452912.htm
http://spainkate.com
https://www.expatica.com

Auxiliares Timeline

Early-Mid January

APPLICATION PERIOD OPENS! MAKE SURE YOU HAVE YOUR LETTER OF RECOMMENDATION, COLLEGE TRANSCRIPTS AND DIPLOMA READY IN ORDER TO APPLY QUICKLY

||

February-March 1st

YOU WILL HEAR BACK FROM THE PROGRAM AND YOUR STATUS IN PROFEX WILL CHANGE TO –ADMITIDA- THIS MAY TAKE AS WELL A MONTH OR SO.

||

Mid-May/June 15th

YOU HAVE A LOW INSCRITA NUMBER, LETS SAY BELOW 1,500, THIS WILL BE ABOUT THE TIME YOU START HEARING BACK FROM THE SCHOOLS AND FINDING OUT IN WHICH REGION YOU HAVE BEEN PLACED. IF YOU HAVE A NUMBER OF INSCRITA BELOW 5,000. YOU'LL HEAR BACK FROM THEM IN AUGUST OR EVEN SEPTEMBER SOMETIMES. YOU WILL HAVE ONLY **3 DAYS TO ACCEPT OR REJECT THE POSITION.**

||

June/July 15th

ONCE YOU HAVE ACCEPTED YOUR POSITION, YOUR SCHOOL WILL SEND YOU VIA EMAIL A **CARTA DE NOMBRAMIENTO,** WHICH YOU NEED TO SHOW AT THE CONSULATE TO APPLY FOR YOUR VISA. CHECK YOUR SPAM TRAY IN CASE YOU DON'T FIND IT!

||

July/August 1st

AS SOON AS YOU GET YOUR **CARTA** DE NOMBRAMIENTO, YOU NEED TO DO YOUR **BACKGROUND CHECK,** FBI, STATE POLICE CHECK, **MEDICAL CHECK.** YOU'LL NEED THESE FOR THE **VISA APPLICATION.** YOU NEED TO MAKE AN APPOINTMENT WITH THE CONSULATE ASAP TO START YOUR **VISA PROCESS.** CHECK YOUR STATE CONSULATE REQUIREMENTS. THERE ARE FEW APPOINTMENTS EACH MONTH.

||

Early September/October 1st

YOU MUST BY THEN, **HEAD FOR SPAIN.** MOST SCHOOLS START OCTOBER 2, BUT SOME OTHERS **SEPTEMBER 12. WRITE TO YOUR SCHOOL ASAP** AND GET YOUR SHIT TOGETHER! WHEN YOU ARRIVE YOU'LL NEED **THE NIE,** THE **EMPADRONAMIENTO,** YOUR **INSURANCE CARD** FROM SCHOOL-FILL OUT THE SCHOOL FORM-AN **APARTMENT** AND **A BANK ACCOUNT.**

I hope this eBook helps some of you through the process of looking for, getting a job or settling down in Spain. This book is definitely one of the simplest ways to find out how you can work and travel Spain and possibly the right to achieve future Spanish residency.

4 Golden Rules Before You Come To Spain

For those brave enough to take the plunge and move to Spain, I can only offer 3 pieces of advice:

1. **LEARN Spanish** and its culture **WELL**
2. **COME** with a **VERY laid-back** attitude, and
3. Bring a **LOT** of savings
4. And Remember! Take care of yourselves and each other!

So watch this space!

About Sean

Who am I?

After graduating from UCLA in 1999, I hit the open road and headed to Spain. I didn't have a specific agenda or goal – just to travel abroad, see some interesting places and meet new people. I didn't realize until then that I wanted to live overseas, but by doing something that I found meaningful. I didn't just write about it, and I don't intend on writing about why you should go work or travel abroad or convince you what's best for you. I figure you should do what you want to do in life, and try to make that work for you. This eBook is just to help you save time, money and pain.

After a bad break-up with my Spanish girlfriend I found myself at a crossroads. I had lived my life in California with the typical guidance a young American gets "Go to the best school possible, get the best job possible that makes the most money, and then get a huge untenable mortgage and live the American dream".

But what is that dream? How can you decide what you want to do if you haven't had the experience yet to know what would make you fulfilled? From Nordstrom's, from College, from your parents who grew up in a different time with different expectations with different opportunities presented to them?

I had been on the road for many years and had finally taken the plunge to solve these tough life questions by starting my own business in Spain. So, Thanks for purchasing and reading my books.

-Sean Dykes

PS- If you want to shoot me or my buddy Colin an email about anything you think it is not accurate, wrong or out-dated, you can find me or Colin on atlantischannel@gmail.com or go to www.colinrivas.com

Do You have a kindle or an iPhone and want to upload a version of this Book to your devices?
We Recommend You Purchase the kindle eBook, now available on Amazon.com
However, the kindle or pdf version does not have all the graphics as in this paperback volume.